GLOSSOP FC
IN THE
FOOTBALL LEAGUE

A Complete Record and Who's Who 1898-1915

Garth Dykes

A *SoccerData* Publication

Published in Great Britain by Tony Brown,
4 Adrian Close, Beeston, Nottingham NG9 6FL.
Telephone 0115 973 6086. E-mail soccer@innotts.co.uk
First published 2009

Cover design by Bob Budd. The medal formerly belonging to Herbert Rothwell is repoduced with
the kind permission of Bryan Horsnell. Player caricatures on the back cover are by the author; the
players are, top, left to right; Cuffe, Kelly, McEwan, McKie, McMillan. Bottom; McMillan,
Robottom, Ross, Tustin.

Photographs to page 95 are from the author's collection. Photographs after pages 117
are © Jim Lockwood/GNE and used with permission.

DEDICATION

To the memory of Ralph Moat
1948 - 2009

Printed and bound by 4Edge, Hockley, Essex
www.4edge.co.uk

ISBN: 978-1-905891-80-1

CONTENTS

This aerial view of Glossop in the 1920s includes the North Road ground at the top of the picture.

AUTHOR'S PREFACE

Considering the fact that it is approaching a century since Glossop F.C. bowed out of the Football League, the task of tracing the early history of the club and its players has been a fascinating, if at times a problematic, task. Nevertheless, it is hoped that what follows will have shed some new light onto the subject, and added something to the overall knowledge of our national game. Certainly, in those far-off days, the 'Peakites' took the Football League by storm, reaching the top flight of English football at the first attempt. That they were unable to retain their elevated status was sad but hardly surprising when it was noted that more than one team in the First Division had average home attendances in excess of the total population of the Glossop district. Despite the extreme generosity of the club's president Mr Samuel Hill-Wood over a very lengthy period, the problems of a small town club were ever present. Even with assistance of several of the very best amateur players of the day, the cream of the club's professional talent inevitably departed Glossop to 'balance the books', leading to a lack of playing success and the eventual demise of the club. During research into the 232 players who qualified for entry into the "Who's Who" section, much new information has been gathered. Glossop were not the best book keepers in their Football League days, their players' registrations, and playing appearances, as logged with the Football League, were not without a number of errors. Every effort has been made, however, to ensure that the information contained in this book is correct, but those familiar with the task of collating football statistics from such an early period will be aware of the pitfalls involved. In this regard, I would like to apologise in advance for any errors or omissions, and I would be grateful to hear from readers who perhaps had ancestors on the club's books, or can add anything to what is already known. I can be contacted via the publisher.

Garth Dykes
Leicester
November 2013

ACKNOWLEDGEMENTS

My sincere gratitude, as ever, to Jim Creasy for his invaluable help during the twelve months that I have spent on this project. His continued delving into the nation's archives has enriched every one of my books, and many other works of football history. I am also most grateful for the assistance of Peter Holme, Collections Officer of the National Football Museum, for access to their records. I am indebted to friends and fellow historians Mike Jackman, Mike Davage, Michael Braham, Robert Reid (Partick Thistle historian), Tom Sutcliffe, Bryan Horsnell, Dr. Steve Phillipps, Gordon Small, Michael Joyce and Stewart Beckett. Jim Lockwood provided photographs of today's GNE, and Jonathan Haggart provided an account of recent events at the club. Anne Bowden and the staff of Glossop Library provided welcome assistance in tracing much research material. Last, but not least, thanks as ever to my dear partner, Ann, who has helped, encouraged and supported my writings for more years than she would probably rather not contemplate!

A HISTORY OF FOOTBALL IN GLOSSOP TO 1915

The name of Glossop in football circles was a household word for a great number of years prior to the First World War. As one of many clubs representing small communities its survival – and a healthy one for many years – owed much to the sporting instinct of its godfather and benefactor, Mr Samuel Hill-Wood.

The club was formed in 1886, as Glossop North End, and owed its existence chiefly to the brothers Baxter, who had introduced the Association code into the district from Darwen, where they had previously lived. There were no leagues in existence then, and all fixtures were naturally of a 'friendly' nature. Some rare struggles were witnessed, however. The meeting with Hadfield was at this time a 'Derby Day' and the attendances at these matches compared favourably with some of those achieved during their spell as a Football League club. Admission to the ground could then be obtained for 1d. and 2d. The players were pure amateurs who paid their own expenses, but judging from a minute passed by the committee in March 1890, it was evident that at times that team selection was of a last-minute nature. The entry in the minute book read as follows: "That any member picked, and not sending word by Thursday night to the secretary of their inability to play, unless in a very unfit state of health, or impossible through the calls of business, will be fined sixpence."

The club finances were never really in a flourishing condition, and another minute passed in May 1890, revealed an unusual item of expenditure: "That J. Littler look after the balls, and that he is paid 2s. 6d. at the end of the season." One of the club's players, W. Gee, was an enthusiastic footballer, and used to walk from Whalley Bridge to Hayfield, and was then met by a horse and trap sent over the moors to carry him to the ground, a distance of eight miles. In season 1893-94 the Glossop North End XI succeeded in winning the cup and championship of the North Cheshire League. It was during the North Cheshire League days that Mr. Hill-Wood became interested in football, and on the disbanding of the Moorfield eleven he joined the North End club, assisting the team as an outside-right. From this point the club made rapid progress, and professionalism was introduced, Mr Hill-Wood generously paying the wages of the players. On September 4th 1894, through the generosity of their patron, a new ground, named the New Pyegrove, was presented to the club, and the Sheffield Strollers attracted a gate of around £12 at the opening ceremony. From this point on, rapid progress was made, and in 1894-95 admission was obtained to the Combination. The club in season 1895-96 finished third in the table with twenty-one points. Only fourteen matches were played, nine were won, three drawn and two lost, with thirty-three goals scored and thirteen conceded. Attendances began to grow, and in a Combination match against Ashton North End £33 was taken at the gates - a record at that time. Under the management of Mr. J.W. Sykes, a Football League linesman, the club gained admission to the Midland League in 1896-97. With William Storer as captain (the Derbyshire and England wicket keeper and former Derby County footballer), the team finished as runners-up to Doncaster Rovers for the championship. In the following season the club finished in fourth place in the Midland League table. Tom Bartley, a clever centre forward who proved a most successful goal scorer, was capped by Wales. He was the first Glossop playing member to receive international recognition. Arthur Goddard represented the Football League against the Irish League at Woolwich in season 1901-02 and Archie Goodall won the last two of his ten Irish caps whilst on Glossop's books in 1904.

Few of the club's supporters, if any, expected that the season of 1898-99 would prove to be the most momentous in the club's history. Application had been made for admission to the Lancashire League, the club had been admitted, and the necessary deposit of £25 had been paid. However, owing to the intended extension of the Second Division of the Football League, the Glossop North End club were invited to make application for one of the vacancies. The outcome was that, along with Barnsley, Burslem Port Vale and New Brighton Tower, they were elected. Naturally, the club were willing to sacrifice their £25 deposit to the Lancashire League and the foresight of the executive in accepting the main chance was justified.

Season 1898-99

The team played brilliantly throughout their first season in the Football League and succeeded in finishing second to Manchester City with 46 points, earning a place in the First Division, to the exclusion of Sheffield Wednesday and Bolton Wanderers. The greatest excitement prevailed throughout the month of April, and it was only the failure of New Brighton Tower at Leicester Fosse, and the success of Glossop against Loughborough Town on the last Saturday of the season that placed Glossop in the runners-up position by a one-point margin over Leicester Fosse. The team that met with such unexpected but most acceptable success was: Williams; McEwen, Rothwell; Colville, Clifford, Killean; Colvin, Gallacher, Donaldson, Price, Lumsden.

The team also enjoyed an excellent run in the FA Cup, defeating New Brighton Tower (4-2), Crewe Alexandra (1-0), Stockport County (2-0) but were then defeated by Newcastle United (0-1) at North Road, where the club had taken up its quarters on admission to the Second Division, the ground having previously been the headquarters of the old Rugby club.

During 1899 the club was formed into a limited liability company.

1898-99, start of season. Back row: Unknown (in bowler hat), Cawson (trainer), unknown (flat cap), Colville, Rothwell, Clifford, Williams, unknown (flat cap, at back), unknown player (possibly Lomax), McEwen, Dale (manager, slightly to front), S Hill-Wood (with homburg). Front: Oliver (director), Gallacher, unknown, Donaldson, unknown, Lumsden. The unknown players in the front row may be Bartley and Tinto.

1898-99, end of season Standing, all persons left to right: Causer (trainer), Miller, unknown (at back), Sutcliffe, Elliott, Colvin, Orr, Colville, Rothwell, Clifford, Williams, Killean, Gallacher, McEwen, Dale (manager), unknown (at back), Oliver (director). Front: Gallacher, Donaldson, Connachan, McCosh, Lumsden

Season 1899-1900

It was decided that to avoid clashing in any degree with the name of Preston North End, long-standing members of the First Division, that the words 'North End' should be dropped from the title of the club, which would in future be known by the simpler title of the Glossop Football Club. At a Council Meeting of the Football Association held in London on 11th August 1899, the change was sanctioned and North End were given permission to change their name to Glossop F.C.

The prospects of the newly named club aroused more than ordinary curiosity in the football world. Having reached the 'charmed circle' of the First Division, it was pointed out that more than one team in the Division could boast of an average attendance in excess of the entire population of the Glossop district. Nevertheless, it was felt that Mr. George H. Dale, secretary and manager of the club, who so greatly distinguished himself last season, would guide the club to at least a fair measure of prosperity in Division One.

Sadly, the season proved to be a disastrous one. To all appearances the team had been materially strengthened, but disaster followed disaster, and at the end of the season the club had lost its place in the First Division, only eighteen points having been obtained. The season opened with a victory against Burnley (2-0) at home, but on the following Monday the team were slaughtered 9-0 by Aston Villa at Villa Park. Another victory was obtained at North Road against Nottingham Forest (3-0) in September, but a full three months elapsed before another was recorded, when Aston Villa were beaten 1-0 on 16th December. Between times, further misfortune in the shape of a hurricane passed over the Glossop district in early November with the football club sustaining the biggest loss. A large stand, recently installed at a cost of £40 was lifted bodily by the gale, overturned and smashed. Most of the fencing around the enclosure was also wrecked. At about the same time, players Colville and Clifford asked for an increase in salary. A meeting of the Glossop committee considered their request unjustified, and following the decision, both players were seen leaving town, taking luggage with them. Happily, they were quickly returned to the fold, but whether their salary demands were met was not made public.

The New Year opened with a trip to Newcastle. In a match played in dense fog, Glossop were leading 3-2 and seemingly heading for their first away win of the season, when the game was abandoned fifteen minutes from time. Mr Hill-Wood was said to be prepared to spend £1,000 to secure players capable of keeping the club in Division One, and in mid season over £600 was spent on three players, Davidson from Third Lanark, Goddard from Stockport County and Carlin from Birkenhead. Despite having, at one point, three matches in hand of the bottom two clubs, Notts County and Preston North End, there was little overall improvement in the team's displays. Blackburn Rovers were beaten 4-2 on Shrove Tuesday, but the side were then without another victory in the final eleven League matches. The melancholy record for the season read: Played 34, won 4, drawn 10, lost 20, goals for 31, against 74, points 18. The club also suffered defeat in the first round of the FA Cup; Stockport County, after drawing two goals each at North Road, won the replay by three goals to nil.

Season 1900-01

A desire to bring about economies in the administration of the club led to the services of Mr. G.H. Dale, secretary and manager of the club for the past two seasons, to be dispensed with. The club was

G.H. Dale

to be run solely by a management committee, of which Mr. Elliott was honorary secretary. A considerable change in the personnel of the team was effected, especially in regard to the forward division with Arthur Goddard the only regular member of the previous season's front line expected to find a place in a quintet strengthened by the signing of Kennedy (Stoke), Crump (late of Derby County), King (Leicester Fosse) and Chesworth (Stockport County). The Stockport club also provided a capable half back in Hall, and for the full back division, Kent (Sheffield United), who had been recommended by Foulke, the Blades' famous goalkeeper.

Of the departures, McEwen joined Bury and there was uncertainty regarding the availability of last season's captain, Rothwell, who in the event appeared in only six matches during the season. The team failed to win their way back into the First Division, finishing fifth in the table with 38 points. Of the 34 matches played, 15 were won, 8 drawn and 11 lost. 51 goals were scored against 33 conceded. Arthur Goddard became the first Glossop player to register a hat-trick in the Football League, netting all of his team's goals in a 3-1 victory against Gainsborough Trinity on 20th October. He finished the season with an ever-present record and scored 14 goals. He was transferred to Liverpool in the close season for £460. He had been signed from Stockport County for £260, a record transfer fee at the time.

Season 1901-02

Back: Oliver (director), Hadfield (director) J Goodall, Colville, McCartney, Birchenough, Norgrove, Durbar, Hall, Elliott (secretary), Charlesworth. Front (seated and kneeling): Goddard, Burgess, Crump, Rae, Parker, Dougal, Berwick (trainer)

Under the tutorship and advice of the old Derby County player, Johnny Goodall, who had taken up residence in the town, it was expect that a marked improvement in the team's results would be shown. In the event, they did less well than in the previous season, finishing in eighth position with 32 points from 34 matches. Ten were won, 12 drawn and 12 lost. Only 36 goals were scored against 40 conceded. In thirteen League matches the team failed to score, although Ivan Thornley, who scored on his debut against Blackpool, showed great promise. Fred Crump led the scoring list with 12 goals in 31 matches. A better run in the FA Cup than last season, when the side went out 1-0 at Stoke, saw the side reach the first round proper, beating St Helens (5-2), Nantwich (3-1), Stockport County (2-0) and Leicester Fosse (1-0) before losing 1-3 against Nottingham Forest.

The Nottingham Evening Post carried a report of the game. Forest travelled by the Great Central route to Glossop, and were followed by a good number of supporters. Snow fell heavily during the night, leaving six inches on the ground. The pitch had been cleared through the efforts of a staff of 70 workmen, but it afforded heavy going. The weather was bitterley cold at the start. Goodall won the toss, and Calvey kicked off for Forest, facing a driving snow storm. Forest took the lead after 10 minutes, when Morris scored following excellent work by Spouncer, Birchenough in the Glossop goal misjudging the shot. Glossop were level 10 minutes later when Hall carried the ball to the left wing, and passed to Goddard, who beat the Forest goalkeeper with a fine shot from 30 yards. Frank Foreman then gave the "Reds" the lead with a splendid shot before half-time. The first period of the second half was marked by Glossop adopting "the one back game", which had the effect of throwing the visiting forwards offside almost every time they attacked. Glossop's Hall and Goodall received injuries and had to leave the field. Morris scored the third goal for Forest with a few minutes remaining. The gate was £65.

Season 1902-03

Back: Pell, Clark, J Goodall, Berwick (trainer), Jack. Front: Burgess, Coates, Badenoch,
Norgrove (at front), McCartney (behind), Murphy

Of the new players signed for the season, quite a few were new to League football, but arrived with the reputation of being very capable players. The best of the newcomers were Clarke, a goalkeeper and Pell a right half back, both from Northampton Town. Coates, from Hyde, had a splendid season missing only two matches. The fact that both Manchester City and Manchester United were in the same Division was expected to result in greatly increased attendances when the two famous clubs visited the North Road enclosure. Projected expenditure was cut down by the abolition of the reserve team, which had been run at a loss since the club started. Mr S. Hill-Wood, who had stood by the club for many years, remained determined that the public of Glossop should have the best of football. Unfortunately, the team sank into the eleventh position after a dismal opening to the season that saw them without a victory after nine League matches. They then rallied, winning six of the next eight matches, but on 11th January they suffered a club record defeat of 10-0 at Chesterfield. The season's record was: Played 34, won 11, drawn 7, lost 16, goals for 43, against 58.

The club again negotiated the qualifying rounds of the FA Cup with wins against Crewe Alexandra (3-0), Wrexham (4-0), St. Helens Recreation (5-0), New Brompton (2-1), before suffering defeat to Stoke by 2-3. The Glossop officials considered that they continued to be unfairly treated by the Football Association, once again being made to qualify for the FA Cup. During the last five seasons they had had only once failed to reach the competition proper, and had only been knocked out by narrow margins by such clubs as Nottingham Forest, Newcastle United and Stoke (twice).

Season 1903-04

For the new season, the ground was carefully overhauled and re-laid, and new drainage installed. In late August the playing pitch said to be "in the pink of condition". The newly formed Glossop United Club, members of the Manchester League, shared the facilities of the Glossop club, when not required by the senior team. A practice match was arranged between the two teams, with the season proper opening on the following Saturday with Burton United the visitors to North Road. The match most looked forward to by the Glossop public, however, was the visit of Manchester United a fortnight later.

Despite the loss of Burgess, their clever and popular full back, who transferred his affections to Manchester City, Glossop re-engaged the majority of the players who did duty in the last campaign. Several new men included J. Hancock (Bradley Swifts), who took the place at right full back in place of Burgess. He had been tried in the last match of the previous season and showed much promise. W. Galley, a half back (Shrewsbury Town), J. Bainbridge (Sunderland Royal Rovers), S. Barnes, an outside left, who had done good work for the now defunct New Brighton Tower Club, and S. Jones (Bristol City) were the other new men who were to be trained by A. Berwick, the professional of Glossop Cricket Club. The first six matches of the season brought the disheartening return of just one point and an adverse goal average of just two scored, and nineteen conceded. The arrival of the veteran Irish international Archie Goodall in January brought about an

Samuel Hill-Wood

overall improvement to the side, who recorded a number of comprehensive victories in the final three months of the campaign, including a 7-0 demolition of Barnsley and a 5-0 victory against Leicester Fosse in the penultimate fixture of the season.

Gainsborough Trinity were the final visitors to North Road, and a win for Glossop might just have been enough to scrape them clear of the last three on goal average, but they failed to make the best use of their chances, suffering defeat by two goals to nil. The absence of Irvine Thornley and Frank Norgrave – transferred to Manchester City – was greatly felt, and the club's final placing of seventeenth obliged them to seek re-election. The season's miserable record read: 34 matches played, 10 won, 6 drawn. 18 lost, goals for 57, against 64, points 26.

Further misfortune, which had for some time been looming on the Glossop horizon now overtook the club. The Football Association caused an inquiry to be held into the club's affairs, several players and four directors were suspended, and the club fined £250. Mr S. Hill-Wood, the founder and great patron of Glossop came to the rescue of the club and subscribed £200 towards the fine, while the public managed to raise the remaining £50. The bare facts of this serious matter surrounded irregularities in the transfer of players Thornley and Norgrave to Manchester City, and in regard to amateur players being paid for their services. The commissioners found that Glossop kept two cash books and two bank accounts, the same "with intent to deceive", according to the report of the commissioners. In addition to paying amateurs, the club handed over cash bonuses to certain of their professionals for re-signing, and further bonuses to the players after certain League matches so as to encourage them in the future. The press of the time considered the sentences imposed as excessively severe, but accepted that their purpose was to deter others from similarly corrupt practices.

Season 1904-05

Back: Berwick (trainer), Synott, Davies, Orr, Sutcliffe (secretary). Centre: Phillips, Gall, Cairns, A Goodall, Murphy, Lawrence. Front: Brown, Boden, Maginnis

With re-admission to the League gained, the campaign began with a new lease of life. Sweeping changes were made. Archie Goodall took over the management of the team, and secured the services of several well-known players. For the forward line they included Fred Spikesley, the England international wingman from Sheffield Wednesday; Cairns, the Scottish junior international from Raith Rovers; Lawrence from Fulham; Gall from Belfast Celtic and Brown from Stalybridge Rovers. For the middle line Phillips (Alloa Athletic), and McGuinness (Belfast Celtic). For the full back berths Synott (Belfast Celtic) and Orr, a former Glossop player, returned after five years away with Manchester City and Fulham. To replace goalkeeper Clarke, transferred to Bristol Rovers, Frank Davies was signed from Derby County. The signings of the trio of Irishmen (Gall, McGuinness and Synott), led to an allegation of 'poaching' by the Irish Football Association, but this proved to be unfounded. Secretary Mr. J.R. Sutcliffe reported an increased demand for season tickets and the season opened with a promising 2-2 draw at Liverpool, new signings Gall and Cairns scoring on their debuts. Just prior to Christmas, Glossop United resigned their membership of the Manchester League, and at a meeting of the League Committee it was revealed that Glossop F.C. had taken over the liabilities of the club. They stated, that under certain circumstances, they were prepared to fulfil United's remaining fixtures. The offer was not accepted, however, due to the league's rules in respect of wage limits for professional footballers. At the turn of the year, a 1-0 away win at Burslem Port Vale was only the second win in ten matches, the side's lack of goals instanced by their record of just fourteen goals scored in seventeen League engagements. The mid term signing of 'Kiltie' Cameron from Renton increased the striking power of the team, lifting the side to a position of twelfth in the table with the following record: Played 34, won 10, drawn 10, lost 14, Goals for 36, against 46, points 30. Jack Boden's form throughout the season had not gone unnoticed; in May he joined Clapton Orient, who were ordered to pay £200 for his transfer.

Season 1905-06

For this season, secretary Mr. J.R. Sutcliffe took over from team manager Archie Goodall, the former Derby County half-back, who was not re-engaged. On August 5th, the first trial match of the season featured two teams of entirely new players, from various parts of the country, who had applied for trials for positions in the new Combination XI that was to be run this season. In August Mr. Sutcliffe advised the *Athletic News* correspondent that: "The team are practicing daily, and are expected to form one of the strongest combinations in the League."

The reasons behind the high expectations were difficult to justify, considering that they had lost the services of several good men in J. Hunt (to Derby County), J. Boden (to Clapton Orient) E. Murphy (to Bury) and T. Cairns, who had returned to Belfast Celtic. Their replacements included Edgar Chadwick, the veteran England international, last season with Blackpool; Whitehouse, the

William Ross

Stoke inside-right; Carr, a diminutive inside-left from Renton, and Ross, outside-left from Grimsby Town. For the half back line, McNab of Motherwell and Mair, the Scottish Junior international of Glasgow Ashfield were signed. A strong reserve team was formed with a view to developing local talent.

The meeting with Manchester United in September 1905 produced a record attendance for the North Road ground, with a reported 10,285 inside. United's unbeaten start to the season probably meant a large number of their supporters were present. Quite how many of them could see anything of the game remains a mystery. Glossop had the well-known Corinthian amateur player and Welsh international Morgan Morgan-Owen available for the game. Tom Phillips was badly injured after 15 minutes play and had to leave the field. Davies was in good form in the Glossop goal, and 70 minutes went by without either team scoring. Then two quick goals, from Beddows and Ball, appeared to give United a comfortable lead. With a few minutes remaining, Cameron scored for Glossop from a pass by Ross, and came close to an equaliser in the final moments.

In terms of Division Two football, and despite the signing of the noted Scotland international J.T. Robertson as player-manager in mid-season, the slippery pole was again descended, 28 points obtaining sixteenth position in the League, a re-admission application only avoided on goal average. It could be said that they were their own worst enemy, instanced by events in March. In view of the team's precarious League position, it was decided to send the players away to Matlock for special training. However, several players committed breaches of club rules and were sent home, their places being filled with reserve team players. The season's record was: Played 38, won 10, drawn 8, lost 20, goals for 49, against 71, points 28. D. Mair made the most appearances, missing only one match, leading goal scorers were Cameron (13 in 32 matches) and Ross (11 in 21 matches).

There were exotic visitors in the F.A. Cup, after Glossop were drawn against Brighton & Hove Albion from the Southern League. Yates gave Brighton the lead in the 53rd minute, and an "open goal" miss by Brown was the nearest the home club came to an equaliser. A subsequent enquiry was held to consider the allegation that Brighton had illegally approached Glossop players before the game. As a consequence, Albion's secretary-manager was suspended for 4 months, and four players, including Glossop's Ross, were each fined £2 for their part in the scam. The match referee was suspended for nine months for "having acted as a football agent and seeking payment for his services in introducing players".

Season 1906-07

Back: Berwick (trainer), Robottom, Cuffe, Tustin, McEwan, Kelly, McDiarmid, Sutcliffe (secretary). Front: Callaghan, McKie, Napier, McMillan, Fyfe, Ross, Mair.

Another season and again Glossop came up smiling, full of determination to do better than before. In August, the Football Association gave Glossop permission to donate the funds realised from their pre-season practice matches to the Glossop Cricket Club, who were struggling with debts of about £340, due to poor gate receipts. The best of the previous season's men who were retained numbered just seven; they were: Frail, goalkeeper; Cuffe, full back; Mair and McDiarmid, half backs; Callaghan, McKie and Ross, forwards. Among the departed were goalkeeper F. Davies to Manchester City; their best forward Cameron to Bolton Wanderers; J. Dargue to the Airdrieonians, D. McCartney to Chelsea and Edgar Chadwick to Darwen. To fill the vacancies, new signings included W.A. Tustin, goalkeeper, late of Kidderminster and with the reputation of: "Being one of the best custodians in the Birmingham League last season." The half backs included Horace Rowbothom, latterly with Brentford; Tom Kelly of Talke United, who was considered one of the most promising half backs in the North Staffordshire League. Also for the intermediate line, Patrick Galvin was signed from Oldham Athletic. The forward line was greatly strengthened by the signing of John McMillan, from Bradford City, who was considered the best of the new captures. New forwards also included James Fyfe from Alloa Athletic and Sam Napier the Irishman from Bolton Wanderers. The season commenced with a trip to Chelsea, whose goalkeeper Mick Byrne – later with Glossop – had a relatively quiet afternoon. At the other end, Glossop's custodian Joe Frail was under siege for ninety minutes. Chelsea's centre forward George Hilsdon scoring five in the Pensioners' 9-2 win. It was quickly obvious that Glossop had once again failed to get together a team worthy of the patronage of their great benefactor, Mr. Samuel Hill-Wood. Throughout the campaign, the team were poor travellers, winning only twice away from North Road. The club could only finish 15th in the table with 32 points, although their record was slightly better than the previous season's record of 28 points. 13 matches were won, 6 drawn and 19 lost. 53 goals were scored and 79 conceded. Sam Napier headed the scoring list with 14 goals in 27 matches. In the FA Cup competition, an offer of £20 plus half of the gate receipts failed to tempt Newhall Swifts, a team from the Burton district, to switch the venue to Glossop. The Swifts held out for £30 and half of the gate money, an amount that Glossop did not feel justified in paying. In the event, Glossop travelled and won 2-1, but they could not repeat the performance when drawn away at Brentford in the next round, losing by 2-1.

Season 1907-08

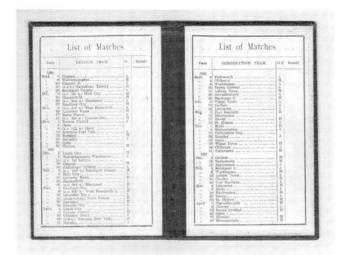

The members card for 1907-08 included the season's fixtures

Practically a new team was secured for the upcoming campaign and enthusiasts in the North Derbyshire town were expecting a much more successful time. Manager Robertson felt that he had assembled a team capable of holding its own against any club in the Second Division, and one that would make a bold fight for promotion. Only five of the previous season's team remained: Tustin, Cuffe, McEwen, Galvin and McMillan. Callaghan and Napier were resigned, but transferred to Manchester City and Linfield respectively. Other notable departures were McKie and Mair to the new Bradford Park Avenue club; McDiarmid to Clyde, Kelly to Denaby United, while Dr. Waddell returned to Cliftonville. The new men included Byrne (Chelsea; goalkeeper); Comrie (Reading; centre half); McGregor (Grimsby Town; right half); Weir (Reading; left half); Gettings (Reading; outside right); Bradshaw (Lancaster Town; inside-right); McKenzie (Portsmouth; centre forward); Copeland (Chelsea; inside left); Gould (Bristol Rovers (inside left) and Tufnell (Worcester City outside left.

Whilst supporters of the club had become accustomed to seeing their favourites occupying a lowly League position, the opening two months of the season were bitterly disappointing. Without a victory in the first eight matches, the side finally roused themselves during the month of December with a 3-0 win against West Stanley in the FA Cup, followed by an astonishing 7-3 win at Chesterfield; a 3-1 home win against Burnley; a 2-1 win against Clapton Orient on Christmas Day and a goalless draw against Oldham Athletic at Boundary Park. On January 11th, a crowd of 6,500 packed into North Road for the first round FA Cup-tie against Division One neighbours, Manchester City. Led by former Glossop favourite Irvine Thornley, City were strong favourites to progress to round two, but they were held to a goalless draw before progressing, thanks to a 6-0 win in the replay at Hyde Road that attracted a crowd of 20,000. In late season, 'doubles' completed against Lincoln City and Chesterfield eased the League position but the final placing of 17th was only obtained on goal average over Grimsby Town to ensure that a re-election application was avoided. Of the 38 matches played, 11 were won, 8 drawn and 19 lost. Goals for: 54, against: 74, points: 30. Jimmy Robertson missed only one League match and headed the scoring list with 17 goals, his total including four in one match against Hull City at North Road on November 9th.

Season 1908-09

Back: W Hankinson, LG Hunter, Raine, Hofton, Kelly, Butler, Gettins, Morrison, WR Sutcliffe (secretary).
Centre: McMillan (trainer), Cuffe, Robertson, S. Hill Wood (chairman), H Stapley, Greechan, Underwood.
Front: McGregor, Weir.

During the close season a few alterations were made to the North Road enclosure. A little extra banking was done behind the goal near to the main entrance, but very careful attention was paid to the playing surface, which was in splendid condition when the first Thursday evening practice game was staged, giving supporters a first look at several new men, in addition to practically the whole of last-season's players who were re-engaged. The most notable departure was that of goalkeeper Tustin, to Brighton & Hove Albion. As the local correspondent noted: "Until they turn out, the Glossop eleven will be a very uncertain quantity." Nevertheless, the new signings coupled with the promise of assistance from several notable amateurs, suggested that they were fairly well prepared for the new season. Butler was retained for goal, with another ex-Stockport County man in A. Warsley signed as understudy. Cuffe and Gettins, of the full backs, were retained with E.A. Harvey of New Brompton and F.H. Milnes of the 'Pilgrims' and ex-Sheffield United the new men. The choice for the half back line included retained players McGregor, Comrie and Weir, with L. Hofton of Denaby United expected to challenge strongly for a place in the intermediate division. There was plenty of choice for the forward line with seven of last season's men retained, whilst newcomers included H.S. Stapley, of West Ham United, the amateur international centre forward; C. Copeland of the 'Pilgrims', inside right; T.H. Underwood, of Brentford, outside left and G. Blackburn, outside right, of Denaby United. The reserves continued in the Second Division of the Lancashire Combination, continuing their efforts to win promotion to the premier section.

Although the club was never seriously involved in the hunt for promotion, they were widely considered to be the best side assembled since Glossop had run through the Second Division in 1898-99. Bolton Wanderers, Tottenham Hotspur and West Bromwich Albion were the strongest sides in the Division. Only one point and goal average separating them in the first three places in the table. Glossop's first meeting with the eventual champions, at North Road on 28th November, was not for the faint hearted. In a bruising encounter, won 2-0 by the visitors, referee Mr. W.

Gilgryst sent off both of Glossop's full backs, Cuffe and Hofton, plus Marsh of Bolton Wanderers. The North Road ground was ordered closed until December 31st, and the commission expressed the opinion that more than four uniformed policemen should have been employed on the ground. A much-improved Glossop defence conceded only 53 League goals in 38 matches and two goals in six FA Cup-ties. H.S. Stapley rounded off a successful season by netting a hat trick against Birmingham in a 3-1 win, taking his season's total to an impressive 19 goals in 31 League matches. Goalkeeper Joe Butler appeared in all matches throughout the season, the first of four 'ever present' campaigns and an outstanding record of 152 consecutive League appearances before joining Sunderland in 1912-13 and winning a League Championship and FA Cup runners-up medal in his first season at Roker Park. Glossop's most successful campaign since 1900-01, when they finished fifth, ended in eighth position in the Second Division. Their record for the season was: Played 38, won 15, drawn 15, lost 8. Goals for: 57, against: 53. Points 38.

Season 1909-10

For once, the customary pre-season optimism appeared to be well justified. Judging from the class of the new men secured, the president, Mr. Samuel Hill-Wood, was expected to come very near, if not realise, his ambition of seeing the 'Peakites' once more featuring in the premier division. The directors retained practically the whole of last season's side: Butler, Hofton, Cuffe, McGregor, Morrison, Wilson, along with the three crack amateurs, H.S. Stapley, J.E.Raine and I.G.Sharpe. Two of last season's regulars were amongst the departed – Jimmy Robertson moved south to join Leyton and Weir was one of three players to join Stockport County. The other two were Gettings and Greechan, who were both seen in the first team on several occasions last season. Elmore, a reserve team player, moved on to Blackpool. Of rather more significance, manager J.T. Robertson resigned his post as team manager and accepted the position of reserve team manager of

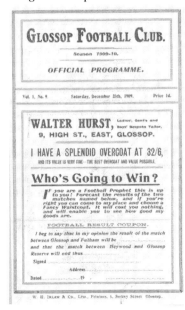

The programme for Glossop's game on Xmas Day 1909

Manchester United. Another missing face was trainer McMillan, who was appointed in a similar position by the Birmingham club. His position was filled by the re-appointment of Alf Berwick, for many seasons the professional of Glossop Cricket Club. Having earlier stated that the president, Mr Hill-Wood, would take charge of team management, a change occurred in August when David Weir was appointed to the post. Weir had played for Bolton Wanderers for ten years as a forward, joining them in 1885. In addition to playing for Lancashire in inter-county games he was capped by England in 1889 against Scotland and Ireland. Of later years he had scouted for Bolton Wanderers, and was felt well suited to his new appointment, to which he was recommended by no less a personage than Mr J.J. Bentley, president of the Football League. Among the new men were three more amateurs, and all of the highest order. T.T. Fitchie, last season with Woolwich Arsenal, and who did much good work at inside-left. The other two were T.C. Porter of Northern Nomads, and A.K. Campbell, of Southampton, both amateur internationals. Other new players signed included G. Henderson, right half from Chelsea; Pryce-Williams, a half back from Wrexham; A. Needham, an inside forward from Crystal Palace; G. Hamilton, right back from Wellington; L.J. Wall, inside forward from Shrewsbury Town and J. Hodkinson, outside left from Lancaster Town. Only one defeat in the first three months of the campaign owed much to the goal scoring exploits of centre forward Harry Stapley, who had registered seventeen League goals by the end of December. Four of them came on the 27th of the month in a 6-2 demolition of Oldham Athletic, who had defender Billy Cook sent off for a "foul charge" on his tormentor-in-chief, Harry Stapley.

In the return match at Boundary Park on New Year's Day an improved defensive display by the Latics saw them take the points in a 1-0 win. This proved to be a pivotal result for both clubs. Oldham Athletic lost only one more match all season and won promotion to the premier division, while Glossop's season fell into sad disarray, a further ten defeats in the final eighteen League matches left the team in a disappointing sixth place in the table with the following record: Played 38, won 18, drawn 7, lost 13. Goals for: 64, against 57, points 43. Goalkeeper Butler was the only 'ever present' throughout the season; Harry Stapley was leading scorer with 23 in 32 appearances. Some consolation for the club's directors was supplied by the reserve team who carried off the championship of the Second Division of the Lancashire Combination with an outstanding season's record of: Played 38, won 29, drawn 5, lost 4, Goals for: 120, against: 35. Points 63. On February 7th, a local hero returned to Glossop. Irvine Thornley, Manchester City's star forward, was married at St James' Church to Miss Emma Sykes of Glossop, youngest daughter of the late Mr John Sykes, former landlord of the George and Dragon Hotel, Woodhead.

Season 1910-11

With all of the amateurs still available and a good supply of local talent, the directors felt that they would have little difficulty in selecting a team capable of putting up a good fight for promotion. The management also resolved to run a strong reserve eleven to meet additional local interest, following their elevation to the First Division of the Lancashire Combination. Two of last season's 'regulars', Morrison and Needham, departed in the close season. The former crossed the border to join Clyde, while Needham had transferred to Wolverhampton Wanderers. By late August, five new men had been signed, all with youth on their side, and said to be of much promise. A.H. Causer, who last season kept goal for Dudley in the Birmingham League, was secured as understudy to Butler. Two recruits from Arbroath were G. Willock, outside right, and E. McDonald inside right. W. Milne, a centre forward from Montrose, and another attack leader or inside forward, A. Tomkinson of Leek United.

With home form inconsistent and with little joy from their travels, it was quickly apparent that any hopes of an improvement on last season's showing was not going to happen. Three wins within the space of four matches in November and December, results that included the first away win at Birmingham, lifted hopes which quickly came down with the Christmas decorations following a 6-0 defeat at Bradford Park Avenue on Boxing Day. A final League placing of 14th reflected the sides' lack of firepower, as in 14 of 38 League matches they failed to find the net although Harry Stapley again led the line effectively, scoring 15 goals in 38 appearances. Goalkeeper Joe Butler again appeared in every match. Clare Wilson's consistent displays at left half took his Glossop career total to 96 matches, form that earned him an upward move to First Division Oldham Athletic during the following season. Of 38 matches played, 13 were won, 8 drawn and 17 lost. 48 goals were scored and 62 conceded.

The reserve team, winners of the Lancashire Combination Division Two championship in the previous season, did less well in the premier division finishing in 17th position in the table with 35 points from 38 matches. In the close season they resigned their membership and joined the newly formed Central League.

Season 1911-12

Practically all of last season's players were engaged, the exceptions being Craigie, who was transferred to Fulham, and Milne, who joined Blackpool. Three new players were signed, the most prominent being Goldie, the Fulham left half, who was reported to have cost "a substantial sum". The other two were F. Groves, an amateur outside right from Barnet Alston, a London club, and J. Moore an inside forward from Cradley Heath of the Birmingham League. In another season of poor support, the side proved quite incapable of holding their own in the first half of the season and only escaped having to apply for re-election to the League by the narrow margin of goal average. Improved performances in the second half of the season, however, included a 3-1 win against the eventual champions, Derby County; a 6-0 defeat of Leicester Fosse, and a 5-2 victory against Grimsby Town in which Moore scored four of the goals. The Birmingham born inside left, who was reintroduced into the League side in late January, ended his first season of senior football with a flourish, scoring 13 goals in 17 matches. He also took over from Harry Stapley as leading goal scorer, totalling 14 in 23 matches. Injury sidelined Stapley, who missed the final five matches of the campaign, but his 13 goals in 33 matches was a vital contribution in a season when the next highest scorer was Berwick with four goals. An eventful encounter with Chelsea at North Road on 6th April ended in defeat by 2-1. Glossop lost the services of W. Stapley with a broken leg after ten minutes play in the second half. In the last minute of the game the referee awarded Chelsea a penalty for hands by Goldie. Goalkeeper Butler saved Whittingham's spot kick, but due to an infringement, the referee ordered the kick to be retaken. The enraged Butler rushed menacingly to the referee, Mr Garner of Barnsley, who without hesitation sent goalkeeper off. Cuffe went into goal and was beaten by Whittingham at the second attempt. When time was called, the referee was several times struck by a howling mob of Glossop supporters, several policemen surrounding the official beat back the crowd with their truncheons. The season's record was: Played 38, won 8, drawn 12, lost 18. goals for: 42, against 56, points: 28. Two players made maximum appearances, goalkeeper Butler and outside left Hodkinson.

Season 1912-13

The most noticeable absentees from last season were goalkeeper Joe Butler, who had completed an impressive club record of 161 consecutive appearances prior to joining Sunderland. Full back Heywood who stepped down into Lancashire Combination circles with Nelson, and Goldie who departed after one season to join Bury. Another departure was that of honorary-secretary, Mr J.R. Sutcliffe in late October. He had served the club for ten years, but his resignation came about because he was unable to see eye-to-eye with the club's management. Continuing lack of support limited recruitment of new players to four, all without League experience. Pick of the bunch was E. Cooper the former Stafford Rangers outside right, whose displays quickly attracted the attention of bigger clubs, Newcastle United paying £1,375 for his services in March 1913. Two months earlier, outside left Joe Hodkinson had been transferred to Blackburn Rovers for a fee of £1,000. Despite losing both wingmen, the side found some form in January and February to draw away from the danger zone. After three seasons in which the side were knocked out of the FA Cup in the first round, the pattern continued (0-2 v Crystal Palace) but being obliged to play in qualifying rounds for the first time since 1907-08, they won against Ripley Town & Athletic by 2-0 and followed by posting their record victory in the competition, 11-1 against Southall, who had taken the lead in the first minute; the soon to be departed Cooper scoring five of Glossop's goals. As was the case in the previous season, Glossop finished in 18th position in the table. Their record being: Played 38, won 12, drawn 8, lost 18. Goals for: 49, against: 68. Points 32. For the second successive season, J. Moore led the scoring list with 17 goals in 35 League matches. He had a particularly successful time against Leicester Fosse, scoring all four goals in the 4-1 win at Filbert Street on Boxing Day, and a hat trick in the 3-0 victory at North Road in the return fixture on 21st March.

Season 1913-14

Back: Barnett, Montgomery, Littlewort, Hampton, W Stapley, Dearnaley, Berwick (trainer), Causer, McEwen (manager), Carney. Front: Turnell, Bowden, Doncaster, Bamford, Knight

If the playing record of the previous season had been nothing to write home about, from a financial point of view it was the most successful in the history of the club, for at the close of the season there was a balance in hand of £1,375. This sum being the combined total of the transfer fees received for Butler, Williams, Hodkinson and Cooper. Another brush with the Football Association was punished with a fine of £100 plus a serious warning as to the club's future conduct, stating that: "If rules are not properly observed in future it will be necessary to order disbandment of the club." Commenting on the inquiry, the local press had this to say: "I cannot see what it matters to the FA if Mr Hill-Wood chooses to find employment in his mill for men who excel at sport." Finances were still in a healthy condition after summer wages and other close season expenses had been met, a substantial balance in hand amounting to around £700 being reported. Despite the relative affluence, manager McEwen's recruiting for the new season was again centred upon players new to League football and sadly the four recruits made only 17 first team appearances between them. Four consecutive defeats in September set the tone for another season spent in the shadow of a re-election application. Some relief came, however, when the FA Cup competition commenced with easy home victories in two qualifying rounds against Hinckley United (by 5-1) and Carlisle United (4-1). The luck of the draw continued with a home tie versus Everton in which goals by Montgomery and Barnett helped secure a famous 2-1 victory against the First Division opponents. Drawn at home again against Preston North End, another First Division side, but one in the lower reaches of the table, another upset was on the cards but a single goal by Preston's centre forward Fred Osborne took North End through to round three. At the end of the season Preston North End were relegated to Division Two where Glossop once again narrowly avoided a re-election application, their season lifted in early April by the appointment of the famous England international Tom Crawshaw, of

Sheffield Wednesday fame, as secretary-manager. As the *Athletic News* reported: "Under his generalship the shoals were cleared." It was a narrow escape, however, the side finishing 17th in the table with the following record: Played 38, won 11, drawn 6, lost 21. Goals for: 51, Against 67. Points 28. Right half J. Montgomery was the only player to complete 38 League appearances during the season. Having lost Jimmy Moore, their leading goal scorer of the past two seasons, to Derby County in a £1,500 transfer in October, the ever-reliable Harry Stapley headed the scoring list with 13 goals in 30 appearances. Bob Thompson, a mid season signing from Preston North End, scored four goals in his third appearance against Barnsley in a 5-1 win on March 14th, and his seven goals in 10 appearances was a vital contribution in the team's escape from the foot of the table.

Season 1914-15

Back: Dearnaley, Montgomery, Allen, Causer, Ward, Martin. Front: Toward, Sharpe, Thompson, Gadsby, Knight.

In the face of much opposition, the Football Association and the Football League both determined to adhere to their programmes, at the same time giving the War Office every facility in the work of recruiting for Lord Kitchener's army. A greater portion of last season's players were re-engaged, although a sign of the times was the loss of centre forward Stuart Doncaster, called up to join the colours. Other outgoing transfers included full back George Hampton to Aston Villa; Albert Barnett to Cardiff City, while the two 'Alfs', A.A. Thompson and A.H. Fletcher migrated south to Woolwich Arsenal. Of the new players signed, the most prominent was Ernie Gadsby, an inside forward who was last season with Worksop Town, but better know as one of the Barnsley forwards in their first FA Cup Final in 1910. Two players from the Castleford Town club were Blakey Martin who was destined to score Glossop's last goal in the Football League, and William Ward, a well-built full back who completed 19 League appearances during the season. Heavy defeats both at home and away by Woolwich Arsenal in the first week of the season and a twelve match run spanning November to

January, when only one win was recorded, saw the side anchored at the foot of the table. Their undistinguished record at this point included a club record defeat, 11-1 at Birmingham on 23rd January. Two weeks later, the first – and only – away win of the season came at Huddersfield Town by a goal to nil. A 2-1 home win against Bristol City followed, but with a reported attendance of just 300 spectators attending, it was obvious that the Glossop public had lost patience with their under performing team. Seven consecutive defeats followed, and the final six matches of Glossop's League existence yielded just three points. Their dismal record for the season was: Played 38, won 6, drawn 6, lost 26. Goals for: 31, against 87. Points 18. Glossop's forwards failed to hit the target in 18 of the 38 League matches contested and the defence was breached in all but four matches. The only player to make maximum appearances was amateur outside left J.H. Knight. Leading goal scorer, with just seven, was R. Thompson. At the Annual Meeting of the Football League in July 1915, the president, Mr J. McKenna, reported that the voting in respect of the two vacancies to be filled in the Second Division, had resulted as follows: Chesterfield 8 votes, Darlington 4 votes, Glossop 1 vote, Leicester Fosse 33 votes, South Shields 11 votes and Stoke 21 votes. Leicester Fosse being re-elected and Stoke taking the place of Glossop, who it was felt had only managed to complete the fixtures of the 1914-15 season due to the continued financial support of their long term benefactor, Mr Samuel Hill-Wood. At the same meeting the president proposed that the normal league competition should be suspended, until it was thought desirable to reinstate it. This was agreed without further discussion. Although Glossop were no longer directly involved, the ruling for the 1915-16 season was that all professional competitions would be abandoned, but three combinations of League clubs would be formed, in Lancashire, the Midlands and London.

Wartime Football 1915 - 1919

A decision was taken to continue in the Southern Section of the Lancashire Combination, and Mr Sam Cadman, the well-known Derbyshire cricketer, was appointed trainer. In the opening fixture against Altrincham, Causer, Cuffe, Carney and W. Stapley were the only players from last season to make an appearance. In January 1916 one of the small stands on the club's North Road enclosure was blown over and wrecked in a gale. In the following month, at Tranmere Rovers, George Hardy, Glossop's full back, fractured his right leg between the knee and ankle and was taken to the Birkenhead Borough Hospital. Glossop's new secretary, in succession to Mr. J.W. Johnson, who resigned on taking up a business appointment in Nottingham, was Mr W.H. Boden of Surrey Street, Glossop. Mr Boden was a well-known figure in Football League and Lancashire Combination circles, for several seasons acting as a linesman in Divisions One and Two. In June 1916 news reached Glossop of the death of Private W. Whitehead, an old playing member of Glossop F.C. who had emigrated to Canada some nine years earlier. He was killed in action whilst serving with Princess Patricia's Regiment.

On August 8th 1917 the Manchester Evening News reported on the sad demise of the Glossop club: "A sporting link with the past is to be severed by the decision to voluntarily wind up Glossop Football Club. Mr G. Ross, of Hadfield, has been appointed liquidator, and the stands, turnstiles, refreshment bars and other properties of the club are to be sold." The article continued: "For a quarter of a century the North Derbyshire club figured in first class football, and such well-known players as Herbert Burgess, Irvine Thornley, Leslie Hofton, Jim Moore and John Cuffe graduated in its ranks. For a good number of years the club was in the Second Division, and in 1899-1900 competed in the First Division. Very meagre public support was accorded to the club after the outbreak of World War One, and this has largely contributed to the discontinuance of the club." Happily, when hostilities ceased, Major Hill-Wood was elected president of Glossop's new limited liability football club with shares valued £1 on offer, with support promised from all quarters. Mr T. Jacobs was appointed secretary, and it was decided to once again apply for membership of the Lancashire Combination. With a view to recruiting good talent, a medal competition was arranged in April 1919. The North Road ground was renovated thanks to the generosity of Lord Dovedale, and was placed at the disposal of the new club. Glossop were back in business.

THE FOOTBALL LEAGUE PLAYERS OF
GLOSSOP NORTH END/GLOSSOP F.C. 1898-1915

NOTES ON THE TEXT

For each player I have attempted to provide the following information: full names, recognised playing position, height and weight, date and place of birth, and date and place of death. It should be mentioned here that the dates of birth and death of some players have been culled from registers that only record such events in three-month periods. Hence the use (for instance) of 'January quarter 1923', denotes a span of January/February/March of that year. Also included are each player's Glossop debut, full career and biographical details, and a breakdown of appearances made and goals scored. Every player who played in a Football League match has been included. Unfortunately, it is the case that FA Cup matches of the period, and particularly the qualifying rounds of the competition, did not generate much interested and subsequently received little press coverage. Certainly in Glossop's case, one would have had a better chance to record the details of their more local cup competitions, such as the Manchester and Lancashire Senior Cup matches. Nevertheless, it has been decided to include known FA Cup appearances and goals scored against each player's record, if applicable.

ABBREVIATIONS

These have been kept to a minimum and are those in general use in works of this type:

App/s	Appearance/s
cs	close season
gl/s	Goal/s
q.v. (quod vide)	denoting a cross reference
FA	Football Association
FL	Football League
WW1	The First World War (1914-18)
KIA	Killed in action

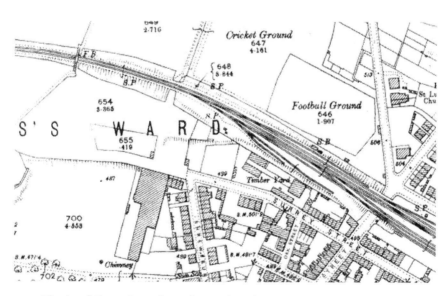

The site of Glossop's North Road ground. Today's ground is a little to the west, along the now-extended Surrey Street.

ALLEN, Albert ' Jack'

Full back
5' 9½" 11st 10lbs
Born: Moston,
Manchester, 16th
October 1891
Died: Crumpsall,
Manchester, 23rd
October 1971
Debut v Fulham
(h) 5.12.1914,
won 1-0
Career: Higher
Blackley.
Barrowfields
1910. Hurst
amateur
December 1912
to May 1921. Glossop amateur September 1914.
(Wartime guest player with Manchester City
September 1915). Southport June 1924. Crewe
Alexandra June 1925. Southport July 1926.
Lancaster Town July 1927.

Four consecutive defeats in November 1914 led to
the introduction of amateur Jack Allen at right full
back for the visit of Fulham on December 5th. In a
display described as "Cool and plucky" the recruit
from non-League football showed much promise in
the welcome 1-0 victory, and he retained his place
throughout the remainder of the season. Moving
on to Manchester City, he played in just three
matches in 1915-16   before the army claimed him,
his service as a Lieutenant including a spell of
fighting in Italy. In post war years, he made 52
League appearances for the City, with 27 matches
in 1922-23 his best seasonal return. He was also
Lancashire Senior Cup winner in May 1921. Two
separate spells with Southport, with a season with
Crewe Alexandra between, precede his transfer to
Lancaster Town, who finished runners-up to
Chorley for the championship of the First Division
in his first season at the Giant Axe. On retirement,
he worked as an insurance agent.

Appearances: FL: 23 apps 0 gls FAC: 1 app 0 gls
Total: 24 apps 0 gls
Honours: Manchester City: Lancashire Senior
Cup winners May 1921.

ARMSTRONG, Adam

Goalkeeper
Born: Chorlton, October quarter 1877
Died: Chorlton, October quarter 1905
Debut v Bury (a) 11.11.1899, lost 1-2
Career: Rochdale. Glossop April 1899.

One of three different goalkeepers fielded during
Glossop's single season in the top flight, when they
finished nine points adrift of Burnley at the foot of
the table. They also had the worst defensive record
of the eighteen clubs in the division, conceding 74
goals in 34 matches. Armstrong deputised twice for

Richard Williams before the ex Everton and Luton
Town custodian lost out when Herbert
Birchenough was signed from Burslem Port Vale.
In his two outings, Armstrong was described as
"Cool and plucky" and he created a highly
favourable impression on his first team debut at
Bury. The match was played in near gale force
winds, and with the assistance of the elements
Bury were two goals ahead at the interval, a score
line that was only kept to a reasonable level thanks
to the outstanding display of the rookie goalkeeper
and his overworked backs, Orr and Rothwell.
Attacking the Cemetery End in the second half,
Glossop's forwards reduced the arrears through
Connachan, but failed to find an equaliser, relying
too much on long range shooting.

Appearances: FL: 2 apps 0 gls Total: 2 apps 0 gls

BADENOCH, George Huntly

Outside right
Born: Castle Douglas,
Kirkcudbrightshire,
9th April 1882
Died: K.I.A., Givenchy,
France, 15th June 1915
Debut v Newton Heath
(h) 19.10.1901,
drawn 0-0
Career: Douglas
Wanderers. Heart of
Midlothian. Glossop 14th
October 1901. Watford
August 1903. Tottenham Hotspur 4th May 1906.
Northampton Town 3rd May 1907 to cs 1909.
Indian Head (Canada).

George Badenoch's first senior club was Heart of
Midlothian who, in season 1900-01 finished next-
to-bottom of the Scottish League Division One, but
won the Scottish Cup, beating Celtic 4-3. In the
close season, many likely players were released as
the "A" Team, a non-paying concern for many
years, was disbanded. The youthful Badenoch was
amongst several promising juniors who prospered
on leaving Tynecastle. A provider rather than a
goal scorer on his own account, his game featured
speed, pinpoint crossing from the wing and
consistency, the first 37 of his 48 Glossop
appearances being made consecutively. He
subsequently enjoyed productive spells with
Watford (80 Southern League matches and nine
goals), but played only once in the Southern
League for the Spurs, before winning the Southern
League championship with Northampton Town in
1909. He later emigrated to Canada, but lost his
life in the trenches while serving with a Canadian
Regiment in WW1.

Appearances: FL: 48 apps 6 gls FAC: 8 apps 2 gls
Total: 56 apps 8 gls
Honours: Northampton Town: Southern League
champions, 1909.

BAINBRIDGE, John Robert 'Jack'

Outside right
5' 10"   12st 0lbs
Born: New Seaham, April quarter 1880
Died: Sunderland, 17th January 1960
Debut v Burton United (h) 5.9.1903, lost 0-1
Career: Silksworth. Sunderland Royal Rovers. Glossop May 1903. Reading 9th June 1904. Portsmouth 3rd May 1906. Southampton 3rd May 1907.
Hartlepools United cs 1910. Horden Athletic.
Glossop's recruiting for season 1903-04 included several players of hefty build, and they included Bainbridge who, by the standards of the day, would have been considered a more likely candidate for the role of full back. He nevertheless proved to be a keen and forceful wingman whose chief asset was his speed off the mark. Despite being without previous League experience, he was a fixture at outside right throughout the season; along with his opposite wingman, Murphy, the pair were the only 'ever present' players during the campaign. A lengthy spell of Southern League football followed, initially with Reading who finished as runners-up for the championship in 1904-05 and additionally shared the Southern Charity Cup with Tottenham Hotspur. A second runners-up position came with Portsmouth in 1906-07, while Southampton finished third in 1908-09, Bainbridge completing 94 League and Cup appearances before returning homewards to join Hartlepools United and resuming his original occupation as a coalminer.
Appearances: FL: 34 apps 4 gls Total: 34 apps 4 gls

BAMFORD, Harold Walley 'Harry'

Left half
5' 10"   11st 7lbs
Born: Hull, October quarter 1886
Died: Le Touquet, 26th November 1915.
Debut v Clapton Orient (h) 25.1.1913, won 3-0
Career: Bitterne Guild September 1907. Southampton cs 1908. Glossop amateur October 1912.

Southampton schoolmaster Harry Bamford joined his local club from Hampshire junior football. He made very infrequent first team appearances in three seasons at the Dell, and was also largely in reserve with Glossop, but proved a capable deputy for left half Jimmy Carney in nine appearances during season 1912-13. Harry Bamford lost his life during the First World War, dying from septic poisoning after being wounded whilst serving as a Second Lieutenant with the Shropshire Light Infantry.
Appearances: FL: 15 apps 0 gls Total: 15 apps 0 gls

BARDSLEY, Edwin

Outside left   5' 8½"
Born: Denton, October quarter 1883
Died: K.I.A., Somme, 18th November 1916
Debut v Barnsley (h) 13.2.1904, won 7-0
Career: Godley St. John's. Hooley Hill. Glossop amateur 8th February, professional 16th February 1904. Stockport County 15th July 1904. Godley St. John's *circa* October 1906.
The first appearance of Bardsley coincided with the Glossop spectators enjoying the pleasant surprise of seeing their team trounce Barnsley by seven clear goals, which was the greatest victory ever achieved by the 'Peakites' in the Football League. Glossop had re-arranged their team for the visit of Barnsley to include Edwin Bardsley, their recruit from Hooley Hill, at outside-left, Murphy moving inside, causing Green to be dropped after scoring just two goals in twelve earlier appearances. Glossop were three goals up in fifteen minutes, and a few minutes before time, from a centre by Bardsley, Boden scored the seventh and last goal. Although the local correspondent felt it out of order to individualise the winning side, he nevertheless felt that Bardsley was due special praise, for in his first appearance he showed that he had the makings of a fine player. Unfortunately, he did not remain with Glossop, moving on to Stockport County in the close season. He assisted his new club to the championship of the Lancashire Combination in his first season. They also played against Glossop in the FA Cup and it actually took four matches – two uncompleted – to settle the Glossop/Stockport tie. The first was abandoned due to fog during extra-time with the score at 0-0. Five days later the sides met again and were level at 0-0 when the tie was abandoned at half time as a result of a snowstorm. When the teams managed to complete ninety minutes, a 1-1 draw at Glossop was followed by a replay at Stockport, Bardsley scoring the only goal of the match against his former colleagues to take his team through to the next round against Wrexham, whom they beat 4-0.
Appearances: FL: 10 apps 1 gl Total: 10 apps 1 gl
Honours: Stockport County: Lancashire Combination Champions 1905.

BARLOW, Arthur

Outside left

Debut v Leicester Fosse (a) 21.2.1901, won 2-1

Career: Everton 26th October 1900. Glossop 25th January 1901.

A mid season recruit from Everton, where he had failed to reach League level, Arthur Barlow was first tried at inside left, but when moved to the extreme flank he was a revelation. Within the space of five matches, spanning March and April 1901, he scored five goals. Two of them came against Blackpool in a 6-0 home win, and two against Burton Swifts in the away and home fixtures, won by Glossop 3-1 and 3-0 respectively. He also netted the winner in the 2-1 defeat of Barnsley. Such performances seemed worthy of another season at North Road, but the season's retained list, which included seven forwards, did not feature the name of Arthur Barlow. His subsequent whereabouts have not been traced, but a player of the same name joined Stalybridge Rovers on 5th June 1902.

Appearances: FL: 12 apps 5 gls Total: 12 apps 5 gls

BARNES, George

Outside left   5' 8"   11st 9lbs

Born: Liverpool, October quarter 1876

Died: Wallasey, October quarter 1946, age 70

Debut v Burton United (h) 5.9.1903, lost 0-1

Career: Rock Ferry August 1897. Darwen November 1897. Bolton Wanderers August 1898. Portsmouth 15th May 1899. New Brighton Tower 3rd May 1900. Glossop 5th July 1903. Tranmere Rovers 27th August 1904. Hoylake 5th March 1907.

Six goals in 31 appearances by George Barnes for Darwen in season 1897-98 failed to keep the 'Barley Bankers' out of the bottom two in the Second Division, but it earned him a move to Bolton Wanderers of the First Division in the close season. Sadly, another relegation battle ensued, and Barnes was released following the club's relegation to the Second Division. His next move was to Portsmouth, whose first playing strip — salmon pink shirts with maroon cuffs and collars — saw them quickly named 'The Shrimps.' It was their first season, and remarkably they won 20 out of 28 Southern League matches and finished runners-up to Tottenham Hotspur. Barnes' up-and-down career continued with a season close to his home with New Brighton Tower, and although they finished fourth in Division Two, three days before the start of the following season they shocked the football world by resigning from the League and disbanding. Some three years on, Barnes arrived at Glossop, but played in only five early season matches, with Murphy, and later Bardsley, dominating the left wing position.

Appearances: FL: 5 apps 0 gls Total: 5 apps 0 gls

BARNETT, Albert

Left half

5' 9"   11st 6lbs

Born: Altrincham, 7th January 1892

Died: Altrincham, October 1941

Debut v Fulham (h) 20.9.1913, lost 0-1

Career: Altrincham. Heywood United January 1911. Bolton Wanderers (trial) December 1911. Macclesfield. Glossop May 1913. Bolton Wanderers (trial). Cardiff City May 1914, fee £50. (Wartime guest player with Manchester United; Stockport County January 1916; Rochdale February 1916). Aberdare Athletic August 1924. Fordson's AFC coach July 1925. Wigan Borough (trial) September 1926.

Albert Barnett was born into a family large enough to field its own football team. In 1910, he and his ten brothers played a challenge match against the Wild family in Manchester. Three years later, Albert commenced his senior career with Glossop. Built on sturdy lines, with a style of play described as "dashing and robust", he played in a little over half of the matches in season 1913-14 when the side finished 17th in the Second Division. He joined Cardiff City just before the Great War, and when they were elected to the Football League in 1920, he made 18 appearances and scored one goal. He next made 22 appearances for Aberdare Athletic, but had dropped out of League football to accept a coaching appointment when he was offered a trial by the Wigan Borough club, at that time operating in the Third Division North. Sadly, in the third match of his trial, at Wrexham, he suffered a broken ankle that effectively ended his career. He then retired to return to his trade as a house plumber.

Appearances: FL: 19 apps 2 gls FAC: 2 apps 1 gl Total: 21 apps 3 gls

BARTLEY, Thomas

Outside right, or inside forward

Born: Flint, July quarter 1874

Died: Newton-le-Willows, Lancashire, 24th December 1951

Debut v Blackpool (h) 3.9.1898, won 4-1

Career: Flint 1890-96. Port Sunlight 1st September 1896. Glossop North End 13th May 1897. Stalybridge Rovers 2nd December 1898.

Llandudno Swifts 12th April 1899. Earlestown 6th September 1901. Ashton Wanderers 1902-03. Earlestown 7th October 1904 (and still with them in 1909).

Tom Bartley's best days with Glossop came before they gained entry to the Football League in season 1898-99. In earliest days, the youthful centre forward, described as "A splendid forager and a fine shot", was a Welsh Amateur Cup finalist with Flint at the age of seventeen. Some six years later, when combining his football with a labouring job in a print works, his goal scoring exploits for Glossop in the Midland League earned him his cap for Wales against England. Glossop recruited heavily for their debut in the Football League, and the centre forward berth was given to Bob Donaldson, the ex-Newton Heath and Luton Town sharpshooter. Bartley was tried on both wings and as inside right within the space of seven early season outings and perhaps unsurprisingly departed in mid term. In September 1905, Glossop, with three exceptions, sent their full League side to Earlestown in connection with a benefit for their former forward. He had settled in Lancashire and played in both the Lancashire Combination and the Lancashire League, working as a wood machinist in a wagon works in later years.

Appearances: FL: 7 apps 2 gls FAC: 1 app 1 gl Total: 8 apps 3 gls

Honours: Wales International, 1 cap v England 1898. Flint: Welsh Amateur Cup Finalist 1891.

BELL, Andrew
Centre forward
Debut v Burnley (a) 19.11.1904, lost 1-3
Career: Maybole F.C. Glossop 14th November 1904.

In two consecutive Football League appearances Andrew Bell failed to shine, finding the step up to Second Division football difficult, having previously operated in the Ayrshire and Renfrewshire League with Maybole F.C. In additional to his debut at Burnley, Bell was tried at outside left for the visit to Blackpool, but was again on the losing side; Blackpool winning 4-1. One of their goals scored by the England International inside forward Edgar Chadwick, who joined Glossop in the following season.

Appearances: FL: 2 apps 0 gls Total: 2 apps 0 gls

BELL, George
Inside left
Debut v Burnley (a) 27.4.1907, drawn 1-1
Career: Glossop amateur September 1906.

Although signed on amateur forms in September of the 1906-07 season, George Bell had a lengthy wait for his debut in the Football League. As deputy for Glossop's celebrated Scotland International player-manager, Jackie Robertson, he had a hard act to follow, but Bell had the satisfaction of assisting his

team to an unexpected share of the points at Turf Moor. During the season, Glossop picked up only eight points on their travels, their dismal 'away' record being three wins, two draws and fourteen defeats.

Appearances: FL: 1 app 0 gls Total: 1 app 0 gls

BELL, Thomas
Centre forward
Born: Kilwinning, 1875
Debut v Gainsborough Trinity (h) 20.10.1900, won 3-1
Career: Kilwinning Eglington 19th June 1895. Abercorn 22nd September 1898. Kilwinning Eglington 30th August 1900. Glossop 12th October 1900. Kilwinning Eglington 31st October 1902.

Coalminer Tom Bell first left his native Kilwinning for a spell with Abercorn, at that time operating in the Second Division of the Scottish League. In his first campaign, Abercorn finished at the bottom of the table with just nine points from 18 matches. In 1899-1900 they improved to finish sixth. In the close season, Bell departed Underwood and the 'Abbies' to return to his first love, Kilwinning Eglington, but he was shortly on the move again, joining Glossop in October 1900. To accommodate the new centre, Fred Crump was moved over to inside left, to the exclusion of Frank Chesworth. A hat trick by Arthur Goddard saw Bell off to a winning start against Gainsborough Trinity, but successive defeats against Walsall and Woolwich Arsenal led to his being dropped, and he made only one further first team appearance at outside left in the Christmas Day 1-1 draw against Chesterfield at North Road.

Appearances: FL: 4 apps 0 gls Total: 4 apps 0 gls

BERWICK, William John
Inside right   5' 9½"   12st 3lbs
Born: Northampton, July quarter 1887
Died: Glossop, October quarter 1948, age 61
Debut v Burnley (h) 2.1.1911, drawn 1-1
Career: Glossop amateur April 1910. Stockport County October 1913. (One guest appearance with Watford in WW1). Everton August 1919 to 1920.

William Berwick, the son of Glossop's trainer, Alf Berwick, began at North Road as a 22 year-old amateur inside forward. He had some time to wait for a first team opportunity, but his chance finally came as deputy for Chris Porter, the former Northern Nomads and Stockport County England amateur international. In a run of eight consecutive matches Berwick, described as "forceful and sturdily built", enjoyed a particularly good outing against the Wolves on 18th February 1911, scoring twice in Glossop's 5-1 victory, their best win of the campaign. A fair amount of first team action followed in 1911-12 – fifteen matches and four goals – but he appeared only once in 1912-13. On leaving Glossop, he did not make a

League appearance for Stockport County, and by February 1915 he was on active service with the 3rd/6th Cheshire Regiment. During four and a half years with the colours, he won four football medals, and acted as captain of the Cheshire's, also the King's Shropshires and the Western Command teams. Resuming after the war, he was listed as a right full back in Everton's playing staff, and he appeared just once, against Bolton Wanderers in a 3-3 draw in November 1919. In summer months, Berwick played amateur cricket at a high level. His father, J.A. Berwick had earlier played in County Cricket for Derbyshire as a lower order left-handed batsman and a left-arm fast-medium bowler. He also represented Northamptonshire in non-first-class cricket, and was professional with the Glossop Cricket Club, for whom his performance of taking eight wickets for seven runs against Sheffield Wednesday C.C. on May 1899 won him a prize of one guinea, offered by a Sunday newspaper.

Appearances: FL: 25 apps 7 gls Total: 25 apps 7 gls

BIRCHENHOUGH, Herbert)

Goalkeeper 6' 0" 12st 0lbs
Born: Haslington, near Crewe, 21st September 1874
Died: Stoke-on-Trent, October quarter 1928, age 53
Debut v Stoke (h) 3.2.1900, lost 1-2

Career: Haslington Villa. Crewe Alexandra September 1892. Nantwich. Sandbach St Mary's. Audley. Crewe Alexandra. Nantwich. Burslem Port Vale 5th April 1898. Glossop 5th January 1900, fee £250. Manchester United 8th October 1902. Crewe Alexandra May 1903.

Within a matter of weeks following his appearance for the Football League, Glossop spent £250 to bring Herbert Birchenhough, the tall, moustachioed goalkeeper, to North Road. Glossop had made a dreadful start to their first season in the top flight and, whilst his presence helped to stabilise a leaky defence, relegation could not be avoided, the team's dismal record being eighteen points and only four wins during the season. Back in Division Two in 1900-01, Birchenhough appeared in all 34 League matches and conceded only 33 goals, being undefeated in twelve matches. He joined Manchester United in October 1902, appeared in 25 League matches and five FA Cup-ties and was allowed to leave in the close season when he rejoined his local club, Crewe Alexandra, for a third spell. When not playing football, he worked as a fitter for a manufacturer of steam engines.

Appearances: FL: 84 apps 0 gls FAC: 6 apps 0 gls Total: 90 apps 0 gls
Honours: Football League v Irish League, November 1899

BLACKBURN, George

Outside right 5' 6½" 11st 0lbs
Born: Worksop, April quarter 1888
Died: Worksop, December 1954, age 66
Debut v Derby County (h) 7.11.1908, won 3-1 (scored two)
Career: Bolton United (A Yorkshire Club) 24th August 1905. Goldthorpe Institute 6th September 1906. Denaby United 4th May 1907. Glossop 4th May 1908. Denaby United July 1909. Bradford Park Avenue November 1909. Huddersfield Town June 1910 to June 1912.

Despite the best possible start to his senior career – three goals in his first two appearances – George Blackburn was afforded few further opportunities in his season at North Road. Returning to his former club, Denaby United, his finishing abilities quickly attracted the attention of the Bradford Park Avenue club, where he replicated his two-goal Glossop debut for his new club at Leeds City in a 3-2 win on 13th November 1909. In the following month he would doubtless have enjoyed scoring twice against his former Glossop colleagues in a 3-3 draw at Park Avenue. Surprisingly, his goal scoring talents did not earn him a regular place in the League side and after six goals in eleven matches he moved on in search of first team football with Huddersfield Town, who had just secured admission to the Second Division of the football League. By coincidence, his debut for Huddersfield was made against his former team mates Bradford Park Avenue, and although he failed to maintain his record of scoring debuts, the 1-0 win was an excellent start to his career at Leeds Road. He remained for two seasons, scoring six goals in 37 League appearances, and one goal in two FA Cup-ties.

Appearances: FL: 5 apps 3 gls Total: 5 apps 3 gls

BODEN, John William 'Jack'

Centre half
5' 10½"
13st 0lbs
Born: Northwich, January quarter 1882
Died: Greenbank, Northwich, 13th March 1946, age 64
Debut v Burnley (h) 2.12.1902, won 2-0
Career: Northwich Victoria.

Glossop November 1902. Clapton Orient 4th May 1905, fee £200. Aston Villa 7th March 1906. Reading 11th June1907. Croydon Common August 1909. Plymouth Argyle June 1911. Gillingham October 1912. Northwich Victoria July 1913 to April 1914.

Jack 'Drummer' Boden, who was born within three miles of the Drill Field, began with Northwich Victoria in their first season in the Manchester League, 1900-01. He had commenced playing football as a goalkeeper, but subsequently became one of the best half backs ever seen at the Drill Field. In his second season he was a medal winner in both the Cheshire Amateur Cup and the Northwich & District Cup, and in November of the following campaign he stepped up to League football with Glossop. Some remarkably fine displays featured seemingly inexhaustible energy and brilliant headwork, and after missing just two first team matches in two and a half seasons, he was transferred to Clapton Orient. He played in Orient's first ever League match, but after 27 appearances and five goals he was on the move again to Aston Villa, but as deputy to Alex Leake he made only 18 appearances, scoring two goals. A trip around the Southern League commenced at Reading and peaked with Plymouth Argyle, who finished one point adrift of champions Queens Park Rangers in season 1911-12. His final playing season was as captain of his first club, Northwich Victoria, and on his return to the Drill Field he scored in the 8-2 win against Hyde on 13th September 1913.

Appearances: FL: 91 apps 4 gls FAC: 4 apps 0 gls
Total: 95 apps 4 gls

BOOTH, Charles

Right half
Born: Glossop, April quarter 1896
Died: Ashton-under-Lyne, October quarter 1966, age 70
Debut v Nottingham Forest (a) 6.3.1915, lost 0-1
Career: Dinting Church. Glossop amateur 5th October 1914.

Three consecutive League outings, the first at Nottingham Forest, followed by two home fixtures against Leicester Fosse and Hull City, was the extent of amateur wing half Charlie Booth's first team involvement in Glossop's swansong as a Football League club. With the side anchored to the foot of the table, the Glossop public had effectively 'voted with their feet' as the attendances for the matches against Leicester Fosse and Hull City were estimated to be just 1,000 and 500 respectively.

Appearances: FL: 3 apps 0 gls Total: 3 apps 0 gls

BOWDEN, Joseph

Centre half/Inside left
Born: Glossop, 8th October 1884
Died: Glossop, 1st March 1958
Debut v Preston North End (h) 1.1.1913, lost 2-3
Career: Thornsett United. Stalybridge Rovers. Thornsett United. Bury April 1906. Rossendale United May 1907. Hyde United January 1908. Rochdale September 1908. Thornsett United November 1908. Glossop amateur September 1910.

Joe Bowden, employed as a washer in a Calico Works, played in four matches in 1912-13 and two in the following season. He had commenced with Thornsett United and was their captain when he joined Bury as a teenager. He scored in his single appearance for the Shakers, but it was his only taste of senior football before he joined Glossop. An all round sportsman, Bowden headed the batting averages of Glossop Cricket Club in 1909. In the same year he began as an opening right-handed batsman with the Derbyshire County Cricket Club, playing in 231 matches between 1909 and 1930. He scored 7,613 runs at an average of 20.57, with a highest score of 120. He scored 1,000 runs in a season twice, his best being 1,221 at 30.52 in 1926.

Appearances: FL: 7 apps 0 gls FAC: 1 app 0 gls
Total: 8 apps 0 gls

BRENNAN, John 'Jack'

Half back 5' 9"   11st 5lbs
Born: Manchester, 13th December 1891
Died: Blackpool, 13th August 1942, age 50
Debut v Lincoln City (h) 5.10.1912, lost 0-1
Career: Cheetham Higher Grade School. Ancoates Lads' Club. Hollinwood United. Manchester City (trial) March 1911. Denton. Glossop amateur October 1912. Bradford City November 1913. Manchester City July 1914. Rochdale cs 1922.

A star in schools football, Jack Brennan assisted Cheetham HGS to the final of both the Manchester Schools League and the England Schools Shield Final in 1906. With Hollinwood United he won the league championship, also the Cawley Cup and the Manchester Amateur Cup. He had undergone trials with Manchester City before joining Glossop on amateur forms in October 1912. A press comment during his thirteen months at North Road indicated that he was a strong and versatile player, equally at home on either flank in the middle line. Moving on to Bradford City, he appeared in eleven First Division matches, and in 56 matches for

Manchester City at either side of the Great War, in which he served with the 20th Battalion of the Yorkshire Regiment. In post war years he represented Great Britain in the 1920 Olympic Games and won his England Amateur cap in the following year.

Appearances: FL: 20 apps 0 gls FAC: 1 app 0 gls Total: 21 apps 0 gls

Honours: England Amateur international, 1 cap 1921. Olympic Games 1920.

BRODIE, Duncan
Right back
Born: Lugar, Ayrshire, 23rd April 1878
Died: 1915
Debut v New Brighton Tower (h) 16.2.1901, lost 0-1
Career: Cumnock Juniors. Partick Thistle 12th September 1898. Lugar Boswell 30th August 1899. Cumnock. Glossop 31st January 1901. Lanemark 23rd April 1901. Abercorn 31st December 1901. Barnsley, trial, September-October 1904. Thornhill.

A brawny Scot who combined football with his occupation as a builder's labourer, Duncan Brodie began with Partick Thistle but appeared in only four Scottish League matches and one Glasgow Cup-tie in season 1898-99 when Thistle were relegated from the top flight having taken only six points from eighteen League matches. Released in the close season, Brodie crossed the border in January 1901 and made his Football League debut with Glossop against New Brighton Tower at North Road. Although he had the misfortune to put the ball through his own goal to give the visitors the two points, Brodie was praised for his display, the *Athletic News* correspondent considering that: "He ought to be of much use to the Derbyshire team". In the event, Brodie appeared in only a further two League matches. Glossop fielded eight different full backs during the course of the season, with the right flank being the most troublesome; a satisfactory partner for Herbert Burgess proving elusive.

Appearances: FL: 3 apps 0 gls Total: 3 apps 0 gls

BROOKS, Joseph 'Joe'

Left back
5' 11"   12st 12lbs
Born: Stalybridge, July quarter 1878
Debut v Walsall (h) 2.3.1901, won 2-0
Career: Stalybridge Rovers amateur. Glossop amateur December 1900. Watford August 1903. Sheffield United 23rd April

1907, fee £275. Stalybridge Celtic August 1912 to cs 1920. Hurst manager *circa* 1921.

After a relatively undistinguished start to his career, Joe Brooks blossomed with Southern League Watford as a powerfully-build left full back who was ever-present in his first two seasons and went on to complete 106 Southern League and eight FA Cup appearances. He also gave good service to Sheffield United of the First Division, completing 126 League appearances and two in FA Cup-ties. Released with a free transfer, he rejoined his hometown club, Stalybridge Celtic. Joe was a keen amateur cyclist in his youth, and when the season opened on Good Friday in 1901, he entered a five-mile scratch race at Burnley and was second to T. Davies. One day later, he was the winner of a similar meeting at Belle Vue, Manchester, leading the field from start to finish. Interviewed after the race, he admitted that playing football for Glossop kept him fit during the winter and, when the cycling season came around, he was in sound health and ready to go with his muscles supple. In 1904 he was the one-mile champion cyclist of England.

Appearances: FL: 4 apps 0 gls Total: 4 apps 0 gls

BROWN, John

Half back
5' 10"   12st 0lb
Debut v Liverpool (a) 3.9.1904, drawn 2-2
Career: Stalybridge Rovers. Glossop 17th June 1904 to May 1906. One of five new forwards signed by Glossop for the 1904-05 season, John Brown did not impress in early season outings at centre forward, but became a fixture in the half back line from mid season. In November of the following campaign, he deputised as attack leader for the injured 'Kilty' Cameron and scored six goals in five matches. His purple patch included both goals in a 2-0 win against Chesterfield, and another two in the following week's 3-3 draw at Burslem Port Vale.

Appearances: FL: 52 apps 8 gls FAC: 5 apps 1 gl Total: 57 apps 9 gls

BULLOUGH, Dennis Reginald 'Denny'
Outside/Inside right
Born: Allerton Bywater, Castleford,
29th November 1895
Died: Bebington, Wirral, 3rd April 1975
Debut v Derby County (h) 5.9.1914, drawn 1-1
Career: Castleford Town. Glossop amateur
May1914. (Wartime guest player with Blackpool &
Arsenal). Stockport County February 1920.
Doncaster Rovers March 1921. Tranmere Rovers
September 1921. Southport December 1921.
Hoylake 1922. Cadby Hall *circa* 1926-33.
Denny Bullough, was a naturally talented athlete
who excelled in a variety of sports. In addition to
football, he played in Rugby League football with
Castleford, and as a track athlete won a number of
Yorkshire Running Championships, and was
reserve for Great Britain in the 4 x 440 yards relay
team at the 1920 Antwerp Olympics. He played in
just two matches for Glossop as an eighteen year-
old amateur inside forward, and in post war
football made his debut in the Second Division
with Stockport County, and scored against Fulham
in a 2-1 win at Edgeley Park in February 1920. In
the relegation season that followed, Bullough made
the first of three rapid moves within the space of
nine months. His best, if briefest spell, came with
Tranmere Rovers for whom he netted five goals in
just nine appearances. While working for Lyons
Cakes he played for their works' team, Cadby Hall,
and later spent 25 years working at Lever Brothers
at Port Sunlight.
Appearances: FL: 2 apps 0 gls Total: 2 apps 0 gls

BURGESS, Herbert

Full back
5' 5" 11st 2lbs
Born: Openshaw,
Manchester,
October quarter
1883
Died:
Manchester, July
quarter 1954
Debut v Liverpool
(h) 28.4.1900,
lost 1-2
Career: Gorton
St Francis.
Openshaw
United. Moss
Side FC. Glossop 5th March 1900. Manchester City
July 1903, fee £250. Manchester United 1st
January 1907, fee £1,400 including four other
players. Retired due to injury cs 1910.
Subsequently held coaching appointments in
Hungary, Spain, Italy, Austria, Denmark &
Sweden. He returned to Manchester in 1932 and in
October 1934 was appointed trainer to Ashton
National FC.

Herbert Burgess was born in a house that stood on
the site of the Whitworth Baths at Openshaw. As a
youth he worked as a blacksmith's striker in a
smithy, which no doubt helped to build his broad
shoulders and athletic frame, despite being of
much less than average height. He was first noted
in the ranks of a junior team, Openshaw United,
and first joined Glossop at the princely figure of 5/-
(25p) per week. He was first tried at half-back, but
against Liverpool in the closing stages of 1899-
1900 he was given a trial at full-back in which
position he showed tremendous promise. Despite
his inches – he only stood 5'5"- he was without
doubt one of the finest backs of his era. After three
years with Glossop he was transferred to
Manchester City, and within half a season he was
selected for the North in an international trial, and
shortly afterwards won the first of his four England
caps. On New Years' Day 1907 he was one of a
quintet of City players who migrated to Old
Trafford where he won a League championship
medal in 1908 before a badly injured knee
enforced his retirement in 1910. He took over a
licensed premises in the neighbourhood of the Old
Trafford ground, but gave it up to move to the
Continent where he became a highly respected
coach.
Appearances: FL: 81 apps 0 gls FAC: 8 apps 1 gl
Total: 89 apps 1 gl
Honours: England International, 4 caps, 1904 to
1906. Football League representative, 7 apps.
Manchester City: FA Cup winners 1904.
Manchester United: FL champions 1908.

BUTLER, Joseph Henry

Goalkeeper
5' 9½"   12st 0lbs
Born: Dawley Bank
January quarter
1879
Died: Stockport,
October quarter
1939
Debut v Lincoln
City (a) 21.3.1908,
won 1-0
Career:
Bamfurlong
Rovers. Stockport
County 17th
October 1899.
Clapton Orient 4th
May 1905. Stockport County 1st February 1906, fee
£100. Glossop 19th March 1908, fee £150.
Sunderland October 1912, fee £700. Lincoln City
May 1914. (Wartime guest player with Rochdale &
Stockport County.)
A great favourite at Stockport, where he received
his League baptism, Joe Butler had three separate
spells there and actually played for them, in

wartime football, 21 years after originally signing. Agile, strong and brave, he made 161 consecutive League appearances for Glossop, and assisted them to reach the quarter-finals of the FA Cup in season 1908-09. The high point of his career, however, was the part that he played in Sunderland's outstanding 1912-13 season. An ever-present following his October arrival, he also played in all ten FA Cup-ties including the narrow defeat in the fiercely contested final against Aston Villa, a result that cost Sunderland the chance of a coveted 'Double.' In a long career, Butler eventually grossed over 450 League appearances. Prior to professional football he had worked as a miner.

Appearances: FL: 161 apps 0 gls FAC: 9 apps 0 gls Total: 170 apps 0 gls
Honours: Sunderland: FL Division One Champions 1913; FA Cup Finalists 1913.
Stockport County: Lancashire Combination Champions, 1905.

BYRNE, Michael Patrick 'Mick'

Goalkeeper 5' 10" 11st 12lbs
Born: Bristol, April quarter 1880
Died: Bristol, December 1931
Debut v Wolverhampton Wanderers (h) 7.9.1907, drawn 1-1
Career: Army football (Grenadier Guards). Bristol Rovers 1902. Southampton August 1903. Chelsea 4th May 1905 to September 1906. Glossop 8th May 1907.

Mick Byrne played in little first team football throughout his varied career, which he combined with army service, a spell in the police force, and work as a barman. With his first club, Bristol Rovers, he failed dislodge Arthur Cartlidge who was considered one of the best goalkeepers in the Southern League. A move to Southampton, where he was signed as deputy to George Clawley, restricted him to just five appearances in two seasons. When opportunity beckoned at Chelsea, he dislocated his shoulder in the first match of the 1906-07 season and didn't play in the first team again. With Glossop, Byrne shared the first team jersey with William Tustin and enjoyed a run of nine consecutive outings in early season, but the arrival of Joe Butler from Stockport County in late season saw the goalkeeping position settled to absolute satisfaction for the following four seasons.

Appearances: FL: 11 apps 0 gls Total: 11 apps 0 gls

CAIRNS, Thomas

Inside right
5' 5" 10st 7lbs
Born: Dundee, *circa* 1880
Died: Tynemouth, Newcastle-on-Tyne, 27th May 1911, age 31
Debut v Liverpool (a) 3.9.1904, drawn 2-2 (scored one)
Career: Distillery. Raith Rovers 18th June 1902. Belfast Celtic. Glossop 7th May 1904. Distillery August 1905. Stalybridge Rovers 29th June 1907. Haslingden 10th April 1908. West Sleekburn 15th May 1908. Choppington St Pauls 22nd September 1908.

On the small side but speedy and skilful, Tom Cairns began brightly with Glossop, but was not at his best on heavy grounds. A little extra weight would have been an advantage, as he was quite easily hustled off the ball by opposing defenders. His lengthy spell of first team football ended when he lost his place at inside right to a fellow Scot, Hugh Simpson. Six years after leaving Glossop, Tom Cairns tragically committed suicide after failing to find work in a local shipyard.

Appearances: FL: 22 apps 2 gls FAC: 4 apps 1 gl Total: 26 apps 3 gls
Honours: Scottish Junior International

CALLAGHAN, Thomas

Outside right
Born: Birmingham, 1886
Died: K.I.A., circa February/March 1917
Debut v Gainsborough Trinity (h) 15.4.1905, won 3-1
Career: Small Heath. Halesowen. Glossop 12th April 1905. Manchester City 14th June 1907. Partick Thistle August 1909. St Mirren November 1911. Partick Thistle May 1912 to 29th March 1913.

A speedy and accomplished outside right who centred well, Tom Callaghan missed only seven matches in his two seasons at North Road, but his transfer to Manchester City saw him cast in a reserve role, his first team appearances amounting to just two in as many seasons. A move to Scotland proved beneficial, as he starred on Partick Thistle's right wing after making his debut in what was the first football match played at the Firhill Stadium on 18th September 1909 versus Dumbarton Harp in a second round qualifying cup-tie. After two seasons at Firhill he joined St Mirren, but was back with the Jags some six months later to take his overall career record with them to 93 matches and ten goals. He was serving as a machine gunner at the time of his death in action, which was reported in the *Manchester Evening News* of Saturday 3rd March 1917.

Appearances: FL: 73 apps 8 gls FAC: 3 apps 1 gl Total: 76 apps 9 gls

Honours: England Junior International v Scotland, season 1904-05

CALLENDER, Reginald Henry 'Reg'

Outside left
Born: Bishopton, near Stockton, October quarter 1892
Died: Armentieres, 5th October 1915
Debut v Leeds City (h) 15.3.1913, won 2-1
Career: Stockton School. St John's College (Cambridge). Glossop amateur March 1913. Derby County March 1914.

Schoolteacher and Cambridge Blue Reg Callender stepped into the breach when the Glossop club found themselves short of a wingman after they had transferred Edward Cooper to Newcastle United. His single appearance brought a welcome 2-1 win against Leeds City, but the Glossop club were fined by the Football Association for playing him without first registering him with the authorities. In the following season the amateur wingman made five appearances for Derby County in March and April, but was unable to lift the side clear of relegation from the First Division. An under-graduate at St John's College, as quite a young player he made his mark in the Varsity Match of 1912, and was considered one of the best outside-lefts to represent Cambridge University for many years. He played in all the England Amateur international matches of 1912-13, and also represented England in matches on the Continent, whilst in the Oxford & Cambridge Universities match against Birmingham, he was reported to be the best player on the field. Although somewhat on the small side, he was very fast and tricky, and his accurate centres were a feature of his play. His most unfortunate and tragic death while on active service in France was caused by an accident with a hand grenade.

Appearances: FL: 1 app 0 gls Total: 1 app 0 gls

Honours: England Amateur International & Cambridge Blue.

CAMERON, William Smith 'Kilty'

Forward
5' 8"   12st 0lbs
Born: New Spynie, Elgin, 15th May 1886
Died: Bolton, 15th October 1958
Debut v Liverpool (a) 31.12.1904, lost 0-2
Career: Burnbank Athletic 1902. Albion Rovers 1903. Renton 1903-04. Glossop 30th December 1904. Bolton Wanderers 5th May1906. Blackburn Rovers 18th April 1907. Bury January 1913, fee £600. Hull City January1914, fee £600. (Wartime guest player with Clydebank September 1915; Dykehead November 1915; Hamilton Academical February 1916; Vale of Leven August 1916; Bury November 1916). Bury manager May 1919 to May 1923. Was suspended from June 1923 to May 1929 following a bribery scandal. Rochdale manager August 1930 to December 1931.

An iron moulder whose hobbies were cricket and cycling, 'Kilty' Cameron showed early promise as a footballer, representing Lanarkshire at the age of seventeen in a match against Glasgow Rangers in May 1903. Glossop was his first Football League club, and his robust displays and eye for goal saw him lead the scoring list in both of his seasons at North Road. Several clubs angled for his signature when he left Glossop, but his parents lived in Bolton, so the Wanderers was his preference. He subsequently became a noted utility man, able to occupy any position on the field, and during his lengthy association with Blackburn Rovers was quoted as saying "I will yet get my chance beneath the bar." It didn't happen, but he did win a Championship medal with the Rovers, and eventually totalled 234 League appearances and 72 goals for his five different English clubs. Turning to management with Bury after World War One, his team were occupying second position in Division Two in January 1923 when allegations of match fixing, dating back to April 1920, came to light. The Football Association duly held an inquiry which led to the permanent suspension of Cameron; directors including the club's Chairman, Mr J.W. Horrocks, and five players. Cameron's ban was lifted in May 1929, and he was appointed manager of Rochdale in August 1930. He resigned in

December 1931 after successive defeats of 9-1 at Tranmere Rovers on Christmas Day, and 6-3 against the same opponents at Spotland on Boxing Day. At the end of the season, Rochdale had collected just eleven points, having failed to win any of their last 26 matches.

Appearances: FL: 51 apps 23 gls Total: 51 apps 23 gls

Honours: Blackburn Rovers FL Division One Champions 1912.

CAMPBELL, Alistair Kenyon 'Alec'

Centre half
6' 2½"   12st 9lbs
Born: Southampton, 29th May 1890
Died: Cosham, Hants, 16th June 1943, age 53
Debut v Bury, FAC 1 (a) 15.1.1910, lost 1-2
Career: King Edward V1 School. Atherley 1907. Southampton amateur 1908. Also played for the Pilgrims and the Pirates in 1909. Glossop amateur September 1909. Southampton December 1913. Bournemouth & Boscombe Athletic cs 1914. (Guest player with West Ham United during WW1). Poole FC July 1926. Chesterfield manager April to December 1927. Basingstoke Town March 1928. Greenwaves (Plymouth) October 1929.

One of several amateur internationals to assist Glossop, but Alec Campbell was best remembered as Southampton's towering centre half at either side of the Great War, in which he served as a trooper with the Hampshire Carabineers. West Ham were anxious to retain his services following guest appearances for them during the hostilities, but he returned to The Dell, becoming the club's first captain in post-war football. He remained until 1926, clocking up just one short of 200 appearances for the Saints, scoring 15 goals. During the Second World War he served as an officer in the Royal Artillery but died of pneumonia in 1943. Very much the all round sportsman, Campbell was a good swimmer and a talented batsman, good enough to represent Hampshire in seven matches in 1908-09.

Appearances: FL: 10 apps 0 gls FAC: 1 app 0 gls Total: 11 apps 0 gls

Honours: England Amateur International. Southampton: FL Division Three South Champions 1922.

CARLIN, John Charles 'Jack'

Inside forward
5' 7"   10st 10lbs
Born: Southport, October quarter 1876
Died: Liverpool, April quarter 1935, age 59
Debut v Sheffield United (h) 2.12.1899, drawn 2-2
Career: Firvale F.C. (Liverpool & District League) August 1893. Tranmere Rovers (trial) December 1893. Firvale F.C. Tranmere Rovers August 1896. Birkenhead August 1899. Glossop 16th November 1899. Barnsley 18th November 1900. Tranmere Rovers 1906.

In what was probably Glossop's best win in Division One – 1-0 against Aston Villa on December 16th 1899 – inside left Jack Carlin impressed the *Athletic News* correspondent who reported: "The inside-left struck me as a most promising youth. He belongs to Birkenhead, and although not particularly clever, he puts in any amount of work, and is always ready." Although the victory against their famous opponents was doubly enjoyable, as it went some way to easing the memory of the humiliating 9-0 defeat at Villa Park, Jack Carlin did not collect another winning bonus, and left after twelve months to join Barnsley.

Appearances: FL: 8 apps 1 gl Total: 8 apps 1 gl

CARNEY, James Michael 'Jimmy'

Wing half
5' 7"   11st 0lbs
Born: Bolton, 4th December 1891
Died: Newport, 23rd November 1980
Debut v Blackpool (h) 5.11.1910, won 3-1
Career: Bolton Wanderers. Blackpool. Glossop October 1910. (Wartime guest player with Blackpool October 1915). Bolton Wanderers 1919. Stalybridge Celtic June 1920. Newport County June 1923 to 1927 when his playing career ended due to a cartilage injury.

A stylish and popular wing half throughout a lengthy spell with Glossop, Jimmy Carney was without League experience when he arrived at North Road. After spending much of his first season in reserve, he became a fixture, mainly at left half, from November 1911 through until April 1915. Although on the small side he was always in the thick of the action, and despite losing four years of his career to the Great War, he gave good service after the hostilities to both Stalybridge

Celtic (72 appearances and 14 goals) and Newport County (118 appearances, 13 goals)
Appearances: FL: 138 apps 6 gls FAC: 6 apps 1 gl
Total: 144 apps 7 gls

CARR, Laurence Hudson Ashdown
Inside left   5' 4½"   10st 4lbs
Born: Clayton, Manchester, April quarter 1887
Died: Southampton, 27th August 1959, age 72
Debut v Leicester Fosse (a) 28.10.1905, lost 1-2
Career: Renton. Glossop 20th May 1905. Renton March 1907. Vale of Leven. Renton April 1908.
Laurence Carr played his early football in Renton, which since the middle of the eighteenth century was heavy involved in the dyeing, bleaching and calico-printing trades. Carr's occupation was in the millinery trade, which he left for spell when attached to Glossop. Although he scored on his second appearance, in a 3-1 home win against Hull City, and despite his nifty footwork and eye for an opening, his lack of any physical advantage proved to be a drawback when faced with robust defenders.
Appearances: FL: 7 apps 1 gl Total: 7 apps 1 gl

CARR, Robert Stanley
Outside right
Born: Collyhurst, April quarter 1881
Died: Chorlton-cum-Hardy, 2nd August 1927, age 46
Debut v Burton United (a) 6.9.1902, lost 1-2
Career: Bolton Wanderers amateur, professional 17th November 1898. St Helens Recreation 31st May 1901. Glossop 9th June 1902.
Carr made his debut in First Division football with Bolton Wanderers as an eighteen year-old amateur wingman. In two early season appearances he figured in a 2-1 win against the Wolves, followed by a 0-1 defeat at Everton. In the same season, the Wanderers suffered relegation for the first time. One of the oldest clubs in the country, they had held continuous membership of the First Division since the commencement of the League. Happily, they bounced straight back in the following season, but Carr did not add to his two League appearances. He was next seen in the colours of St Helens Recreation, but after finishing seventh in the Lancashire Combination Division One they withdrew their membership, and Carr moved on to Glossop. He was one of only two new forwards signed; the other one, Morrow of Ayr Parkhouse, did not feature in the League side, and Carr did little better, despite appearing in the opening three fixtures of the season, all of which ended in defeat.
Appearances: FL: 4 apps 0 gls Total: 4 apps 0 gls

CAUSER, Arthur Haden

Goalkeeper   5' 9"   11st 3lbs
Born: Wolverhampton, October quarter 1884
Died: Wolverhampton, 8th March 1927, age 42
Debut v Burnley (a) 7.9.1912, lost 1-2
Career: Wolverhampton Clutha F.C. Wellington Town August 1906. Dudley Town June 1909. Glossop May 1910. (Wartime guest player with Sheffield Wednesday October 1915; Rochdale December 1915 and Stockport County August 1917). Preston North End February 1919, fee £200. Shrewsbury Town June 1922.
Arthur Causer waited long and patiently for his chance in League football, as he spent his first two seasons as deputy for Joe Butler, Glossop's star goalkeeper who made a record 161 consecutive League appearances before joining Sunderland. Removed from the shadows, Causer seized his opportunity to maximum effect, missing only five League matches in Glossop's final three seasons. Whilst training as an Artillery man at the Fulwood Barracks during the WW1 period he played for Preston North End, who signed him immediately after the League had reduced his transfer fee from £500 to £200, a sum that the player received in lieu of a benefit. Preston came very close to relegation in Causer's first season at Deepdale, but he conceded only three goals in the final five League matches to steer his team to safety. Although not ideally built for his position, he was extremely agile and was rarely in difficulties, despite being unafraid to take risks when leaving his line. He completed 46 League appearances for Preston, ending his career in non-League football with Shrewsbury Town. Arthur Causer is often quoted as being the only player to have played for two Football League teams called North End. This is incorrect, however, as Glossop dropped 'North End' from their title in August 1899.
Appearances: FL: 110 apps 0 gls FAC: 6 apps 0 gls
Total: 116 apps 0 gls
Honours: England Junior international.

CHADWICK, Edgar Wallace

Inside left
5' 6"   10st 7lbs
Born: Blackburn,
14th June 1869
Died: Blackburn,
14th February 1942
Debut v Gainsborough
Trinity (h) 2.9.1905, won
1-0 (scored)
Career: Little Dots FC
1884. Blackburn Olympic
1886. Blackburn Rovers
cs 1887. Everton July
1888. Burnley 2nd June 1899. Southampton 24th
August 1900. Liverpool 3rd May 1902. Blackpool
21st May 1904. Glossop 20th May 1905. Darwen
13th July 1906, retired 1908. Coaching
appointments with The Hague & Harlem FC
(Holland) 1908. England Amateur Team coach
November 1908. Stonehurst College coach October
1912. One final playing appearance at outside left
for Blackburn Rovers during wartime season 1916-
17, at the age of 47.

A season with Glossop rounded off the outstanding
career of the lightweight inside forward Edgar
Chadwick. When the veteran international scored
the only goal of the game on his debut for Glossop,
the *Manchester Courier's* correspondent
considered that: "He seems to possess the
attributes of Tennyson's brook." After a season
with Blackburn Rovers he joined Everton for the
1888-89 season and their debut in the newly
formed Football League. He stayed at Goodison for
eleven seasons, making exactly 300 League and
Cup appearances, scoring 110 goals. Along the way,
he won a League Championship medal and
appeared in two FA Cup Finals. He won seven
England Caps, scoring against Scotland in April
1892 after just 35 seconds. In the FA tour to
Germany in November 1899, he scored ten goals in
three matches. During his spell in the Southern
League with Southampton, he won a
Championship medal, but an FA Cup winners'
medal continued to elude him as he was on the
losing side in the 1902 Final, as he had been in his
two Finals with Everton. Edgar's cousin, Arthur
Chadwick, played for and managed several League
clubs and won two England caps while a
Southampton player. On retirement, Edgar
returned to Blackburn and his original trade of
baker.

Appearances: FL: 35 apps 5 gls FAC: 1 app 0 gls
Total: 36 apps 5 gls
Honours: England International, 7 caps, 1891 to
1897. FL Representative, 2 apps. FA Tour to
Germany November 1899. Everton: FL Champions
1891. FA Cup Finalists 1893 & 1897. Southampton:
Southern League Champions 1901, FA Cup
Finalists 1902.

CHESWORTH, Frank

Inside left
Born: Nantwich, October quarter 1873
Died: Manchester, January quarter 1907, age 33
Debut v Newton Heath (h) 1.9.1900, won 1-0
Career: Nantwich. Stockport County 17th
December 1898. Glossop 4th May 1900. Stockport
County 19th July 1901. Nantwich 11th September
1902 to July 1904. Witton Albion. Stretford.

In his first spell with Stockport County, inside left
Frank Chesworth's 18 goals in 28 matches was a
major contribution in a season when the
Lancashire League championship was won. He also
scored one of the goals that helped his team beat
Glossop by 3-0 in the FA Cup replay on November
1st 1899. Along with wing half Tommy Hall,
Chesworth joined Glossop in May 1900, following
their relegation from the First Division in the
previous season. A personal highlight was his
scoring two goals against his previous colleagues in
a 6-0 win on December 1st. Later in the season, he
scored the first of Glossop's three goals in the
return fixture at Stockport that Glossop won 3-1.
Perhaps unsurprisingly, Stockport County sought
his transfer in the close season, where he exactly
replicated his performance of the previous season
– six goals in 28 League appearances. In what
proved to be his final appearance, Stockport took
the field with only seven men against Chesterfield
Town on April 19th. Four players had managed to
miss their train to Chesterfield, and to make
matters even worse, the unfortunate Chesworth
suffered broken ribs during the match, leaving
Stockport with only six men. Heroics by goalkeeper
Joe Butler, later to star with Glossop and
Sunderland, kept the losing margin down to 8-1.

Appearances: FL: 28 apps 6 gls FAC: 1 app 0 gls
Total: 29 apps 6 gls

CLARKE, David Cleland

Goalkeeper
5' 11"   13st 0lbs
Born: Sligo, 21st
May 1878
Debut v Burton
United (a)
6.9.1902, lost 1-2
Career:
Northampton
Town 1900.
Glossop 27th May
1902. Bristol
Rovers 30th June
1904. West Ham
United 10th July
1906. Bradford
Park Avenue May
1909. Southend United June 1910. Bristol Rovers
cs 1911.

Glossop lost one good goalkeeper when they transferred Herbert Birchenough to Manchester United in October 1902. Thankfully, the man signed as his understudy, David Clarke, proved a more than adequate successor. Although the transfer of full back Herbert Burgess to Manchester City weakened Glossop's defence in Clarke's second season, the Irish goalkeeper recovered well from a shaky opening to the campaign to remain ever present throughout the season. He returned to Southern League football after leaving Glossop, his only other Football League involvement being with Bradford Park Avenue, for whom he made seven appearances in 1909-10.

Appearances: FL: 67 apps 0 gls FAC: 5 apps 0 gls Total: 72 apps 0 gls

CLAY, George

Inside right   5' 6"   10st 10lbs
Born: Preston, October quarter 1888
Debut v Bristol City (h) 3.9.1913, lost 1-4
Career: Preston North End amateur. Hindley Central. South Liverpool. Glossop May 1913.
A second opportunity in League football was presented to lightweight inside forward George Clay following his return of 23 goals for South Liverpool's championship winning team of 1912-13. Sadly, he was unable to clinch a first team spot with Glossop, finding Second Division defences a great deal more difficult to penetrate than those in the Second Division of the Lancashire Combination. South Liverpool having scored 94 goals in 34 matches in taking the title in 1912-13. George Clay was employed as a labourer in the electrical trade, when not playing football.
Appearances: FL: 6 apps 0 gls Total: 6 apps 0 gls

CLIFFORD, Thomas

Centre half
5' 11"   12st 0lbs
Born: Kilbirnie, Ayrshire, 14th August 1874
Died: K.I.A. on the Somme, 19th January 1917, age 42, when serving as a Private in the 6th/7th Royal Scots Fusiliers.
Debut v Blackpool (h) 3.9.1899, won 4-1
Career: Annbank. Newton Heath 5th December 1896. Ayr 13th April 1898. Glossop North End 31st May 1898. Luton Town 30th July 1900. Celtic 28th August 1901. Beith September 1903. Motherwell 1904. Nottingham Forest 12th May 1905.
One of any number of talented footballers whose skills were honed in the tiny Ayrshire village of

Annbank. Stated to be an outside-left when signed by Newton Heath, his height and weight suggested that he might have been better suited to a defensive role. He did not graduate to first team football with the 'Heathens', but as Glossop North End's centre half he marshalled his defence to great effect in the initial promotion season. Virtually ever-present from mid season, he missed only two matches, following a sending-off and fourteen days suspension from February 27th. In the following relegation season, with the team shipping goals at an alarming rate, Lupton, whose first outing was an unqualified success, retained the centre half position for the remainder of the campaign. At the time of Tom Clifford's death on the Somme, his home address was given as Rankiston, Ayrshire.
Appearances: FL: 40 apps 1 gl FAC: 4 apps 0 gls Total: 44 apps 1 gl

CLOUGH, George William

Outside left   5' 8"   11st 0lbs
Born: Barton Irwell, January quarter 1882
Debut v Bristol City (h) 27.12.1904, lost 0-1
Career: Clifton F.C. Glossop amateur December 1904.
Four League matches within the space of seven days over the Christmas period left little recovery time for players with relatively minor injuries, and an enforced change in the forward line saw George Clough introduced for his Football League debut against Bristol City in place of Tommy Cairns. Hailing from Clifton Junction, near Prestwich, the amateur wingman was billed as "Very speedy and a good shot" but he failed to shine in a front line that was dismissively considered by one observer as: 'a poor lot'. Things did improve in the following week when 'Kilty' Cameron joined from Renton, his ten goals in 19 appearances guiding Glossop away from the lower reaches of the table. George Clough, who worked as a bricklayer, did not appear at senior level again.
Appearances: FL: 1 app 0 gls Total: 1 app 0 gls

COATES, Frederick 'Fred'

Left half
Born: Sheffield, 16th November 1879
Died: Glossop, 22nd May 1956, age 76
Debut v Leicester Fosse (a) 1.4.1902, drawn 1-1
Career: Hyde FC. Glossop 22nd March 1902 to June 1904.
Tenacious   tackling coupled with excellent distribution made Fred Coates a key member of Glossop's middle line for

two seasons. Sadly, as Glossop found themselves in the dreaded 'bottom three' of the League at the close of the 1903-04 season, sweeping changes were made with only four of the previous season's players retained. Archie Goodall took over the management of the team but his newly assembled squad failed to deliver, finishing twelfth in the table. Coates' whereabouts post-Glossop have not been traced, but his off the field employment as a wood sawyer continued.

Appearances: FL: 64 apps 3 gls FAC: 4 apps 1 gl
Total: 68 apps 4 gls

COLVILLE, George

Right half
Born: Tarbolton, Ayrshire *circa* 1876
Died: Glossop, July quarter 1928, age 51
Debut v Blackpool (h) 3.9.1898, won 4-1
Career: Annbank July 1895. Blackpool 10th June 1896. Hibernian October 1896. Annbank 6th October 1897. Glossop North End 4th May 1898. Fulham December 1903 to cs 1904. Annbank. Port Glasgow Athletic cs 1908.

George Colville began with Annbank, which, at the turn of the century, was described as a one-street village, but it certainly turned out many class footballers. Its Peeble Park pitch was sometimes named 'The Precipice' – usually by disgruntled opponents, but Annbank played as well away as they did at home. During his career in League football Colville was variously described as: "Quite inoffensive and genial," which probably referred to life off the pitch; in a length spell with Glossop, George Colville was regularly praised. A typical comment being: "A more consistent and hard working player never donned the Glossop colours." Certainly the club met with a serious loss when he suffered a broken leg in season 1901-02. A brother, James, was a Newton Heath player in season 1892-93.

Appearances: FL: 105 apps 2 gls FAC: 7 apps 0 gls
Total: 112 apps 2 gls

COLVIN, Robert 'Bobby'

Forward
5' 4½"   10st 0lbs
Born: Kirkconnel, 5th December 1876
Died: Liverpool, October quarter 1940, age 63
Debut v New Brighton Tower (a) 24.9.1898, drawn 2-2
Career: Coatbridge. Oldham County 22nd January 1897. Liverpool 6th November 1897. Glossop North End 4th May 1898. New Brighton Tower 3rd July 1899. Luton Town 13th May 1901. Queens Park Rangers 7th May 1902. Swindon Town cs 1903. Maxwelltown Volunteers. African Royal 1st November 1907.

Bobby Colvin's first English Club was Oldham County. The newly formed 'Counts' endured a difficult first season, and Colvin was one of an influx of new players, mostly Scotsmen, who arrived in mid season. Results did not improve, and in November 1897 the club folded. Within days, Colvin became a Liverpool player. A skilful and elusive performer, best suited to a role on the wing, he joined Glossop having failed to establish himself at Anfield, making only three League appearances. His single season at North Road saw the side promoted to the First Division, but Colvin was not amongst the players retained at the end of the season. He subsequently made 34 League appearances in his two seasons with New Brighton Tower, but his best season was 1901-02, when he made 28 Southern League appearances for Luton Town.

Appearances: FL: 16 apps 2 gls FAC: 2 apps 1 gl
Total: 18 apps 3 gls

COMRIE, James 'Jimmy'

Centre half
5' 10"   13st 0lbs
Born: Denny, 31st March 1881
Died: KIA while serving with the 1st/7th Battalion Northumberland Fusiliers in 1916
Debut v Leeds City (a) 2.9.1907, lost 1-2
Career: Dunipace. Third Lanark January 1904. Reading 18th May 1906. Glossop 15th May 1907. Bradford City 18th September 1908. Lincoln City November 1910. Grantham October 1911. Stenhousemuir November 1911. Reading May 1912 (Boston Swifts loan January-May 1914).

Jimmie Comrie crammed much into a comparatively short life. He began in senior football with Third Lanark in mid season 1903-04 and made four first team appearances for the side that won the championship of the Scottish Division One and reached the semi-final of the Scottish Cup. He then made 50 League and 13 Cup appearances in the following two seasons and scored 13 goals in 1905-06, seven of them coming in two matches against Queen's Park when he was fielded at centre-forward. The first of two separate spells with Reading followed, in which he totalled 127 Southern League appearances. In a little over a season with Glossop the ideally built pivot was strong defensively and showed a flair for combining with his forwards. After just three matches of the 1908-09 season he was transferred to Bradford City, but he did not appear regularly until season 1909-10. His final Football League club was Lincoln City who were relegated from Division Two in season 1910-11 and failed to win re-election.

Appearances: FL: 38 apps 1 gl FAC: 2 apps 0 gls
Total; 40 apps 1 gl
Honours: Third Lanark: Scottish Cup winners 1905; finalists 1906.

CONNACHAN, James
Forward 5' 8" 11st 12lbs
Born: Glasgow, 29th August 1874
Debut v Leicester Fosse (h) 18.2.1899, lost 1-3
Career: Glasgow Perthshire. Duntocher Hibernian. Glasgow Perthshire. Celtic 1st March 1897. Airdrieonians 24th October 1898. Newton Heath 28th October 1898. Glossop North End 6th February 1899. Leicester Fosse 2nd May 1900. Nottingham Forest (trial) 1901. Morton October 1901. Renton August 1902. Britannia (Canada) 1906. Dumbarton Harp December 1907, retired cs 1908.

In October 1898 the Newton Heath official programme reported that James Connachan had been signed. The editor also enlightened his readers as to the correct pronunciation of their new centre forward's name – "Kon-a-Kan". In one of his early outings at Clayton, the *Manchester Guardian* considered that: "Connachan showed dash, but was lacking in almost every respect." He certainly did a great deal better on joining Glossop North End, his four goals in eleven matches towards the close of season 1898-99 assisting his team to the runners-up position behind Manchester City in the Second Division. Sadly, in their single season in Division One Connachan failed to maintain a level of performance that had seen him score in consecutive matches against West Bromwich Albion, Everton and Bury. His final season of League football was spent with Leicester Fosse in Division Two, fielded in every

forward position except outside left, he scored six goals in 29 appearances.

Appearances: FL: 28 apps 8 gls FAC: 2 apps 2 gls
Total: 30 apps 10 gls

COOPER, Edward

Outside right
5' 7" 11st 0lbs
Born: Walsall, 28th May 1891
Died: Walsall, 7th July 1976, age 86
Debut v Lincoln City (h) 5.10.1912, lost 0-1
Career: Stafford Rangers, Glossop May 1912. Newcastle United March 1913, fee £1,375. (Wartime guest player with Bradford Park Avenue September 1917). Notts County June 1920, fee £500. Stafford Rangers November 1921. Burton All Saints August 1923. Cannock Town August 1925. Darlaston September 1926.

In a career interrupted by Army service in France with the West Yorkshire Regiment, Edward Cooper began his senior career with Glossop and had not completed one season when Newcastle United paid what was then a very significant sum for his transfer. The highlight of his brief stay with Glossop was his scoring of five goals in the record 11-1 victory against Southall in the fifth qualifying round of the FA Cup at North Road on December 14th, 1912. Initially operating as understudy to Newcastle's famous England international outside-right Jackie Rutherford, Cooper's senior opportunities were limited, but at either side of the Great War he totalled 45 League appearances and scored two goals. Moving on to Notts County in June 1920, he failed to hold down a first team place after appearing in four of the first six matches of the season. A bricklayer by trade, Cooper returned to non-League football, initially with his former club, Stafford Rangers.

Appearances: FL: 24 apps 5 gls FAC: 3 apps 5 gls
Total: 27 apps 10 gls

COPELAND, David Campbell

Forward
5' 7" 11st 9lbs
Born: Ayr, 2nd April 1875
Died: Erdington, 16th November 1931, age 56
Debut v Grimsby Town (a) 28.9.1907, lost 0-4
Career: Ayr Parkhouse. Walsall 10th May 1897. Bedminster 13th May 1898. Tottenham Hotspur 5th

May 1899. Chelsea 2nd May 1905. Glossop 8th May 1907. Ayr Parkhouse.

In all competitions, David Copeland totalled 303 appearances and scored 110 goals for the Spurs. He joined Chelsea in May 1905 and scored on his debut in a 9-2 win against Glossop on 1st September, but on 3rd November he suffered a broken leg at Burslem Port Vale and didn't play again that season. Former Chelsea team-mate Jack Robertson, Glossop's player-manager, recruited Copeland from Stamford Bridge in May 1907 but he was said to lack mobility and made only two first team appearances. His occupation was an unusual one (a maker of golf balls), and his death was too, as he expired while chopping wood.

Appearances: FL: 2 apps 0 gls Total: 2 apps 0 gls

Honours: Tottenham Hotspur, FA Cup winners, 1901. Southern League champions 1900. Played in an International Trial match in 1903 for the Anglo-Scots v Home Scots.

COSTELLO, John

Right back   5' 8"   11st 6lbs
Born: Blakely, Manchester, April quarter 1890
Died: Of wounds received on active service in the Dardanelles, *circa* June/July 1915
Debut v Fulham (h) 20.9.1913, lost 0-1
Career: Altrincham. Rochdale 1911-12. Longfield F.C. (Blackley). Glossop amateur September, professional November 1912. Stockport County August 1914.

John Costello played only once for Rochdale in the season that they won the championship of the Lancashire Combination. He subsequently showed enough promise to earn a professional contract with Glossop after making his first five appearances as an amateur. He was destined, however, to spend much of the season in the reserves, with George Hampton the usual partner to the long serving Cuffe in the rear division. Costello did not appear in Second Division football with Stockport County. The Census report of 1911 listed his occupation as a labourer. His death was reported in the Manchester Evening News of 3rd July 1915. He had served as a sergeant in the Plymouth Battalion of the Royal Marine Infantry. His home was in Barker Street, Harpurhey.

Appearances: FL: 7 apps 0 gls Total: 7 apps 0 gls

CRAIGIE, Charles Niddrie.

Right half   5' 8"   11st 3lbs
Born: St. Clement, Dundee, 1886
Debut v Gainsborough Trinity (a) 9.10.1909, won 3-1
Career: Dundee Violet (for five seasons). Forfarshire County. Glossop October 1909. Fulham July 1911.

Charlie Craigie departed Havercroft Park after five seasons with Dundee Violet and fitted seamlessly into Glossop's middle line, the side remaining undefeated in his first eight appearances. A steady and reliable player, he kept his place in the side by consistently good form. A sixth place finish was considered a successful season, and practically all of the season's players were retained, the exceptions being Milne, who went to Blackpool, and Craigie to Fulham. In the following month, a move in the opposite direction brought full back Jock Goldie to Glossop from Fulham

Appearances: FL: 32 apps 3 gls FAC: 1 app 0 gls Total: 33 apps 3 gls

CRUMP, Frederick 'Fred'

Forward
Born: Smethwick, January quarter 1877
Died: Walsall, January quarter 1952, age 74
Debut v Newton Heath (h) 1.9.1900, won 1-0
Career: Stourbridge. Derby County 27th June 1899. Glossop 4th May 1900. Northampton Town 20th May 1902. Stourbridge. Stalybridge Rovers 27th September 1904. Stockport County 13th May 1905. Brighton & Hove Albion 4th May 1908. Walsall August 1909. Darlaston.

Fred Crump began with Derby County, his senior career commencing with a modest six appearances and one goal. At either centre forward or inside, he was a dashing forward with a fine shot, not easily shaken off when heading for goal. He headed Glossop's scoring list in both of his seasons at North Road, scoring 15 goals in 35 matches in 1900-01 and following with 14 in 35 matches in 1901-02, when the next highest scorer managed only seven. Crump was similarly effective with his second Football League club, Stockport County, scoring 29 goals in 89 matches. His senior career wound up with a season in the south with Brighton & Hove Albion for whom he scored five goals in 20 matches. He then returned to Birmingham League football with Walsall.

Appearances: FL: 64 apps 26 gls FAC: 4 apps 3 gls Total: 68 apps 29 gls

CRUMP, Herbert

Right half
Born: Wellington, Shropshire, 10th May 1890
Died: Wolverhampton, 11th January 1973, age 82
Debut v Blackpool (h) 21.9.1912, won 2-0
Career: Glossop September 1912

One of no fewer than nine different players fielded at right half during the course of season 1912-13 when 27 players appeared during the League programme, and wholesale changes of line-up did nothing to halt the side's alarming involvement in the battle to avoid a re-election application.

Appearances: FL: 6 apps 0 gls Total: 6 apps 0 gls

CUFFE, John Alexander

Full back
5' 9½"   12st 0lbs
Born: Timbreborngie,
New   South   Wales,
Australia,   26th   June
1880
Died: Burton-on-Trent,
16th May 1931
Debut v Burnley (h)
16.12.1905, drawn 1-1
Career: Talbot Villa.
Glossop amateur August
1905,   signing
professional 3rd May 1906 to 1914. (Wartime guest
player with Rochdale and Oldham Athletic).
Glossop's record appearance holder, by a very wide
margin, Cuffe had all the attributes necessary for
full back play. "A vigorous and fearless tackler" was
one verdict, another commenting that he was:
"Exceptionally fast; resourceful; kicked strongly;
tackled effectively." Often linked with possible
moves to bigger clubs, he remained loyal to
Glossop, combining his football career with that of
a county cricketer with Worcestershire, as a right
hand batsman and slow left arm bowler. He
performed the 'double' in 1911 and altogether
scored 7,476 runs at an average of 22.25 and took
738 wickets at an average cost of 25.47. After
retiring as a player he continued as a first class
umpire. He died in tragic circumstances, found
drowned at Burton-on-Trent, shortly after taking
up an appointment as coach to Repton School.
Appearances: FL: 279 apps 3 gls FAC: 16 apps 1 gl
Total: 295 apps 4 gls

DARGUE, James Henderson

Inside left
Born: Blantyre, Lanarks, 1882
Died: Townhead, Glasgow, 3rd May 1937
Debut v Burnley (h) 16.12.1905, drawn 1-1
Career: Burnbank Swifts. Hamilton Academical.
Glossop December 1905. Airdrieonians June 1906.
Heart of Midlothian May 1907. Bristol Rovers 4th
May 1908. Royal Albert September 1909. Hamilton
Academical October 1913.
A recruit from Scottish Second Division football,
James Dargue joined a struggling Glossop team in
mid season 1905-06. Said to be a clever inside
forward of typically Scottish style, on the debit side
he was said to: "lack steadiness in front of goal".
After seven consecutive League appearances, of
which only one was won, he ended his season in
the reserves. He subsequently gave good service in
a season each with Airdrieonians (eight goals in 30
matches), and Heart of Midlothian (five goals in 25
matches). He next sampled Southern League
football with Bristol City (two goals in 37 matches).
Dargue returned to Douglas Park for his final
season of senior football with the Hamilton

Academical, scoring once in 14 appearances.
Outside of the game he worked as a coal miner.
Appearances: FL: 7 apps 0 gls Total: 7 apps 0 gls

DAVIDSON, Alexander Lauder

Centre forward
Born: Armadale, 27th September 1878
Died: Bolton, October quarter 1929, age 51
Debut v Notts County (h) 18.11.1899, drawn 0-0
Career: Beith. Third Lanark 20th May 1899.
Glossop North End 11th November 1899, fee "nearly
£300". Manchester City 26th March 1900. Reading
3rd May 1901. West Ham United 17th December
1902. Luton Town 24th February 1903. Fulham.
New Brompton. Kilmarnock. Aberdeen. Stockport
County 4th March 1905. Atherton Church House
25th September 1905. Bolton Wanderers 1906.
Wigan Town 29th January 1906. Nelson 23rd
November 1906. Macclesfield. Denton.
Four goals in nine appearances for Third Lanark in
the early weeks of the 1899-1900 season attracted
the attention of English clubs, but Alex Davidson's
move to Glossop was not amicable, Glossop being
censured by the FA following an inquiry. On
arrival, the *Athletic News* ventured the opinion
that Davidson played with the intention of getting
toward goal by the quickest route. He was also said
to be clever in extracting himself from difficult
positions, but his line holding abilities were not a
strong point. His debut was made on a foggy day,
the game kicking off ten minutes early. As the
Athletic News reported "Davidson was the
cynosure of all eyes," but the goalless encounter
with Notts County, fellow strugglers in Division
One, was a big disappointment to the 4,000
Glossopians assembled. A fine individual goal
against Aston Villa in the unexpected 1-0 victory in
December 1899 was the high point of his relatively
brief stay at North Road. The lowest point came
when he was suspended for one month for striking
two Nottingham Forest players after the match at
Nottingham on January 13th. His career thereafter
did not lack variety and although his overall ratio
of goals to games – roughly one goal in three
appearances – was a quite reasonable return, he
struggled to hold down a first team place
throughout much of his senior career, his best
return being 11 goals in 26 Southern League
appearances for Reading.
Appearances: FL: 13 apps 1 gl Total: 13 apps 1 gl

DAVIES, Frank

Goalkeeper
5' 11"   12st 1lb
Born: Birkenhead,
January quarter 1882
Debut v Liverpool (a) 3.9.1904,
drawn 2-2
Career: Birkenhead.   Derby
County 6th May1902. Glossop 14th

June 1904 to March 1906. Manchester City 20th June1906 to October 1909.

Signed by Derby County as understudy to Jack Fryer, the Rams' vastly experienced goalkeeper with three FA Cup final appearances, Frank Davies impressed in a trial at the Baseball Ground. The *Athletic News* reporting: "F. Davies, a tall young fellow from Birkenhead, kept a splendid goal on his trial and saved a penalty as coolly as a veteran." Called upon only once for first team action, in the final match of season 1902-03, he was signed for Glossop by Archie Goodall, the club's new team manager. Installed as first choice goalkeeper, Davies did not disappoint, being ever-present in his first season, and continuing his run of consecutive outings to 52 before injury halted his sequence. He departed Glossop rather abruptly in early March 1906. The step taken as a result of Glossop's signing of two new goalkeepers, Lindsay of Sunderland, and Frail, late Stockport County, on the 2nd March. Transferred to Manchester City in the close season, Davies made only six first team appearances, never really recovering from a disastrous start in which he conceded 13 goals within the space of two days. A 4-1 home defeat by Woolwich Arsenal on his debut, being followed by a 9-1 thrashing at Everton.

Appearances: FL: 61 apps 0 gls FAC: 5 apps 0 gls Total: 66 apps 0 gls

DAWSON, G. A.
Outside right
Debut v Fulham (h) 5.12.1914, won 1-0
Career: Glossop amateur 31st November 1914.

Two appearances as deputy for Ralph Toward on Glossop's right wing resulted in a 1-0 home win against Fulham and, in the following week, a 1-2 defeat at Stockport County. In Glossop's final season of League football they won only six of their 38 Division Two fixtures and finished six points adrift at the foot of the table.

Appearances: FL: 2 apps 0 gls Total: 2 apps 0 gls

DEARNALEY, Irvine
Left back
Born: Glossop, 18th February 1877
Died: Ashton-under-Lyne, 14th March 1965, age 88
Debut v Gainsborough Trinity (a) 28.12.1908, lost 1-3
Career: Glossop amateur in 1897, registered for Football League matches 28th October 1905. Pilgrims F.C. amateur.

Elder brother of Robert Harold, who also appeared at full back, but who was called upon only once in an injury crisis over the Christmas period in 1908. Obviously a versatile performer, he was noted as goalkeeper for the reserve team in season 1901-02, when a *Glossop Chronicle* match report, in prose that were less than deathless, described his failed effort to save a shot as follows: "Wilmington (of

Accrington Stanley) sent in a shot which the home tenter (Dearnaley) partially mulled, and the leather rolled into the net." Irvine was a better cricketer than a footballer, being a professional with Derbyshire C.C.C. in 1900, and an amateur from 1905-07. He also played for, and was secretary of the Glossop Cricket Club, and in June 1912 scored 136 against Crompton in a Central Lancashire League match. He had been associated with Glossop North End F.C. before they gained entry into the Football League, and in a lengthy association, he was noted as a director of Glossop F.C. in June 1913.

Appearances: FL: 1 app 0 gls Total: 1 app 0 gls

DEARNALEY, Robert Harold

Left back
5' 9½"
10st 11lbs
Born: Glossop, October quarter 1886
Died: Sheffield, 24th October 1951
Debut v Leeds City (h) 5.2.1910, won 2-1
Career: Glossop amateur May 1906. Pilgrims F.C. amateur 1909.

A locally born amateur full back, whose occupation was listed as a builder, painter and glazier. Bob Dearnaley signed his first amateur form at nineteen years of age, and was largely a reserve throughout, his 54 appearances spanning six seasons, with 18 matches in season 1914-15 his best seasonal return. In December 1915 he was reported to be employed in munitions and playing football for the works' team. He did not reappear in senior football after the First World War. Bob Dearnaley was an accomplished cueist and in March 1915 was the winner of the Footballers' Billiard Tournament, played at the Manchester rooms of Messrs. Orme & Sons. The tournament was staged in aid of local relief funds, and a cup for the winner of the competition was donated by Mr. W.H. Davies, a director of Manchester United. Dearnaley beat A.E. Lashbrooke, of Oldham Athletic, in the second round by 200-156, including a break of 39, the highest break of the tournament at that point. In the closely contested final he beat the Manchester United player Enoch 'Knocker' West by 350-339.

Appearances: FL: 55 apps 0 gls FAC: 2 apps 0 gls Total: 57 apps 2 gls

DONALDSON, Robert 'Bob'

Forward
5' 8"   12st 10lbs
Born: St Clement, Dundee, 10th September 1870
Debut v Blackpool (h) 3.9.1898, won 4-1 (scored one)
Career: Dundee Our Boys. Airdrieonians. Blackburn Rovers May 1891. Newton Heath May 1892. Luton Town 16th December 1897. Glossop North End 3rd May 1898, along with two other players for a combined fee of £200. Ashford FC August 1899.

When Bob Donaldson moved from Airdrieonians to Blackburn Rovers in May 1891 it was said that he received £50 down and wages of £2.10s.0d. (£2.50p) per week, a great deal of money over a century ago. A former apprentice moulder, Donaldson was one of the hardest-working centre forwards in the game. He was sometimes accused of holding onto the ball too much, but in doing so he took the majority of the knocks in the days when the game was altogether more physical and robust than it is today. In 1922 a former Newton Heath colleague recalled something of the old centre forward's methods: "Bob Donaldson used to wait in the goalmouth for free kicks to fall over his head. Then he rushed in and anything or anybody in the way had to go down." (It should be mentioned here that the regulation stipulating that the goalkeeper could only be charged when in contact with the ball did not come into operation until 1894.) Despite his robust approach, the *Cricket and Football Field*, a Bolton based newspaper, had the following to say about the old centre forward in March 1901: "Everybody had a good word for Bob; opponents, though fearing him, respected him." He was the scorer of Newton Heath's first ever League goal, and was the first to score a hat trick for them. He also scored in Glossop North End's first Football League fixture and his 18 goals was a significant contribution in a season when promotion to the First Division was achieved. Had he remained for a second season, Glossop might have avoided relegation, as they were the lowest scoring team in the League in 1899-1900 with only 31 scored in the 34-match League programme.
Appearances: FL: 32 apps 18 gls FAC: 2 apps 1 gl
Total: 34 apps 19 gls

DONCASTER, Stuart

Centre forward
5' 8½"   11st 12lbs
Born: West Burton, Nottinghamshire, April quarter 1890
Died: Preston Victoria, Australia, 1957
Debut v Blackpool (h) 6.12.1913, lost 1-2 (scored)
Career: Gainsborough County School. Buxton. Stourbridge May 1911. Aston Villa May 1912. Glossop December 1913. (Guest player with Matlock season 1915-16).

A move up from Birmingham League football with Stourbridge, to Aston Villa of Division One, saw the young and bustling centre forward cast in a reserve role, with the celebrated Harry Hampton (242 goals in 376 appearances) a fixture at the forefront of the Villa attack. A move to Glossop in December 1913 afforded more opportunities, his speedy and enthusiastic displays making him a handful for opposing defenders. His accurate marksmanship was also borne out by his excellent return of seven goals in 15 outings. Census reports revealed that Stuart Doncaster was serving with the Coldstream Guards in 1911, and in August 1914 the *Athletic News* reported that he had called up to join the colours.
Appearances: FL: 15 apps 7 gls FAC: 2 apps 0 gls
Total: 17 apps 7 gls

DOUGAL, George

Outside left
Born: Eyemouth, 1876
Died: Grimsby, April quarter 1941, age 65
Debut v West Bromwich Albion (a) 2.9.1901, won 1-0
Career: Hibernian 9th May 1896. Manchester City 9th March 1898. Glossop 3rd May to December 1901.

George Dougal began with Hibernian and missed only one match in his first season when the Hibs finished runners-up to local rivals Hearts for the championship. He was transferred to Manchester City and scored in his second appearance against Lincoln City. At the end of the season he appeared in the Manchester Senior Cup Final against Stockport County, but City had omitted to register him to play in the competition. City won 4-0, but the final had to be replayed and Stockport County took the trophy by winning 2-1. In 1898-99 Manchester City won the championship of Division Two, with the legendary Billy Meredith the scorer of 29 goals in 33 matches.

On the opposite flank, George Dougal netted seven goals in 31 appearances. Rather surprisingly for a wingman, Dougal was reported to be: "Good, but slow", but he gave good value to the City, scoring 13 goals in 75 League appearances. Sadly, he failed to settle with Glossop, his final appearance being in the FA Cup at Leicester Fosse on December 14th. He was then reported to have returned homeward to Eyemouth, resuming his trade as a cooper.

Appearances: FL: 9 apps 0 gls FAC: 3 apps 1 gl Total: 12 apps 1 gl

Honours: Manchester City, FL Division Two champions, 1899.

DURBER, Peter

Defender
Born: Wood Lane, Staffordshire, June 1873
Died: Newcastle-under-Lyne, 16th March 1963, age 89
Debut v West Bromwich Albion (a) 2.9.1901, won 1-0
Career: Wood Lane. Audley Town. Stoke 13th June 1896. Southampton 12th May 1898. Stoke 2nd May 1900. Glossop 26th August 1901. Northampton Town 5th May 1902 to 1908.

With an occupation described as "A coal miner hewer" it was not surprising to also read that the Staffordshire-born defender had a fine physique. In his first spell with Stoke he appeared in 30 League and Cup matches, but he left the potteries, and the coalmines, to join Southampton in May 1898. In two seasons he appeared in 43 Southern League matches and nine FA Cup-ties, and in 1900 played in the final of the FA Cup at Crystal Palace, and also appeared in an international trial match. He then returned to Stoke, adding a further 35 League and Cup appearances to his record before joining Glossop. In a full back partnership with Herbert Burgess, Durber missed only one match throughout the season that ended with Glossop in eighth position in Division Two. A final season with Northampton Town wound up his senior career and by 1911 he had quit football and returned to his birthplace at Wood Lane. He was working as a coalminer and later became a publican in the potteries. In May 2010, his 1900 FA Cup runners-up medal was sold at auction for £2,400.

Appearances: FL: 33 apps 0 gls FAC: 3 apps 0 gls Total: 36 apps 0 gls

Honours: Southampton: Southern League champions 1899, FA Cup finalists 1900. International Trial, South v North.

DYKE, Joseph
Outside right
Born: Biddulph, April quarter 1872
Died: Stoke-on-Trent, June 1961
Debut v Barnsley (h) 18.4.1903, drawn 2-2 (scored one)
Career: Stoke F.C. September 1902. Newcastle Swifts (Staffordshire) loan. Glossop 9th April 1903.
One of two players signed from Newcastle Swifts, Patrick Fielding was the other, both players were given a trial in the League side in the penultimate fixture of the 1902-03 season. In the 2-2 draw against Barnsley, Dyke scored the first goal from outside right. The forward line, however, lacked cohesion and Dyke was not alone in being criticised for being too individualistic.

Appearances: 1 app 1 gl Total: 1 app 1 gl

EARNSHAW, John
Right back
Debut v Bradford City (h) 1.3.1904, won 2-0
Career: Glossop February 1904. Ripley Athletic 20th September 1904. Alfreton Town 21st January 1906.
John Earnshaw was added to the Glossop ranks in the late stages of the 1903-04 season, as the team battled to avoid a re-election application. Taking over at right full back at the expense of Joe Hancock, Earnshaw formed a good understanding in partnership with Frank Norgrave and initially the team's performances lifted. Undefeated during the month of March, hopes were raised, but four defeats in the final five matches dashed all hopes, Glossop finishing next-to-bottom, agonisingly just one point adrift of Blackpool and Stockport County who finished 15th and 16th respectively. With re-election gained, sweeping changes were made, only four of the previous season's players were retained, and John Earnshaw was not one of them.

Appearances: FL: 9 apps 0 gls Total: 9 apps 0 gls

EASTHAM, John Bilsborough 'Jack'

Full back   5' 10"   12st 0lbs
Born: Blackburn, January quarter 1883
Died: Stalybridge, 3rd May 1932
Debut v Grimsby Town (a) 23.9.1905, drawn 1-1
Career: St Peter's School, Blackburn. Blackburn Rovers 15th March 1901. Glossop 23rd September 1905.

Southampton 5th May 1906 to 1912.
Injuries restricted locally born full back Jack Eastham to 48 League appearances, as the celebrated Bob Crompton's partner, in four plus years with Blackburn Rovers. He commenced his football career at the age of eighteen while working as a foundry iron turner. Joining Glossop in

September 1905, he initially found stiff competition from both Kier and Cuffe for the right full back role, but ended the season with 16 consecutive appearances having finally seen off the competition. On Boxing Day he was called up, in an emergency, to play in goal against Chelsea at North Road. Despite the unaccustomed role, he was considered blameless in the 4-2 defeat. A lengthy spell in the south followed, during which he became captain of Southampton. He completed 161 Southern League appearances (four goals) and 14 FA Cup appearances, and was awarded a benefit match against Portsmouth in September 1911. He retired at the end of the season and returned to the Blackburn area. Later he was licensee in Preston, Blackpool, and Stalybridge, where he died at the Boar's Head Hotel in 1932.

Appearances: FL: 27 apps 0 gls Total: 27 apps 0 gls

ELMORE, George

Forward
Born: Northwich, July quarter 1880
Died: K.I.A.,1st July 1916
Debut v West Bromwich Albion (h) 26.10.1907, won 2-1 (scored one)
Career: Witton Albion. Broadheath. Manchester United (trial) December 1902. West Bromwich Albion 1st January 1903. Bristol Rovers. Witton Albion 9th September 1904. Altrincham 24th August 1905. Glossop 25th October 1907. Blackpool May 1909. Partick Thistle August 1910. St Mirren 1912. Witton Albion August 1914. St Bernard's August 1915.

George Elmore's debut for Glossop was made against West Bromwich Albion, his first Football League club, and one that had released him after just four first team appearances. The fact that he scored the winning goal for Glossop against his former colleagues must have been especially satisfying. After playing in most matches in his first season, the signing of amateur international centre forward Harry Stapley in August 1908 consigned Elmore to the role of deputy, and he proved a worthy one, scoring six goals in just 11 League appearances. A season with Blackpool followed, and his six goals in 34 appearances included two against his former team mates in the 3-2 win at North Road in April 1910. Joining Partick Thistle in August 1910, Elmore had an excellent first season, in all matches scoring 16 goals, including a hat trick in a 7-2 win against St Bernard's in the Scottish Cup. He was rather less successful in his second season – six goals in 22 League matches – but he was in the Jags team that reached the final of the Glasgow Cup and picked up a finalists' medal, Rangers winning 1-0 at Celtic Park before an attendance of 58,000 spectators! Two seasons with St Mirren followed in which he scored 17 goals in 62 League matches. He left Love Street following the Buddies relegation from the

First Division in 1914. Two years later, George Elmore was killed in action in the First World War while serving as a Lance/Corporal in the 15th Battalion of the Royal Scots Regiment.

Appearances: FL: 35 apps 14 gls Total: 35 apps 14 gls

EVANS, Lorenzo

Outside left
5' 8½"   11st 0lbs
Born: Newton Heath, June 1878
Died: Poulton-le-Fylde, 6th February 1945, age 66
Debut v Burnley (h) 2.9.1899, won 2-0
Career: Newton Heath Athletic. Manchester Grammar School September 1890 to July 1895. St Anne's Rovers. St Anne's Amateurs. Blackburn Rovers amateur September 1898. Glossop amateur July 1899. Blackpool amateur cs 1900 to cs 1903.

A reserve wingman with Blackburn Rovers with just two first team appearances, Lorenzo Evans found more opportunities on joining Glossop for their debut in the First Division of the Football League. Handily versatile, he appeared on both wings, and made odd starts as centre forward and inside left. He moved on after Glossop's relegation from the top flight and next joined Blackpool, for whom he made 56 League appearances and scored six goals. He was an architect by profession.

Appearances: FL: 19 apps 3 gls Total: 19 apps 3 gls

EVENSON, Isaac 'Ike'

Centre half
Born: Manchester, 16th November 1877
Died: Stockport, April quarter 1936, age 58
Debut v Gainsborough Trinity (a) 5.11.1898, won 4-2
Career: Tonge amateur. Glossop North End 17th October 1898. Wigan County 18th November 1899. Stockport County 6th April 1901. Leicester Fosse July 1903. Luton Town. Clapton Orient 4th May 1905. West Bromwich Albion 29th April 1907, fee £225. Plymouth Argyle 5th May 1908 to cs 1910. Stalybridge Celtic.

Two consecutive appearances in Glossop North End's first season as a Football League club launched the career of Ike Evenson. Initially

operating in the half back line, he was successfully switched to a forward role during his Stockport County spell. Heading their scoring list in their first season at Edgeley Park, 1902-03. Moving on to Leicester Fosse, he was their leading scorer in season 1903-04, and in two seasons totalled 20 goals in 52 League and Cup matches. In Clapton Orient's first season in the Football League, 1905-06, he was the first Orient player to score a hat trick, in a 3-3 draw against Chesterfield on 23rd September 1905. When Orient's player-manager, Billy Holmes, was suspended by the Football League during investigations into bribery and match-fixing, Evenson took over for a three-month spell as acting player-manager. After 67 League and Cup appearances and ten goals he was transferred to West Bromwich Albion, for whom he scored one goal in eight League appearances, taking his overall League figures to 149 matches and 32 goals. Two seasons of Southern League football with Plymouth Argyle wound up his senior career.
Appearances: FL: 2 apps 0 gls Total: 2 apps 0 gls

FARRINGTON, George S

Centre forward   5' 8"   10st 12lbs
Born: Burslem, July 1882
Died: Newcastle-under-Lyme, June 1960, age 77
Debut v Burslem Port Vale (h) 26.4.1902, lost 0-1
Career: Stoke Priory. Glossop April 1902. Hanley Swifts 2nd July 1902. West Bromwich Albion March 1903. Hanley Swifts 22nd December 1904. Smallthorne 24th July 1905. Preston North End 19th January 1907. Smallthorne 5th July 1907.
Briefly with Glossop as season 1901-02 drew to its close, George Farrington was tried at centre-forward in the season's final fixture, but failed to shine in a disappointing 0-1 defeat. Almost exactly a year later, he played in one match for West Bromwich Albion against Derby County and scored once in a 3-0 win. Considered too lightweight for the role of centre forward at the highest level, he returned to non-League circles. A third opportunity, in First Division football, came when he joined Preston North End midway through the 1906-07 season. North End had scored their 1,000th goal in the Football League in March 1907, but Farrington did not add to the total in two appearances, the last of which was a 2-2 draw against already relegated Stoke at Deepdale.
Appearances: FL: 1 app 0 gls Total: 1 app 0 gls

FIELDING, Patrick

Centre forward
Born: Tunstall, 1st December 1877
Died: Bucknall, Stoke-on-Trent, 8th October 1958, age 81
Debut v Barnsley (h) 18.4.1903, drawn 2-2
Career: Newcastle Swifts (Staffordshire). Glossop April 1903.
One of two forwards signed on trial from Newcastle Swifts – J. Dyke was the other – both were tried in the penultimate fixture of the season against Barnsley. Although Fielding lacked nothing in effort, and Dyke scored Glossop's first goal, neither player was considered up to the required standard.
Appearances: FL: 1 app 0 gl Total: 1 app 0 gls

FISHER, James

Inside right
5' 5"   11st 7lbs
Born: Denny, Stirlingshire, 23rd December 1876
Died: Edinburgh, 8th February 1921
Debut v Preston North End (a) 28.11.1903, lost 0-3
Career: Vale of Forth. King's Park February 1892. East Stirlingshire 19th June 1895. St Bernard's 12th May 1896. Aston Villa 11th May 1897. Celtic 27th August 1898. Preston North End (loan) 28th January 1899. East Stirlingshire (loan) 2nd December 1899. Celtic February 1900. King's Park 18th August 1900. Newton Heath 12th October 1900. King's Park 14th February 1902. Vale of Leithen 4th December 1902. Fulham cs 1903. Glossop November 1903. Woodville United September 1904. Grays United September 1905.
A short and stocky inside forward of ripe experience, James Fisher's best spell in English football came with Newton Heath, for whom he scored three goals in 46 League and Cup appearances. Despite his earlier association with Aston Villa and Fulham, Fisher was said to be "not very conspicuous" on his debut for Glossop at Deepdale. Preston North End maintained their undefeated record (eleven wins and one draw) on their way to the championship of the Second Division while Glossop's downward spiral continued, resulting in their first application for re-admission to the Second Division.
Appearances: FL: 3 apps 0 gls Total: 3 apps 0 gls

FITCHIE, Thomas Tindal

Inside forward
5' 9"   12st 4lbs
Born: Edinburgh, 11th December 1881
Died: Streatham, London, 17th October 1947
Debut v Barnsley (h) 4.9.1909, won 3-0
Career: Hazlerigg School (Clapton). Wingfield House 1894. South London Schools 1897. West Norwood 1898. Woolwich Arsenal November 1901 to October 1906. Tottenham Hotspur April 1902. London Caledonians. Fulham 1904 to 1907. Queen's Park January 1905. Rangers September 1906. Norwich City November 1906. West Norwood December 1906. Brighton & Hove Albion October 1907. Woolwich Arsenal September 1908. Glossop amateur September 1909-11. Fulham October 1912 to 1913. London Caledonians January 1914 to 1915. Additionally appeared with The Pilgrims and English Wanderers.

Although a Scot, Thomas Fitchie had his home and business, with a leading firm of athletic outfitters, in the south. A player with a striking individuality; his raven locks, their blackness accentuated by the paleness of his complexion, were alone sufficient to arrest the attention of the crowd. It was, however, his sharp, thrilling, weaving sprints, scintillating ball jugglery, allied to his industry and skill in combination, which drew spectators to him. Despite winning four full caps for Scotland, his business career always came first, and football afterwards. An amateur player throughout, on many occasions during the course of his career he was on the books of more than one club at any given moment. Playing just for the love of the game, whether turning out for top professional clubs or amateur teams around his home in Clapham Common. He first hit the headlines as a youthful prodigy when playing for South London Schools against Westminster Schools for the Corinthian Shield, when he scored 17 goals out of the 29 registered by his side. He did even better in a return fixture, scoring 20 out of 32! Joining Woolwich Arsenal as a 20 year-old, he scored twice on his League debut against Gainsborough Trinity on 8th February 1902 and eventually totalled 27 goals in 56 League appearances for the Gunners, a major part of his career record of 38 goals in 105 League appearances. During his spell with Glossop, he partnered journalist Ivan Sharpe on the left wing and his scintillating footwork led to Sharpe dubbing him "The prince of dribblers." He was out of action for several months in his first season with Glossop, after suffering a fractured ankle on 3rd November 1909, when playing in Philadelphia for the Pilgrims during their tour of America. In summer months Fitchie played cricket for the Heathfield club and was said to be an uncommonly good fielder. He was also a fair billiards player and showed an aptitude for most sports.

Appearances: FL: 41 apps 9 gls FAC: 2 apps 0 gls Total: 43 apps 9 gls
Honours: Scotland International, four caps, 1905-07. London Caledonians: Three Isthmian League medals.

FLETCHER, Alfred Henry 'Alf'

Half back 5' 11"   12st 1lb
Born: Pen Hill, Ripley, 6th September 1892
Died: Glossop, 28th February 1984, age 91
Debut v Bradford Park Avenue (a) 7.2.1914, lost 1-2
Career: Darnall Old Boys. Ilkeston United. Glossop May 1913. Arsenal May 1914. (Wartime guest player with Derby County November 1915). Heanor Town. Chesterfield Municipal August 1919. Shirebrook July 1922. Kettering Town 1923. Glossop July 1926.

Coal miner Alf Fletcher appeared only twice for Glossop in season 1913-14, but his performance in the season's final match, against Woolwich Arsenal, obviously impressed the Gunners' directorate, who signed him some four weeks later. He spent almost all of his season at Highbury in the Reserve team, only three first team appearances being included in his season's record of 53 matches and three goals. He was offered terms by Arsenal when normal League football resumed after the Great War, but opted to return to Derbyshire. In his first season, he assisted Chesterfield Municipal to the championship of the Midland League, but made only four first team appearances when Chesterfield became members of the Football League Division 3 North in season 1921-22.

Appearances: FL: 2 apps 0 gls Total: 2 apps 0 gls

FRAIL, Martin Joseph 'Joe'

Goalkeeper
Born: Burslem, Staffs, 25th January 1869
Died: Hanley, Stoke-on-Trent, 4th September 1939
Debut v Leicester Fosse (h) 3.3.1906, drawn 0-0
Career: Burslem Port Vale (debut) November 1891. Gorton Villa October 1894. Glossop North End 30th April 1895. Derby County 10th May 1897. Chatham 3rd June 1898. Middlesbrough 18th May 1900. Luton Town 15th May 1902. Brentford cs 1903. Stalybridge Rovers January 1904. Middlesbrough 19th May 1904. Stockport County 2nd November 1905. Glossop 2nd March 1906.

A goalkeeper whose style was once described as: "Calm, collected and clever." While this seemed a fair judgment of his abilities between the posts, his off-the-field activities were in direct contrast. Joe Frail was Burslem's first goalkeeper in the Football League but was suspended for the remainder of season 1893-94 when he failed to turn up at Rotherham Town in October and failed to provide a satisfactory explanation. When he first signed with Glossop in April 1895, he was down on his luck and described as being: "On the tramp." He presented himself as a goalkeeper, but had never been heard of in Lancashire and Derbyshire football circles. A hastily arranged trial was arranged in the grounds of Glossop's great benefactor, Mr Samuel Hill-Wood, whose Moorfield estate had both cricket and football pitches. At the time, whenever a new player came to Glossop for a trial, the gardeners, coachmen, gamekeepers, butlers etc., connected with the estate were called out for a game, and the aspirant for a place in the Glossop team had to undergo a private trial. The teams were formed from the Glossop club's professionals and the house staff. Frail was placed in goal, and gave such a marvellous display in the practice game that he was immediately signed on. He was later considered one of Middlesbrough's best-ever goalkeepers, conceding less than a goal-a-game throughout 74 League and Cup appearances, during which he assisted his team to promotion to the First Division in season 1901-02, with only 24 goals conceded in 34 League matches. He was later dismissed by the Brentford club after a row with their manager on the journey back from an FA Cup defeat at Plymouth Argyle in December 1903. Joe Frail assisted five League clubs and totalled 125 appearances, the bulk of which were made with Burslem Port Vale (29 matches) and Middlesbrough (62 matches).
Appearances: FL: 16 apps 0 gls Total: 16 apps 0 gls

FREEMAN, Job
Outside right
Born: Wellington, Shropshire, 26th June 1881
Died: Llanelly, 7th April 1948, age 66
Debut v Doncaster Rovers (h) 24.2.1903, won 3-0
Career: Shrewsbury Town. Wellington Town. Glossop January 1903. Wellington Town 16th May 1904. Chester. Hamilton Academical June 1909 to cs 1910.
Job Freeman was selected for his first match in Glossop's colours in the first round of the Manchester Senior Cup against Manchester City at Hyde Road on February 1902. Heavy rain and a storm caused the game to be postponed, delaying his debut until ten days later, against Doncaster Rovers in Division Two. The weather had not improved; a wretched afternoon with a cold, raw, wind and drizzling rain saw Glossop kick off

towards the Station goal in the teeth of the storm. Although Glossop won 3-0, Freeman was given comparatively few chances on the home right wing, and when at last a chance came, the young wingman put his shot wide. His career took an upturn when he scored 54 goals for Chester in season 1908-09. Officials from the Hamilton Academical club had witnessed his performances in September 1908, leading to his move to Douglas Park in June of the following year. Unsurprisingly, he was much less prolific in his season with the Accies, but nine goals put him at the head of their goal scorers for the season. Another player with Glossop connections, Joe Irvine, scored five goals in the same campaign. Freeman was not retained at the end of the season when it was said that Lincoln City were interested in recruiting him.
Appearances: FL: 2 apps 0 gls Total: 2 apps 0 gls

FYFE, James

Inside left
5' 8"   12st 0lbs
Born: Alva, Clackmannonshire, 1882
Debut v Gainsborough Trinity (h) 22.9.1906, won 3-1
Career: Alloa Athletic 27th February 1899. Dunblane 6th October 1899. Alloa Athletic 30th August 1901. Glossop 19th May 1906.
A recruit from Scottish Combination football, James Fyfe left the Recreation Grounds, Alloa, after a lengthy association with the Clackmannanshire club, which he combined with his occupation as a joiner. A bright start to his Glossop career saw the well built inside left score three goals in his first four appearances in Division Two, but he appeared only once after the turn of the year, scoring on his final senior appearance in the 2-1 FA Cup defeat at Brentford.
Appearances: FL: 11 apps 4 gls FAC: 2 apps 1 gl
Total: 13 apps 5 gls

GADSBY, Ernest 'Ernie'

Forward
5' 7½"
11st 12lbs
Born: New Whittington, July quarter 1884
Died: Don Valley, January quarter 1963, age 78
Debut v Grimsby Town (a) 26.9.1914, lost 0-1

Career: New Whittington Exchange. Chesterfield Town 5th May 1904. Denaby United 15th May 1908. Mexborough Town. Barnsley May 1909, fee £20. Bristol City December 1910. Castleford Town. Worksop Town. Glossop May 1914. New Whittington Exchange August 1919. Clay Cross Town. Clay Cross Zingari. Bentley Colliery February 1922.

The Gadsby family could have fielded their own football team, as Ernie was one of eleven brothers who all played the game. One of them, Walter, was a full back with Chesterfield Town, and father of Kenneth, the Leeds United full back who toured South Africa with the FA Party in 1939. Ernie played in 15 matches and scored twice for Chesterfield Town but was considered too individualistic and was released into non-League football. He was offered a second opportunity by Barnsley and took full advantage scoring 12 League goals in 33 appearances and three in nine FA Cup matches, including one in the semi final replay against Everton. He appeared at inside right in the Final against Newcastle United at Crystal Palace that ended in a 1-1 draw, and also in the replay at Everton that Newcastle won 2-0. Midway through the following season he joined Bristol City, but after ten appearances and one goal he departed to Castleford Town. He joined Glossop from Worksop Town and scored in his second appearance, a 2-2 home draw against Huddersfield Town. He retained his place at inside left throughout the remainder of the season despite a disappointing record as a goal scorer, his other four goals being scored as 'doubles' in a 3-0 win against Bury, and again in Glossop's last Football League victory, 3-1 against Clapton Orient on 5th April 1915.

Appearances: FL: 32 apps 5 gls FAC: 2 apps 1 gl
Total: 34 apps 6 gls
Honours: Barnsley: FA Cup Finalists, 1910.

GALL, Leon Gambetta

Outside right
5' 7"   10st 8lbs
Born: Alloa, 1878
Debut v Liverpool (a) 3.9.1904, drawn 2-2 (scored one)
Career: Gainsborough Trinity 15th September 1896. South Shields 23rd May 1899. Doncaster Rovers 16th May 1900. Wellingborough Town 24th June 1901. Luton Town 15th May 1902. Belfast Celtic. Glossop 12th May 1904 to February 1905. Shelbourne September 1905. Belfast Celtic September 1906. Distillery. Doncaster Rovers.

Leon Gall joined Glossop some three months after he had represented the Irish League against the Scottish League at Love Street, Paisley. He was joined at North Road by Hugh Maginnis, the Linfield wing half, who had also featured in the Irish League side alongside Gall, who was immediately impressive, scoring at Liverpool on his debut in the season's opener at Anfield. His form faded in mid season, however, and he lost his right wing berth to William Prentice, a mid-season signing from Shettleston. In February 1905 his contract was cancelled in agreement with the club, a press release stating that the player wished to return to Ireland, as he considered that he had not been able to justify the big reputation that he had gained in his native country. Gall's career, which did not lack variety, commenced with Gainsborough Trinity, for whom he scored two goals in 13 League appearances.

Appearances: FL: 19 apps 2 gls FAC: 4 apps 0 gls
Total: 23 apps 2 gls
Honours: Irish League Representative

GALLACHER, William 'Willie'

Forward
Born: Glasgow, *circa* 1869
Debut v Blackpool (h) 3.9.1898, won 4-1 (scored one)
Career: Vale of Leven. Bootle 1892. Luton Town 4th April 1897. Glossop North End 6th May 1898, along with two other players for a combined fee of £200.

In two seasons with Glossop, Willie Gallacher sampled the joy of promotion and the despair of relegation. A good all-round forward and a regular throughout both campaigns, he was a fine and accurate crosser from the wing, and was not slow to shoot when the opportunity arose. Although details of his birth and death have proved elusive, in a December 1899 match report, the *Athletic News* correspondent suggested that Gallacher was approaching the veteran stage, having "been in harness for many years." In earlier days, he scored nine goals in 22 appearances for Bootle, and seven goals in 30 appearances for Luton Town.

Appearances: FL: 54 apps 18 gls FAC: 4 apps 1 gl
Total: 58 apps 19 gls

GALLEY, William Thomas

Left half 5' 9½"   11st 0lbs
Born: Nantwich, January quarter 1881
Died: Crewe, October quarter 1941, age 60
Debut v Burton United (a) 5.9.1903, lost 0-1
Career: Nantwich Town. Shrewsbury Town. Glossop July 1903. Bolton Wanderers (trial) 12th September 1904. Shrewsbury Town 28th November 1904. Chester 5th July 1905. Crewe Alexandra 25th September 1907.

For season 1903-04, Glossop retained just seven of the previous season's men and eleven newcomers were signed. One of the new players, William Galley, was at left half as the season opened with a disappointing 1-0 home defeat by Burton United. Much worse was to follow as the next two matches – away at Bristol City and at home to Manchester United – both ended in 5-0 defeats. After eight matches and three points from a possible sixteen, the axe was wielded and Galley lost his place to Fred Coates. He made only three further first team appearances, but his last one, a 3-3 home draw against Bolton Wanderers was sufficiently impressive for him to be offered a two-month trial at Burnden Park, but this did not lead to a permanent engagement.

Appearances: FL: 11 apps 0 gls Total: 11 apps 0 gls

GALVIN, Patrick

Centre half   5' 7½"   11st 0lbs
Born: Glossop, 19th October 1882
Died: K.I.A. France, 17th October 1918
Debut v Chesterfield (h) 13.10.1906, won 3-1
Career: Glossop Central (Champions of Glossop & District League). Glossop 18th October 1901. Barrow 1904. Brynn Central 29th April 1904. Stalybridge Rovers 11th April 1905. Oldham Athletic 7th February 1906, fee £15 plus half of proceeds from a friendly match between the two clubs at Hudson Fold, Oldham. Glossop 19th May 1906, appointed player-coach March 1907. Rochdale 1st September 1908. Eccles Borough September 1910.

Paddy Galvin was first associated with his hometown club on the eve of his nineteenth birthday, and later in his career he returned to North Road after a variety of experience that commenced in the Second Division of the Lancashire Combination with Barrow. Returning from Oldham Athletic in May 1906, he did not command a regular place in the side until tried at centre half. One appraisal at this time considered him to be: "A hard worker who never tired; cool and collected when defending and quick to seize an opportunity in attack." In his second season with Rochdale, they won promotion from the Second Division of the Lancashire Combination and additionally won the Lancashire Junior Cup, beating Eccles Borough 3-2 at Burnden Park, Bolton, on Easter Monday 1910. Galvin lost his life while serving with the Royal Dublin Fusiliers, and was buried at the Highland Cemetery, La Cateau, France. He had earlier been awarded the Military Medal for bravery in action.

Appearances: FL: 20 apps 4 gls FAC: 1 app 0 gls Total: 21 apps 4 gls

GETTINS, Charles Edward 'Eddie'

Left back
5' 9"   11st 7lbs
Born: Darlaston, April quarter 1883
Died: Stockport, January quarter 1925, age 41
Debut v Leeds City (a) 2.9.1907, lost 1-2
Career: Gainsborough Trinity 7th September 1899. Middlesbrough May 1903. Reading 10th May 1905. Glossop 15th May 1907. Stockport County May 1909. Haslingden.

Eddie Gettins commenced with Gainsborough Trinity and in a stay of four years appeared in 110 Division Two matches and scored 29 goals. His move to Middlesbrough coincided with the club's move to their new ground, Ayresome Park, and Gettins was at outside right when Sunderland were the first visitors on 12th September 1903. The attendance was estimated to be 30,000, but Sunderland spoilt the party by winning 3-2. In two seasons, Gettins completed 43 League appearances and scored five goals. Two seasons of Southern League football with Reading preceded his transfer to Glossop. Initially fielded at outside right, he was switched from attack to defence when McEwan was injured in early season, and he slotted into his unaccustomed role so well that he retained the position thereafter. After two seasons he was transferred to Stockport County, for whom he appeared in 62 League matches and five FA Cup-ties. His career aggregate figures were 257 League appearances and 34 goals.

Appearances: FL: 41 apps 0 gls Total: 41 apps 0 gls

GIBBON, Thomas

Goalkeeper
5' 9"   11st 8lbs
Born: West Hartlepool, 24th March 1891
Died: Luton, 12th April 1975, age 84
Debut v Fulham (h) 20.9.1913, lost 0-1
Career: Hartlepool St Joseph's. Houghton Rovers. Glossop May 1913. Merthyr Town 1914. (Wartime guest player with Hartlepools United April 1919). Dundee July 1920. Luton Town June 1922. Queens Park Rangers August 1924. Mid-Rhondda United November 1924. Torquay United December 1926. Ebbw Vale. Thames Association trainer October 1929. Newport County trainer cs 1932.

On arrival at Glossop, Tommy Gibbon was billed as "A young and promising custodian from Houghton Rovers, members of the North-Eastern League." The former shipyard plater was signed as cover for Arthur Causer, but found few first team opportunities. He then assisted Merthyr Town at either side of the Great War, appearing in all matches in 1919-20. He subsequently enjoyed much first team football in Scotland and the Southern League, including 41 appearances for Dundee in season 1920-21 and 69 Third Division South appearances in two seasons with Luton Town. His final playing season was with Torquay United, who headed the Southern League, Western Section, table in 1926-27 and were elected to the Football League Division Three South in the close season.

Appearances: FL: 4 apps 0 gls Total: 4 apps 0 gls

GODDARD, Arthur

Outside right
5' 9½"
11st 7lbs
Born: Heaton Norris, 14th June 1878
Died: Liverpool North, April quarter 1956, age 77
Debut v Sheffield United (h) 2.12.1899, drawn 2-2
Career: Christ Church FC. Heaton Norris Albion. Stockport County 1898. Glossop 21st November 1899, fee £260. Liverpool 25th April 1902, fee £600. Cardiff City cs 1914 to 1920.

Flying wingman Arthur Goddard scored in both of his first two outings for Stockport County in April 1898, and his displays in two FA Cup meetings with Glossop in November of the following year led to his £260 transfer to North Road. A run of 65 consecutive League matches was only halted by his appearance for the Football League against the Irish League at the Manor Ground Plumstead on 9th November 1901. The Football League won 9-0 with Goddard's inside partner Steve Bloomer the scorer of four goals. Some five months later he was transferred to Liverpool where he won championships of the First and Second Divisions in twelve years of sterling service. Fast and fluent in style, he captained the side and recorded 388 League appearances and scored 75 goals. He also made a second appearance for the Football League in 1909, captaining the side that beat the Irish League 8-1 at Boundary Park, Oldham. Moving on

to Cardiff City, he assisted them to finish third in the First Division of the Southern League in 1914-15, and fourth in 1919-20 when football returned to normality after the First World War. He was later in business as a greengrocer in Liverpool.

Appearances: FL: 77 apps 22 gls FAC: 5 apps 2 gls Total: 82 apps 24 gls

Honours: FL Representative, 2 apps 1901-09
Liverpool: FL Division One Champions 1906. Division Two Champions 1905.
International Trial, North v South, at the Crystal Palace, March 1900.

GOLDIE, John Wyllie 'Jock'

Half back
5' 8"   11st 2lbs
Born: Hurlford, Ayrshire, 10th November 1889
Debut v Hull City (a) 9.9.1911, lost 0-2
Career: Hurlford Thistle. Fulham 25th May 1908. Glossop June 1911. Bury September 1912. Kilmarnock (loan) January 1916. Dundee (loan) February 1918.

Kilmarnock May 1920. Clyde (loan) October 1922. Banned for life from football in August 1923.

Although the transfer fee was never revealed, Glossop were said to have paid "a substantial sum" for the transfer of Jock Goldie, who did not find his best form with Glossop until fielded at centre half. Early season outings in both wing half berths had not seen him at his best, but as pivot he tackled with great determination and distributed the ball to advantage. At either side of the Great War he made 154 appearances for Bury, but three years after leaving Gigg Lane he was banned for life. Allegations of bribery and match fixing in the games against Coventry City in April 1920 surfaced following extreme disharmony amongst the board of the Bury club, leading to a commission of inquiry by the Football Association. Their findings resulted in several board members, manager W.S. Cameron (q.v.) and four players, including Jock Goldie, being suspended permanently, one player being suspended for twelve months. Other family members were Archie Goldie, who won a Division Two championship medal with Liverpool in 1896, and William, whose honours included a Division One championship medal with Liverpool in 1901, and two Southern League championships with Fulham, 1905-07.

Appearances: FL: 33 apps 0 gls FAC: 1 app 0 gls Total: 31 apps 0 gls

GOODALL, Archibald Lee 'Archie'

Centre half
Born: Belfast, 3rd January 1865
Died: Barnet, 29th November 1929
Debut v Manchester United (a) 16.1.1904, lost 1-3
Career: Liverpool Stanley. St Jude's. Preston North End 1888. Aston Villa October 1888. Derby County 26th September 1889. Plymouth Argyle May 1903. Glossop January 1904. Wolverhampton Wanderers 20th October 1905.
Archie Goodall joined his brother John at Glossop, the centre-half arriving after a relatively short stay with Plymouth Argyle. He made his first appearance in Glossop's colours at Manchester United and, as the *Athletic News* reported: "It was not his fault that the game was lost." Despite his long career, Archie was still a capable footballer, in feeding his forwards and assisting in defence he did well and as one observer noted: "It is hoped that his labour will lift the club from the dire straits it is in at the moment." In earlier days he assisted both Preston North End and Aston Villa in the season that the Football League was launched, 1888-89. In ten unruly and boisterous seasons with Derby County he was often at odds with his club and football's authorities, seemingly able to start an argument in an empty room. That said, he

was an outstanding footballer, scoring 85 League and Cup goals in 238 appearances for the Rams, figures more remarkable considering that his usual playing position was that of centre half. As a Music-hall artist, he toured both Europe and America with a strongman act.
Appearances: FL: 26 apps 13 gls FAC: 4 apps 1 gl
Total: 30 apps 14 gls
Honours: Ireland International 10 caps, 1899-1904. Derby County: FA Cup Finalists 1898 & 1903.

GOODALL, John

Forward   5' 9"   11st 12lbs
Born: Westminster, London, 19th June 1863
Died: Watford, 20th May 1942, age 78
Debut v Burslem Port Vale (h) 9.2.1901, lost 1-2
Career: Kilmarnock Burns Athletic. Great Lever. Preston North End August 1888. Derby County 8th April 1889. New Brighton Tower 27th October 1899. Glossop 2nd February 1901. Watford player-manager May 1903; manager-trainer June 1909. Racing Club Roubaix player-manager June 1910. Mardy player-manager May 1912, retired 1913.
Elder brother of Archie (q.v.), both were sons of Scottish parents, their father a corporal in the Scottish Fusiliers. Archie was born in Belfast, and a sister in Edinburgh. John was born at Westminster, when his father was quartered there, but moved to Kilmarnock as an infant, and spoke

with a Scottish accent as a consequence. He started in senior football with Preston North End in the first season of the Football League. The team that passed into soccer history as The Invincibles" commenced by scoring twice within three minutes of the kick-off against Burnley at Deepdale, and won the game 5-2. In the 22-match tournament they were undefeated, scoring 74 goals and conceding just 15. They completed the first-ever 'Double' when they beat Wolverhampton Wanderers 3-0 at the Kennington Oval, John Goodall scoring one of the goals. He was also the highest goal scorer in the Football League that season with 21 goals in as many matches. In the biggest transfer of the late 19th Century, Goodall, considered the *doyen* of English forwards, signed for Derby County, in time for the second season of the Football League. An outstanding inside or centre forward, although not a prolific marksman, he excelled in combination and was master of the defence splitting pass, providing much of the ammunition for the legendary marksman, Steve Bloomer. In fourteen seasons with the Rams, Goodall amassed 423 League and Cup appearances and scored 52 goals. In attempts to improve their flagging fortunes and lack of support, New Brighton Tower signed him but after just six matches and two goals he was on the move again, arriving at Glossop at the age of 37. Hardly as nimble as formerly, but with such a sound knowledge of the game and sure touch on the ball, he passed the landmark of a century of League goals in Glossop's colours, when he netted twice against Gainsborough Trinity in a 4-2 win on 27th December 1902. Watford's new owner, Ralph Thorpe, was instrumental in recruiting him as player-manger, and he duly led the side to the championship of the Southern League Division Two in his first season with an unbeaten record. He made 69 Southern League and seven FA Cup appearances and scored 17 goals, playing on until the age of 44. Among other talents, John Goodall was a professional county cricketer with Derbyshire and Hertfordshire, and represented England at bowls. Additionally, he was a prize-winning cage-bird breeder with a shop in Watford.

Appearances: FL: 34 apps 8 gls FAC: 8 apps 2 gls
Total: 42 apps 10 gls

Honours: England International 14 caps, 1888 to 1898. FL Representative, 4 apps. Preston North End: FL Champions 1889. FA Cup winners 1889. Derby County FA Cup finalists 1898. Watford: Southern League Division Two champions 1904.

GOODWIN, Ralph
Right back   5' 8½"   11st 7lbs
Born: Norton-in-the-Moors, Staffordshire,
14th July 1885
Died: Stockport, January quarter 1963, age 82
Debut v Chesterfield (h) 13.10.1906, won 3-1
Career: Tunstall Park. Glossop 31st August 1906. Stalybridge Rovers 20th September 1907. Stockport County 6th April 1908. Preston North End June 1919, fee £250. Stockport County September 1920.
In his first season of League football, Ralph Goodwin showed enough promise to keep Glossop's record appearance holder Cuffe out of the side for a run of fourteen consecutive matches in the first half of the season. He was allowed to depart to Stalybridge Rovers in the close season, but Stockport County moved in to sign him before the close of the campaign. One of the most powerful and resourceful full backs in the Second Division, he was to complete 188 League and Cup appearances for County, and a further 136 during wartime. He finally left Edgeley Park after differences in regard to a benefit; Preston North End paying £250 for his transfer, but he failed to settle at Deepdale, making only seven League appearances before returning to Stockport. He was to make just one final appearance, in December 1920, and then retired to run an athletic sports outfitter's business.
Appearances: FL: 14 apps 0 gls FAC: 1 app 0 gls
Total: 15 apps 0 gls

GOULD, William 'Willie'

Outside left
5' 8"   10st 8lbs
Born: Burton-on-Trent,
July quarter 1884
Died: Bebington, Cheshire,
18th November 1951, age 67
Debut v Leeds City (a)
2.9.1907, lost 1-2
Career: Stafford Street School. Burton Schoolboys. Burton Star. Burton United 1903. Leicester Fosse 19th June 1905. Bristol Rovers 10th May 1906. Glossop 6th May 1907. Bradford City 18th September 1908. Manchester City May 1909. Tranmere Rovers May 1912.
Employed in a local brewery at the time of his Football League debut, fast and tricky wingman Willie Gould made an excellent start, scoring eight goals in 38 matches for his hometown team, Burton United. A move to Leicester Fosse brought few opportunities, but he played in every League and Cup match for Southern League Bristol Rovers in 1906-07. In a large turnover of players, Glossop signed eleven new men for season 1907-08 and Gould was one of the best of the newcomers, his hat trick against West Stanley in the fifth qualifying round of the FA Cup earning Glossop a

plum home tie against Manchester City, and a welcome pay day when the match went to a replay at Hyde Road. In the following season, Gould played in just one match, scoring against Bradford Park Avenue in a 1-1 draw on September 12th. A few days later he was on the move to Bradford, but joined the City, for whom he scored two goals in 18 matches. Manchester City was his final port of call in senior football, and although he had a lengthy wait for a first team opportunity, he had the satisfaction of scoring two goals in the final six matches of the season as City clinched the championship of Division Two. He spent the years leading up to the Great War with Tranmere Rovers and scored seven goals in 31 matches in the championship winning season of 1913-14. In the following campaign, he was one of the goal scorers in Tranmere's record victory in the FA Cup – 13-0 v Oswestry Town on 10th October 1914.

Appearances: 32 apps 6 gls FAC: 3 apps 3 gls Total: 35 apps 9 gls

Honours: Tranmere Rovers, Lancashire Combination Champions 1914.

GREECHAN, James

Inside left
5' 8"   11st 7lbs
Born: Glasgow, 1883
Debut v Oldham Athletic (h) 25.4.1908, drawn 0-0
Career: Petershill. Hibernian July 1903. Bo'ness. Brentford 11th May 1906. Clapton Orient 21st September 1907. Glossop 24th April 1908. Stockport County May 1909. Carlisle United cs 1910. Albion Rovers. Bathgate

James Greechan was described as "An inside left of much promise" when he joined Hibernian in the summer of 1903. In June he had played for Glasgow Juveniles against Edinburgh at Easter Road, when connected with the Petershill club. He was next with Bo'ness, considered to be one of the foremost provincial teams in the East of Scotland. He first crossed the border to join Brentford of the Southern League, and arrived at Glossop after seven months with Clapton Orient, for whom he scored 11 goals in 33 League and Cup matches. Seemingly reserving his best form for FA Cup matches, Greechan starred in Glossop's run to the quarter final of the FA Cup, scoring winning goals in the 1-0 home win against Stockport County, and more famously from the penalty spot in the 1-0 win at Sheffield Wednesday. Transferred to Stockport County in May 1909, along with two other Glossop players, Weir and Gettins, Greechan scored four goals in 16 Division Two matches, and one in two FA Cup-ties. He left to join Carlisle United who resigned from the Lancashire Combination in May 1910, prompted by financial considerations, and

commenced operations in the North Eastern League.

Appearances: FL: 19 apps 3 gls FAC: 5 apps 2 gls Total: 24 apps 5 gls

GREEN, William

Inside-left
Debut v Bolton Wanderers (a) 14.11.1903, won 1-0
Career: Glossop United. Glossop November 1903. Denton F.C. February 1905.

It seems reasonable to assume that William Green was signed on the back of his performances for the newly-formed Glossop United club, members of the Manchester League. United had opposed a Glossop X1 in a pre-season friendly, and they also had a ground sharing agreement with the senior club, playing their home matches at North Road. The dapper and moustachioed Green enjoyed a fair amount of League action, ten of his 15 appearances being made consecutively from November onwards. He scored in home and away fixtures against Leicester Fosse, his final goal coming in the 5-0 home win in the penultimate Division Two fixture of the season.

Appearances: FL: 16 apps 3 gls Total: 16 apps 3 gls

GRIMES, William John 'Billy'

Winger
5' 6"   11st 0lbs
Born: Ickleford, Herts, 27th March 1886
Died: Arlesey, Beds, 6th January 1936
Debut v Grimsby Town (a) 28.9.1907, lost 0-4
Career: Hitchin St John's. Hitchin Town. Watford 29th May 1906. Glossop 6th May 1907. Bradford City 12th December 1908, in exchange for Clare Wilson. Derby County March 1910. (Wartime guest player with Tottenham Hotspur). Luton Town July 1919 to cs 1920.

Billy Grimes commenced with Watford, appearing in all five forward positions in 1906-07, scoring four goals in 16 Southern League and FA Cup matches. First tried at centre forward by Glossop, he was quickly switched to outside right, scoring his first goal in a 2-2 draw against Blackpool on 12th October. He retained his position throughout, and was second highest goal scorer with nine League goals in 33 matches. He lost his right wing place to the amateur international Jim Raine in season 1908-09, and moved on in mid term to join Bradford City of Division One. After 17 League appearances and one goal, he joined Derby County who, in the space of four seasons were relegated once and promoted twice. Grimes' contribution being an impressive 161 League appearances. He made a further 12 appearances in the wartime Midlands Section 1915-16 before the club closed down for the duration. He then played as a guest with Tottenham Hotspur, and spent his final season in post war football in the Southern League with Luton Town.

Appearances: FL: 45 apps 10 gls FAC: 3 apps 0 gls Total: 48 apps 10 gls

Honours: Derby County FL Division Two Champions 1912 and 1915.

GROVES, Frederick William 'Freddie'

Outside right
5' 9"   11st 4lbs
Born: Shadwell, London, 13th January 1891
Died: Hove, January quarter 1965
Debut v Bradford Park Avenue (a) 23.9.1911, drawn 1-1
Career: Barnet Alston. Glossop amateur May 1911. Woolwich Arsenal amateur August 1912, professional October 1913. Brighton & Hove Albion February 1920, fee £500. Arsenal cs 1920. Brighton & Hove Albion July 1921. Charlton Athletic June 1924 to cs 1925.

Freddie Groves contested the right wing position with Billy Law in season 1911-12, but after run of nine consecutive matches in early season, which featured five draws and four defeats, Law took over and retained the position for the remainder of the campaign. Once described as a tricky customer along the touchline, but one who did not shoot often enough, he nevertheless gave good service to both Woolwich Arsenal (50 appearances and six goals) and Brighton & Hove Albion (53 appearances and two goals). Approaching the sunset of his career he appeared in only seven matches for Charlton Athletic before his release at the age of 34.

Appearances: FL: 9 apps 0 gls Total: 9 apps 0 gls

HALL, Thomas 'Tommy'

Half back
Born: Macclesfield January quarter 1877
Died: Stockport, 8th April 1955, age 78
Debut v Newton Heath (h) 1.9.1900, won 1-0
Career: Macclesfield. Stockport County 17th June 1896. Glossop 4th May 1900. Stockport County 15th October 1902, to cs 1907.

Fair-haired wing half Tommy Hall left Stockport County after four years, moving on at the close of a most successful season, 1899-1900, in which they won the championship of the Lancashire League. They additionally knocked Glossop – at that time a First Division side - out of the FA Cup, Hall scoring one of the goals from the penalty spot in the 2-2 draw at North Road. In the following week he assisted his team to win 3-0 in the replay. Stockport were elected to the Second Division of the Football League in the close season, but Glossop moved in to sign two of their best players, Tommy Hall and Frank Chesworth (q.v.). Hall appeared for Glossop in all three half back positions and occasionally at full back in two seasons, illustrating a very useful two-footed adaptability. In October 1902 he returned to assist Stockport County, who failed to win re-election to Division Two at the close of the 1903-04 season. Their stay in the Lancashire Combination proved short lived, as they won the championship at the first time of asking, with a seven-point margin over runners-up Liverpool Reserves. Additionally, and by coincidence, they again knocked Glossop out of the FA Cup, winning 1-0 after a replay that followed two earlier attempts to settle the tie, one abandoned due to fog, the other due to a snowstorm. In his second spell at Edgeley Park, Hall completed 76 League appearances and scored six goals, plus 21 FA Cup appearances and three goals. On 2nd February 1907, fixture between the Reserve teams of Stockport County and Glossop was set aside for Hall's benefit, at that time he was captain of the County's Reserve team. Census records of the time gave his occupation as a 'Concreter' in the construction industry.

Appearances: FL: 53 apps 2 gls FAC: 5 apps 1 gl Total: 58 apps 3 gls

HAMPTON, George

Right back
5' 8½"
11st 2lbs
Born:
Wellington,
Shropshire, April
quarter 1890
Died:
Birmingham,
March 1951
Debut v Burnley
(a) 18.4.1910,
won 1-0
Career: Aston
Villa amateur.
Wellington St George's. Glossop amateur May
1909. Aston Villa June 1914, fee £150. Shrewsbury
Town May 1915. Willenhall 1919-20.
George Hampton was a fixture in Glossop's
defence for a number of seasons, after he had won
the right back position from Jimmy Heywood from
the mid point of his second season at North Road.
Crisp tackling and with a fine degree of
consistency, his outstanding displays during
season 1913-14 earned him a move to the season's
Championship runners-up and semi-finalists,
Aston Villa. At Villa Park he joined his elder
brother, the goalkeeper's nightmare, Harry
Hampton, who scored 242 goals in 376
appearances, and was capped four times by
England. George by contrast spent much of his
single season at Villa Park in the Reserves, playing
in just three First Division matches.
Appearances: FL: 110 apps 1 gl FAC: 7 apps 0 gls
Total: 117 apps 1 gl

HANCOCK, Joseph

Right back
5' 10"   12st 4lbs
Debut v Gainsborough
Trinity (a) 25.4.1903,
drawn 1-1
Career: Bradley F.C. 5th
October 1900. Bradley Swifts
11th September 1901. Glossop
17th April 1903.
Described as: "A smart,
sturdy chap who looked
every inch a footballer", Joe
Hancock seized his
opportunity when given a
trial in the final fixture of the
1902-03 season, and
commenced the following
campaign as first team right
full back. He took over a position in the side that
had been dominated by Herbert Burgess, who had
departed to Manchester City in the close season.
Despite a shaky start, Hancock showed steady

improvement alongside his more experience
partner, Frank Norgrave.
Appearances: FL: 26 apps 0 gls Total: 26 apps 0 gls

HARRISON, Thomas
Left half
Born: Glossop, January quarter 1885
Died: Glossop, December 1962
Debut v Gainsborough Trinity (a)
25.4.1903, drawn 1-1
Career: Glossop April 1903.
A greatly altered Glossop team travelled to
Gainsborough for the final fixture of season 1902-
03. In the previous week, in the 2-2 home draw
against Barnsley, J. Dyke and P. Fielding had been
given their debuts in the Football League, and for
the Gainsborough match T. Harrison and J.
Hancock were similarly introduced. A report of the
match suggested that Gainsborough should have
won with ease, being much the better team in
midfield, they were, however, woefully weak in
front of goal. A quarter of an hour before the finish,
Jacklin scored for the home side, but the joy of the
home crowd was short lived, as a clever individual
effort from Irvine Thornley quickly equalised the
scores. Of Glossop's two new men, Hancock
appeared to be the best prospect, and in the event
he was retained and played in most matches in the
following season. Harrison did not add to his
solitary outing in the Football League.
Appearances: FL: 1 app 0 gls Total: 1 app 0 gls

HARVEY, Ernest Alfred
Right back   5' 8½"   14st 0lbs
Born: Whittington, near Chesterfield, October
quarter 1883
Died: Chesterfield, 10th February 1959, age 75
Debut v Fulham (a) 2.9.1908, won 3-2
Career: Royal Navy football. New Brompton 19th
October 1906. Glossop 4th May 1908. Hyde FC.
Massively built full back Ernest Harvey was
certainly one of the heaviest players to represent
Glossop in the Football League. The former sailor,
and later goods clerk, spent much of his single
season at North Road in the reserve side, with
Hofton and Cuffe the favoured rear pairing. He had
commenced with New Brompton, and on joining
Glossop, was introduced by the *Athletic News* as:
"A well built fellow, who comes with the reputation
of being one of the best full backs in the Southern
League." His season at North Road started badly
when he was carried off the field after being
injured at Wolverhampton on his fourth
appearance. He did return for one more League
game at Birmingham on 19th December, but at the
end of the month his season came to a premature
and painful end following alleged violent scenes
that took place at Worksop on New Years Eve. The
team were there for special training, but the
unfortunate Harvey finished up in Sheffield

Infirmary with a burst eyeball. A directors' inquiry immediately suspended manager J.T. Robertson, Morrison and James Robertson, and although the findings of the hearing were not subsequently disclosed, all three of the suspended players were in the side that played against Burnley on January 2nd.

Appearances: FL: 5 apps 0 gls Total: 5 apps 0 gls

HENDERSON, George Turnbull

Right half
5' 7"   11st 7lbs
Born: Gorbals, Glasgow, 2nd May 1879
Died: Birmingham, 27th January 1930
Debut v Hull City (a) 9.4.1910, lost 2-4
Career: Queen's Park. Dundee 22nd January 1902.   Rangers November   1902. Middlesbrough   June 1905,   fee   £130. Chelsea   April   1905. Glossop May 1909.

George Henderson began with Queen's Park, but made only one appearance – versus Hearts in an Inter City League match – in May 1901. He joined Dundee in the following season and moved swiftly on to the Rangers where he appeared in three Scottish Cup Finals and was capped by his country in 1904. An accomplished stylist in the middle line and a fine tackler he later starred in the Football League with Middlesbrough and Chelsea. He was one of two Scottish internationals who joined Glossop in the summer of 1909, the other being the famous amateur T.T. Fitchie, ex-Woolwich Arsenal. Sadly, Henderson failed to shine in his season at North Road. In a side that finished sixth in the Second Division, Craigie, Morrison and Wilson were the main occupants of the three half back positions throughout the season.

Appearances: FL: 6 apps 0 gls Total: 6 apps 0 gls
Honours: Scotland International, 1 cap v Ireland 1904. Rangers: Scottish Cup winners 1903; finalists 1904 and 1905.

HENDERSON, James Thomas

Forward
Born: Bootle *circa* 1894
Debut v Bury (a) 21.3.1914, lost 0-1
Career: Everton 'A' Team. Bootle F.C. Derby County Reserves cs 1913. Glossop March 1914. (Wartime guest player with Liverpool). Bristol Rovers September 1919. Derby County 1920.

Signed by Derby County from Bootle on the strength of his play in trial matches at the start of the 1913-14 season, Henderson was said to have impressed in the Rams' Reserve side prior to joining Glossop in March 1914. With a hard shot in either foot and a goodly turn of speed, the 20 year-old inside forward made an immediate impact, scoring four goals in his first eight Division Two matches in the final months of season 1913-14. He began the following campaign in the League side, but after six matches lost his place in a struggling side, destined to finish at the foot of the table. The war interrupted his fledgling career, and although he resumed in post war football, he played only once for Bristol Rovers in the Southern League, and did not appear in Derby County's first team.

Appearances: FL: 23 apps 7 gls Total: 23 apps 7 gls

HERBERT, William Edward 'Billy'

Inside right
5' 8½"   11st 7lbs
Born: St. George in the East, London, October quarter 1888
Died: Stoke-on-Trent, July quarter 1928
Debut v Huddersfield Town (a) 1.4.1911, lost 0-1
Career: Walthamstow Grange. Barnet Aston. Woolwich Arsenal 1909. Glossop March 1911. Gravesend United. Stoke December 1912. Bolton Wanderers November 1919, fee £1,500. Wigan Borough September 1921 to May 1922.

Billy Herbert's career in League football commenced with Glossop, after he had failed to reach senior level with Woolwich Arsenal. A forceful attacker, equally at home in either inside forward position, he was quickly snapped up by Stoke. In a lengthy association with them, spanning the Great War, he won two Southern League championships and was a prolific scorer during wartime football. Bolton Wanderers paid £1,500 to take him to Burnden Park, and he duly scored at Everton in his first match. He scored seven goals in 34 League matches before a final move in senior football took him to Wigan Borough. His transfer fee was undisclosed but was said to be a record fee paid by a club in the Northern Section of Division Three. Initially working well in tandem with Bert Freeman, the former Arsenal, Burnley and England international centre forward, sadly he sustained a knee injury and an abortive come-back in April ended during a preliminary run-out prior to kick-off.

Appearances: FL: 17 apps 3 gls FAC: 1 app 0 gls Total: 18 apps 3 gls
Honours: Stoke: Southern League Division Two champions 1910 and 1915.

HEWITT, John
Inside-right
Debut v Leicester Fosse (h) 9.4.1904, won 5-0
Career: Manchester City. Glossop April 1904.
A reserve team forward recruited from Manchester City as part of the deal that took Irvine Thornley to Hyde Road. Hewitt was without League experience, and although he was reported to have "Done some useful work in the first half" he was not selected again. His debut saw Glossop and Leicester Fosse fighting desperately for points at the foot of Division Two. Although Glossop defeated Fosse by five clear goals – Archie Goodall netting a hat trick – they were less successful in their next match, losing at home by 2-0 against Gainsborough Trinity in the season's final fixture and being obliged to apply for re-election as a consequence.
Appearances: FL: 1 app 0 gls Total: 1 app 0 gls

HEYWOOD, James 'Jimmy'

Full back
5' 6½"   11st 2lbs
Born: Stockport, January quarter 1881
Died: Stockport, 24th September 1964, age 83
Debut v Barnsley (a) 8.1.1910, lost 0-3
Career: Stockport County 7th May 1904. Blackburn Rovers 6th April 1907. Glossop January 1910.

Nelson cs 1911.
Jimmy Heywood commenced with the 'Hatters', and quite appropriately worked in the local industry as a 'hatter finisher'. A short but strongly built defender, Heywood was cool, plucky, quick to recover and was altogether a lively force at full back. His Stockport partnership with Arthur Waters was considered one of the best, as well as the smallest, in the Second Division. He arrived at Glossop, to fill the place of the injured Leslie Hofton, as a 29 year-old with a wealth of experience, despite his progress with Blackburn Rovers being limited due to the full back positions at Ewood being dominated by Bob Crompton and Arthur Cowell. After a lengthy run of first team football with Glossop, he lost his place at right back to George Hampton at the mid point of season 1910-11. He departed in the close season to assist Nelson in the Lancashire Combination, and in season 1913-14 he was still turning out with the Seedhill club.
Appearances: FL: 39 apps 0 gls Total: 39 apps 0 gls

HOARE, Gordon Rahere
Forward 5' 11"   12st 3lbs
Born: Blackheath, Kent, 18th April 1884
Died: Putney, London, 27th October 1973
Debut v Stockport County (h) 11.12.1909, won 1-0 (scored)
Career: Westcombe Park. West Norwood 1906. Woolwich Polytechnic. Bromley. Woolwich Arsenal May 1907. Glossop amateur December 1909. Bromley. The Pilgrims. Woolwich Arsenal 1910. Glossop amateur February 1912. Queen's Park November 1913. West Norwood April 1913. Bromley November 1913. Queen's Park December 1913. Arsenal March 1914. Northfleet United August 1914. West Norwood. (Wartime guest with Fulham and Manchester City {September 1916}. Fulham December 1919.
Along with Harry Littlewort (q.v.), Gordon Hoare was a Gold Medal winner in the 1912 Olympic Games, scoring twice in the final against Denmark who were beaten 4-2. Amongst a collection of early medals, Hoare was twice a championship winner with Westcombe Park, and assisted Woolwich Polytechnic to win the championship of the London League. He began in senior football with Woolwich Arsenal, scoring 13 goals in 34 appearances. He arrived at Glossop a matter of days after returning from America, where he had taken part in the Pilgrims' tour. He stepped straight into the League side to replace Harry Stapley who was playing against Holland for the England Amateur eleven. Hoare scored on his debut against Stockport County, but did not play regularly until signing for a second spell from February 1912, his best seasonal return being nine goals in 25 League matches in season 1912-13. He played only twice in League matches for Fulham, but netted 23 goals in as many games in wartime season 1916-17, including five in one match against Reading. A multi talented sportsman, Hoare was a good golfer, swimmer and a keen cyclist. He was aged 89 when he died at Putney in October 1973.
Appearances: FL: 51 apps 16 gls FAC: 2 apps 1 gl Total: 53 apps 17 gls
Honours: England Amateur International, 13 caps. Gold Medal winner in the 1912 Olympic Games.

HODKINSON, Joseph 'Joe'

Outside left
5' 8"   10st 6lbs
Born: Lancaster, April quarter 1889
Died: Lancaster, 18th June 1954, age 65
Debut v Blackpool (h) 2.4.1910, drawn 2-2
Career: Lancaster St Mary's. Lancaster Town. Glossop September 1909. Blackburn Rovers January 1913, fee £1,000. Lancaster Town April 1923, retired January 1925.

Said to be "One of the cleverest and fastest wingers in the League", Joe Hodkinson was a remarkable footballer, either individually or in combination, and his centres from the wing were invariably accurate and well timed. He starred on Glossop's left wing for four seasons and earned the club a very useful fee when joining Blackburn Rovers in January 1913. Shortly after his upward move, he appeared in two internationals and one inter-league match. The former labourer in a Lancaster linoleum works was a teetaller and non-smoker and he enjoyed a lengthy career with the Rovers, spanning 244 League and Cup appearances and 20 goals.

Appearances: FL: 84 apps 6 gls FAC: 5 apps 1 gl Total: 89 apps 7 gls
Honours: England International, 3 caps 1913 to 1919. Victory international, 1 appearance 1920. FL Representative, 3 appearances. 1913-14.
Blackburn Rovers: FL Division One champions 1914.

HODSON, Robert J

Inside forward
Debut v West Bromwich Albion (a) 24.2.1906, lost 0-6
Career: West Hartlepool. Glossop (trial) February to April 1906.

Robert Hodgson's trial got off to the worst possible start, as Glossop were soundly thrashed at West Bromwich Albion on his first appearance. He was switched from inside right to inside left for the following week's home match against Leicester Fosse, and a disappointing goalless draw resulted. A final outing at Burnley, some two months later, resulted in a 1-0 defeat, his performance at centre forward said to be: "lacking in the finer points of the game."

Appearances: FL: 3 apps 0 gls Total: 3 apps 0 gls

HOFTON, Leslie Brown

Full back
5' 9"   12st 0lbs
Born: Sheffield, 8th March 1888
Died: Bridlington, 3rd February 1971
Debut v Fulham (h) 29.4.1908, lost 1-2 (scored)
Career: Kiveton Park FC. circa 1904. Worksop Town 27th June 1906. Denaby United 4th May 1907. Sheffield United amateur. Glossop 28th April 1908. Manchester United July 1910 to May 1913, fee £1,000. Mexborough Town August 1913. Manchester United September 1919. Denaby Main January 1922.

Excellent judges of the game compared Leslie Hofton to Herbert Burgess, who also began with Glossop and went on to play for England. A former Worksop coalminer, Hofton gave every indication of following a similar path until he was injured whilst playing for the Football League. He had cost Manchester United £1,000 – a very substantial fee at that time – and two months after his departure, Glossop complained to the Football League that they had not been paid the transfer fee. It transpired that the player needed a knee operation, but an amicable settlement was reached when Hofton made a remarkable recovery from his operation. He was transfer listed by Manchester United in May 1913 with a fee of £500 on his head but there were no takers. Some six years later he returned to Old Trafford. He was living in Sheffield and when United played the Wednesday in September 1919 he made known his whereabouts and offered his services. After a trial he was resigned and, although he played only once in the League team, he captained the Reserves to the Central League championship in season 1920-21.

Appearances: FL: 53 apps 7 gls FAC: 6 apps 0 gls Total: 59 apps 7 gls
Honours: Football League representative, 2 appearances in October 1911.

HUNT, Herbert

Centre forward
Debut v Burnley (h) 2.12.1902, won 2-0 (scored one)
Career: Glossop November 1902 (And registered again as an amateur February 1904)

Along with Irvine Thornley, Herbert Hunt supplied much of the goal threat in Glossop's attack in season 1902-03. Hunt's signing enabled Thornley to move over from centre forward to his preferred position at inside right, from which position he netted all but one of his season's total of 16. After a distinctly promising start to his League career, it was surprising that Hunt was not offered terms for another season. He did, however, sign an amateur form with the club in February 1904, but did not feature in the League side again.

Appearances: FL: 16 apps 7 gls FAC: 1 app 0 gls
Total: 17 apps 7 gls

HUNT, John
Wing half
Born: Probably Sheffield
Debut v Stockport County (h) 27.2.1904, won 5-1
Career: Alvaston & Boulton. Derby Hill's Ivanhoe 7th August 1900. Derby County March 1902. Ripley Athletic August 1902. Glossop February 1904. Derby County 19th August 1905.

A foot injury sustained by Pell left him unable to take his usual place at right half-back for the visit of Stockport County. To fill the vacancy, a trial was given to John Hunt, described as "A fine built youth from Ripley Athletic." His introduction by no means weakened the Glossop side who had most of the play in the first half and led 2-0 at the interval and ran out easy winners by 5-1, which might have been increased had the home forwards been more accurate with their finishing. Hunt, on his first appearance, made a good impression and retained his place for the mid-week visit of Bradford City, who were beaten by 2-0.

Appearances: FL: 3 apps 0 gls Total: 3 apps 0 gls

HYDE, Wilfred
Centre forward
Born: Ashton-under-Lyne, October quarter 1881
Died: Roby Street Hospital, Manchester, 14th June 1943, age 62
Debut v Burton Swifts (h) 5.4.1901, won 3-0
Career: Glossop January 1901.

Glossop rearranged their forward line for the Good Friday visit of Burton Swifts, the team at the bottom of Division Two. Frank Chesworth was left out, his place at inside left being taken by Fred Crump. Hyde making his Football League debut at centre forward. An attendance of about 4,000 put in an appearance. Glossop had little difficulty in recording a 3-0 win, which might have been even better had Hyde accepted a glorious chance in front of goal. The young centre forward, who worked as a wheelwright, was not given another opportunity in the first team.

Appearances: FL: 1 app 0 gls Total: 1 app 0 gls

IRVINE, Joseph 'Joe'
Outside left
Born: Renfrew area 1882
Debut v Burnley (a) 3.12.1904, lost 1-3 (scored)
Career: Belfast Distillery. Port Glasgow Athletic. Johnstone 23rd June 1900. Abercorn 28th December 1901. Thornliebank July 1904. Glossop 12th November 1904 to cs 1906. Hamilton Academical June 1909. Morton 1910. Linfield. Johnstone June 1912.

When the newly signed former England international wingman Fred Spiksley failed to sparkle on Glossop's left wing, a less celebrated replacement was Joe Irvine, whose experience was limited to Irish and Scottish Second Division football. With youth on his side, however, Irvine had an impressive start to his Glossop career, scoring on his debut and proving equally effective on the left wing or inside. On leaving Glossop he was untraced until signing for Hamilton Academical in June 1909, where another player with Glossop connections, Job Freeman (q.v.) headed the scoring list with nine goals. Joe Irvine's contribution, in his single season at Douglas Park, was five goals in 25 Scottish League matches

Appearances: FL: 48 apps 6 gls FAC: 1 app 0 gls
Total: 49 apps 6 gls

JACK, Robert 'Bob'

Outside left
Born: Alloa, 4th April 1876
Died: Southend, 6th May 1943
Debut v Manchester United (a) 27.9.1902, drawn 1-1
Career: Alloa Athletic 1893. Bolton Wanderers 13th May 1895. Preston North End 6th June 1901. Alloa Athletic 28th July 1902. Glossop 26th September 1902. Burslem Port Vale. Plymouth Argyle 1903, manager cs 1905-06. Southend United player manager 4th July 1906 to cs 1910. Plymouth Argyle manager cs 1910 to April 1938.

In his first season with Bolton Wanderers, Bob Jack helped his club to reach the semi-final of the FA Cup, in which they lost to Sheffield Wednesday after a replay. In his second season, eleven goals in 28 League matches made him the season's highest scorer, all his goals being scored from the outside left position. Before departing to Preston North End, he was involved in relegation from Division One in 1898-99, and promotion in the following season as runners-up to Sheffield Wednesday. He had not played regularly in his final season at Burnden Park, but in total he appeared in 110 League matches and 15 FA Cup-ties for the Trotters, scoring 29 goals. Preston North End were contesting their first ever season in Division Two, and Bob Jack was just one of thirteen new players signed following their relegation. They finished third in the table with 42 points, but well adrift of the runners-up Middlesbrough (51) and the champions, West Bromwich Albion with 55 points. In the same season, Glossop took three points from North End, and it was Glossop where he continued his League career, following a very brief return to his first love, Alloa Athletic. The strong running wingman missed only one match following his debut at Manchester United and was certainly the best wingman on the books throughout the season, full of dash and spirit and the scorer of some useful goals, including 'doubles' against Manchester City and Stockport County. In the close season he moved into Southern League football with Plymouth Argyle. The first-ever professional match played by Plymouth Argyle was a Western League fixture at West Ham on 1st September 1903 that was won 1-0. Less than a week later, their debut in the Southern League brought another win against Northampton Town by 2-0. In 1905, Bob Jack was appointed player-manager, but after just one season in his new role he accepted the offer of a similar appointment with Southend United. He returned to Home Park as manager in 1910, a position that he held for the next eighteen years. In the days when only one club was promoted from the Third Division, Argyle finished second for six consecutive seasons between 1921 and 1927, finally and deservedly winning the championship of the Southern Section in season 1929-30. Bob Jack's three sons all appeared in League football with Bolton Wanderers, the most celebrated, David, scored the first goal in a Wembley Cup Final, and scored 161 goals in 324 League and Cup matches for the Wanderers. An England international, he later managed Southend United and Middlesbrough. In September 1936, father and son set up what was considered a unique record. On the 3rd of the month, Bob Jack had seen his team beat Doncaster Rovers 7-0, while David's team, Southend United, thrashed Newport County 9-2 on the same day. Sixteen goals by father and son's clubs on the same day is a record unlikely to be replicated, and surely a unique family affair.

Appearances: FL: 30 apps 6 gls FAC: 4 apps 0 gls
Total: 34 apps 6 gls

JACKSON, John Thomas
Centre forward
Born: Padiham, January quarter 1877
Died: Chorley, June 1954, age 77
Debut v Wolverhampton Wanderers (a) 23.9.1899, lost 0-4
Career: Padiham. Blackburn Rovers 22nd November 1897. Chorley 23rd December 1899. Glossop Central August 1907.
The scorer of ten goals in 25 League appearances for Blackburn Rovers in season 1898-99, Jackson failed to replicate his achievements on moving to Glossop in September of the following season. In each of his three appearances – versus the Wolves, Stoke and Sunderland – both he, and the team, failed to find the net. Three successive defeats giving an early glimpse of the relegation form prevalent in Glossop's swift exit from the top flight.

Appearances: FL: 3 apps 0 gls FAC: 1 app 0 gls
Total: 4 apps 0 gls

JONES, James
Inside left
Debut v Leicester Fosse (h) 6.10.1900, won 3-1
Career: Berry's Association. Glossop 5th June 1900.
Although billed as 'a left outside' by the *Athletic News* in August 1900, James Jones made his two Glossop appearances in the inside berth, as deputy to Frank Chesworth. The youthful recruit from Berry's Association was not prominent in his two appearances, despite having scored freely for Berry's in the previous season. Berry's, incidentally, were usually referred to as 'The Blacking Team' as they were the works' team of a Manchester based manufacturer of boot and shoe polish. They were one of the better amateur teams in the Manchester area, their reserve team being the first-ever opponents of Oldham Athletic in a friendly match in September 1899.

Appearances: FL: 2 apps 0 gls Total: 2 apps 0 gl

JONES, Richard 'Dickie'
Forward 5' 10"   12st 6lbs
Born: Liverpool, 1874
Debut v Wolverhampton Wanderers (a) 23.9.1899, lost 0-4
Career: Liverpool White Star Wanderers. Barnsley 4th August 1897. Glossop 16th September 1899, fee £25. Barnsley January 1900.
Dickie Jones joined Barnsley for what proved to be the club's last season in the Midland League, and assisted them to the runners-up position. Football League entry was obtained in 1898, and his 10 goals in 30 Division Two matches included the first ever hat trick by a Barnsley player in a Football League match, scored in the 7-2 win against Small Heath on 14th January 1899. In September of the same year he joined Glossop but failed to find his best form and returned to Oakwell in mid season, taking his career total with the Reds to 73 League and Cup matches and 21 goals. Some sources suggest that he was loaned back to Glossop in October 1900, but the player who made two appearances in that month was James Jones (q.v.)

Appearances: FL: 7 apps 0 gls FAC: 1 app 0 gls
Total: 8 apps 0 gls

JONES, Stephen
Centre forward   5' 10½" 12st 0lbs
Born: Aberdare, *circa* 1877
Debut v Burton United (h) 5.9.1903, lost 0-1
Career: Aberdare. Bristol City 9th July 1901. Glossop August 1903.
Stephen Jones left the Aberdare coalface to join up with Bristol City, whose shareholders decided to apply for admission to the Second Division of the Football League, feeling that a wider field than the

Southern League was required for their operations. Jones was signed as a half back, but he commenced as centre forward, and scored on his debut against Stockport County in a 3-0 win in City's first home match in the Football League. His role quickly became that of understudy to T. Boucher, the ex-Bedminster and Bristol Rovers centre forward. In addition to his two goals in five League matches, Jones played in three FA Cup-ties and scored one goal. On joining Glossop in August 1903, Jones was one of three new forwards who made their debuts in the disappointing 0-1 home defeat against Burton United. After six matches, that yielded just one point, only two goals had been scored and nineteen conceded. Sweeping team changes were made for the Lincoln City match on 24th October and the first win of the season, by five goals to nil, justified the re-shuffle. Jones did not add to his six early season appearances.

Appearances: FL: 6 apps 0 gls Total: 6 apps 0 gls

KEIR, Charles
Full back
Born: Cambuslang, 1881
Debut v West Bromwich Albion (a) 11.3.1905, lost 0-1
Career: Cambuslang Rangers. Glossop 10th March 1905.
A talented Scottish junior, Charles Keir showed sufficient promise in six matches in the closing months of the 1904-05 season to be offered a contact for the following term. In the early stages of the 1905-06 season he contested the right full back slot with Jack Eastham, but problems in defence continued throughout the campaign, only Burslem Port Vale conceding more than Glossop's debit column figure of 79. The unfortunate Keir's final appearance coincided with one of the worst displays of the season, a 6-0 thrashing at West Bromwich Albion on 24th February 1906.

Appearances: FL: 14 apps 0 gls FAC: 1 app 0 gls Total: 15 apps 0 gls
Honours: Scotland Junior International.

KELLY, Thomas

Half back
5' 10"   11st 3lbs
Born: Tunstall, April quarter 1884
Died: K.I.A., Gallipoli, May 1916
Debut v West Bromwich Albion (a) 3.11.1906, lost 1-5
Career: Denaby Main. Talke United (North Staffordshire League). Glossop 5th June 1906. Denaby United 10th July 1907. Grimsby Town 3rd March 1909. New Brompton. Silverwood Town June 1913.

"A force to be reckoned with" was one appraisal of Thomas Kelly, who was not the most skilful performer in the middle line, but one who was untiring, hard to get past, and effective in the air. Kelly was considered the most promising right half in the North Staffordshire League, and although he had to wait until November for his first chance in the League side, he then retained his place in the middle line throughout much of the rest of the season. A second opportunity in League football came with Grimsby Town, and similar solid performances saw him play in 25 matches, scoring three goals.

Appearances: FL: 23 apps 1 gl FAC: 1 app 0 gls Total: 24 apps 1 gl

KENNEDY, David Douglas
Inside right
Born: Seghill, Newcastle-on-Tyne, October quarter 1878
Died: Northumberland South, March 1947
Career: Jarrow. Glossop 29th March 1902. Dykehead August 1904.
Debut v Preston North End (h) 12.4.1902, won 3-1 (scored one)
Initially signed on trial from Jarrow, David Kennedy did enough in three late-season matches to earn a contract for the following season, being one of four of the previous season's forwards on the retained list. The late September signing of two new men, Eddie Murphy and Bob Jack, both of whom played in most matches throughout the season, saw Kennedy cast in a reserve role, adding only a further two League outings to his record.

Appearances: FL: 5 apps 1 gls FAC: 1 app 0 gls Total: 6 apps 1 gl

KENNEDY, John 'Jack'
Inside right
Born: Edinburgh, 1873
Debut v Newton Heath (h) 1.9.1900, won 1-0 (scored)
Career: Hibernian April 1895. Stoke 9th March 1898. Glossop 4th May 1900.
A considerable change in the personnel of the Glossop team was effected following their relegation from the top flight in 1900. Secretary-manager Mr. G.H. Dale was shown the door, the club being run by a management committee whose recruiting campaign included four new forwards. The most distinguished being Jack Kennedy, the Scotland international inside right from Stoke, whose role as partner to Arthur Goddard was expected to give Glossop a right wing pairing as strong as anything in the division. Stylish and polished in typical Scottish style, Kennedy proved very adept at making openings for others and he kept his place in the side throughout the season, showing consistently good form. He remained on Glossop's books for a further two seasons, but was

out of the first team picture for almost a year, adding only five League appearances to his record. In earlier days, Kennedy scored 25 goals in 85 Scottish League matches for Hibernian and was capped against Wales at Wrexham in a 2-2 draw on March 20th 1897. He joined Stoke in March 1898 and scored nine goals in 62 League matches and three goals in eight FA Cup-ties.

Appearances: FL: 34 apps 6 gls FAC: 1 app 0 gls Total: 35 apps 6 gls

Honours: Scotland International, 1 cap, 1897. Scottish League Representative, 1 app. Hibernian: Scottish Cup finalists 1896.

KENT, William Edward
Left full back
Born: Middlesbrough, January quarter 1875
Debut v Newton Heath (h) 1.9.1900, won 1-0
Career: Middlesbrough Grange. North Eastern Railway. Middlesbrough Grange. Jarrow 17th May 1897. Sheffield United 16th August 1899. Glossop 11th August 1900.

William Kent appeared in only two late season League matches for Sheffield United in April 1900 and was not retained in the close season. He commenced with Glossop as first team left back in partnership with Willie Orr, and held his place for fourteen consecutive matches. He lost out when the emerging Herbert Burgess was switched from wing half to full back, and his outstanding displays ensured that he retained the position.

Appearances: FL: 14 apps 0 gls Total: 14 apps 0 gls

KENYON, James 'Jimmy'
Outside right
Born: Glossop, January quarter 1888
Died: Glossop, 14th March 1949, age 61
Debut v Notts County (a) 11.10.1913, drawn 2-2
Career: Whitfield Church Guild. Glossop Central. Stockport County 16th September 1908. Bradford Park Avenue August 1910. Rochdale October 1910. Millwall May 1911. Glossop (trial) October 1913. Hurst later in October 1913. Stockport County May 1914. (Wartime guest player with Glossop, Rochdale, Hurst & Manchester City). Hurst September 1919. Glossop.

Locally born wingman Jimmy Kenyon played only one League match, on trial, for his hometown club. He left Glossop Central to embark on a wandering career that amounted to little first team action – 23 League appearances and five goals – the majority of which made in the colours of Stockport County. A career highlight was his season with Rochdale who won the championship of the Lancashire Combination, his contribution being 19 League and Cup goals. After spells with Hurst and Glossop in post war football, he retired and became landlord of the Commercial Inn, Glossop.

Appearances: FL: 1 app 0 gls Total: 1 app 0 gls

Honours: Rochdale, Lancashire Combination champions, 1911.

KILLEAN, Edward 'Ted'
Utility 5' 9" 11st 6lbs
Born: Blackburn, July quarter 1874
Died: Fylde, October quarter 1937, age 63
Debut v Burnley (h) 2.9.1898, won 2-0
Career: Army football (3rd Coldstream Guards). Blackburn Rovers August 1894. Glossop North End 16th November 1898, fee £70. Southampton 28th November 1900. New Brompton (loan) 16th October 1901. Southampton November 1901. Blackpool December 1903.

Ted Killean made 97 first team appearances for Blackburn Rovers. As a player of dual capacity, he began in the forward line but settled at wing half, where his constructive work and prompting were best utilised. Glossop also took full advantage of his versatility, fielding him in no fewer than six different outfield positions in his second season at North Road. A move south proved unrewarding, as he was unable to break into a strong Southampton side and spent a brief loan spell with New Brompton. He returned to his native Lancashire in December 1903 to join Blackpool, but appeared in only three League matches.

Appearances: FL: 54 apps 4 gls FAC: 2 apps 0 gls Total: 56 apps 4 gls

KING, Robert S 'Rab'

Outside left
Born: Wishaw, *circa* 1876
Debut v Newton Heath (h) 1.9.1900, won 1-0
Career: Wishaw Thistle 1893. Dykehead 21st June 1895. Airdrieonians 14th August 1895. Leicester Fosse 24th July 1897. Glossop 4th May 1900. Leicester Fosse 23rd July 1901. Dykehead 11th July 1902. Hamilton Academical. Dykehead August 1904.

Rab King joined Glossop from Leicester Fosse, for whom he had scored 28 goals in 81 appearances. He was unable to replicate his earlier form with Glossop, and lost his first team place after appearing in the first fourteen matches of the season, and appearing only twice thereafter. One of the two goals that he scored for Glossop was against his former team, and he rejoined Fosse for a second spell, taking his overall record with them to 124 League and Cup appearances and 39 goals, but was dismissed in February 1902 for an assault on the club's trainer. An elder brother, Alex, was an inside forward with Hearts and Celtic in the 1890s and was capped six times by Scotland.

Appearances: FL: 16 apps 2 gls Total: 16 apps 2 gls

KNIGHT, John Herbert

Outside left
5' 5½"   10st 1lb
Born: Blackley,
Manchester, *circa*
April 1889
Died: Salford,
January quarter
1958
Debut v Hull City (h)
1.11.1913, won 2-1
Career: Heaton
Park. Crewe
Alexandra. Glossop
October 1913. Royal
Welsh Regiment.
Royal Warwickshire
Regiment.
Manchester
Regiment. (Wartime
guest player with Oldham Athletic August 1915 to
March 1916). Preston North End January 1920.
Wigan Borough May 1921 to 1922.

Reckoned to be one of the smallest forwards in the
game, John Knight excelled as a sprint runner, an
asset that he used to full advantage during an
excellent spell with Glossop. He commenced on the
right wing, but a few weeks later was tried on the
opposite flank with such success that he retained
the position, his last 54 League appearances being
made consecutively. Glossop were offered £800 for
his services in 1914-15 but declined. Early in the
following season he was working just outside
Middleton, and elected to assist Oldham Athletic.
After a lengthy spell of soldiering in the East, he
joined Preston North End in January 1920.
Although he appeared in North End's FA Cup
semi-final team at Hillsborough in March 1921, he
did not realise expectations at Deepdale, appearing
in only three League matches. He joined Wigan
Borough for their first season in the Football
League, but was unfortunate to be injured on his
debut at Nelson and was restricted to 15
appearances in what was his final season of League
football.
Appearances: FL: 65 apps 6 gls FAC: 3 apps 0 gls
Total: 68 apps 6 gls

KNIGHTON, Tom

Inside left
Born: New Tupton, Derbyshire, December 1893
Died: Chesterfield, 15th February 1966, age 72
Debut v Lincoln City (a) 12.9.1914, lost 1-2
Career: Glossop amateur September 1914.
Manchester United amateur September 1915.
(Wartime guest player with Watford, Tottenham
Hotspur and Grimsby Town). Lincoln City amateur
September-October 1919.

Amateur inside forward and timber merchant's
clerk Tom Knighton spent a year with Glossop, but

two consecutive early season matches was the sum
total of his first team involvement. His place at
inside left was taken over by Ernie Gadsby, who
held the position for the remainder of the season.
Knighton played only once for Manchester United
in wartime football, but when based at
Berkhamsted with the Officer Training Corps, he
made seven appearances and scored three goals for
Watford. In the same season (1915-16) he also
played in four matches for Tottenham Hotspur,
scoring twice; at this time his civilian occupation
was that of a schoolteacher. Seven goals in 12
matches for Grimsby Town between 1917 and 1919
brought his wartime record to 12 goals in only 24
matches, but he failed to shine in a brief, post war,
trial with Lincoln City, appearing twice without
scoring.
Appearances: FL: 2 apps 0 gls Total: 2 apps 0 gls

LAW, William 'Billy'

Winger
5' 8½"   11st 0lbs
Born: Walsall, July
quarter 1882
Died: Wolverhampton,
28th June 1952, age 70
Debut v Leeds City (a)
25.9.1909, won 2-1
Career: Rushall
Olympic. Walsall.
Scarborough. Doncaster
Rovers 27th June 1904.
West Bromwich Albion
1st June 1905. Watford
1st June 1906. Queens Park Rangers 4th May 1908.
Glossop July 1909 to 1914.

Initially in reserve with Glossop, despite having
appeared in plenty of first team football elsewhere,
Billy Law's immediate prospects were made
difficult, with amateur international wingmen Ivan
Sharpe and Jim Raine the regular selections in
1909-10. Seen at his best in the sprint when his
inside partner was able to draw the defence and
put the ball into his stride, Law was not a goal
scorer, but his ability to centre accurately on the
run provided numerous opportunities for his
inside men. In earlier days, he joined West
Bromwich Albion when Doncaster Rovers dropped
out of the Second Division, but his best spell was
with Watford, being a regular on their left wing for
two seasons, scoring seven goals in 63 Southern
League matches. In November 1915 he was noted
playing for the works' team of Queen's Ferry
Munitions.
Appearances: FL: 95 apps 4 gls FAC: 2 apps 0 gls
Total: 97 apps 4 gls

LAWRENCE, Everard Thomas

Outside left
5' 10"   11st 10lbs
Born: Kettering,
October quarter 1878
Died: Northampton,
April quarter 1954,
age 75.
Debut v Burslem Port
Vale (h) 10.9.1904,
drawn 0-0
Career:
Wellingborough 1897.
Northampton Town
31st May 1898.
Kettering Town 1st
June 1900.
Northampton Town
19th August 1901. Woolwich Arsenal 1st May 1902.
Fulham cs 1903. Glossop 4th June 1904. Elsecar
Athletic 30th June 1905. Market Harborough Town
20th December 1905. Kettering Town 21st August
1906. Kettering Working Men's Club 2nd
September 1907.

Nine goals in 28 games for Northampton Town
earned Everard Lawrence a move to Woolwich
Arsenal, who came close to winning promotion in
1902-03, finishing third in Division Two. In 20
League matches for the Gunners he scored three
goals. He next joined Fulham, who had been
promoted to the First Division of the Southern
League, and in a season at the Cottage scored two
goals in 18 Southern League matches, and one goal
in seven FA Cup-ties. After a bright start with
Glossop – he scored four goals within the space of
three weeks in early season – his form dipped and
he was replaced by a new signing, Joe Irvine from
the Scottish junior club, Thornliebank.
Appearances: FL: 11 apps 4 gls FAC: 3 apps 0 gls
Total: 14 apps 4 gls

LINDSAY, Albert Fowles

Goalkeeper
Born: West Hartlepool, 26th September 1881
Died: West Hartlepool January quarter 1961, age
79
Debut v Burnley (a) 21.4.1906, lost 0-1
Career: Park Villa. St James'. West Hartlepool.
Sunderland 17th June 1902. Luton Town 14th May
1904. Glossop 2nd March 1906. Sunderland Royal
Rovers 1st November 1906.

Albert Lindsay started out as a centre half in his
Hartlepool days, but it was as a goalkeeper that he
joined Sunderland in June 1902. He faced a
thankless task at Roker Park, understudying the
masterly and invariably fit Ned Doig, Sunderland's
Scottish international custodian, who appeared in
456 matches in a stay of fourteen years. Lindsay
left Sunderland on the day that 'Tal' Lewis was
signed from Sheffield United, but a change of

fortune came with the move to Luton. He was the
regular goalkeeper in 1904-05 making 33 Southern
League appearances. With Glossop, however, he
played in only two Second Division matches, with
Davies and Frail sharing the position for much of
the season. Lindsay returned to the north-east
where he was employed as a shipyard labourer.
Appearances: FL: 2 apps 0 gls Total: 2 apps 0 gls

LITTLEWORT, Henry Charles 'Harry'

Half back
5' 11"   12st 6lbs
Born: Elmsett,
Suffolk,
7th July 1882
Died: Edmonton,
Middlesex, 21st
November 1934
Debut v Burnley (a)
18.4.1910, won 1-0
Career: West
Norwood   October
1905 to 1910. Crystal
Palace amateur 1906.
Fulham   amateur
March 1909. Shepherds Bush cs 1909. The
Pilgrims. Reading amateur January 1910. Glossop
amateur February 1910. Arsenal 1919.

Once described as a "delightful footballer, with an
extensive repertoire of moves", Harry Littlewort
was an ideally built wing half back who played
regularly for Glossop for two seasons up to 1912,
the year in which he won an Olympic Gold Medal
for Great Britain, who beat Denmark 4-2 in the
final. He remained in the unpaid ranks throughout,
initially studying for a law degree, but later
working as a sports journalist with the News
Chronicle.
Appearances: FL: 82 apps 3 gls FAC: 3 apps 0 gls
Total: 85 apps 3 gls
Honours: England Amateur International, 10
caps 1912-14. Great Britain, Gold Medal winner in
the Olympic Games of 1912.

LOMAX, Henry 'Harry'

Right back
Born: Darwen, 1876
Died: Darwen, April quarter 1966, age 89
Debut v Blackpool (h) 3.9.1898, won 4-1
Career: Darwen 25th May 1895. Glossop North
End 14th August 1897, registered for Football
League matches 7th May 1898 to January 1899.

Nineteen year old Harry Lomax was billed as: "A
local lad of great promise" when he commenced
with Darwen in May 1895. In two seasons with the
Barley Bankers he made 29 Division Two
appearances before joining Glossop North End,
who were contesting their second season in the
Midland League. Lomax was one of four players
retained for the following season when North End

made their debut in the Football League, and he was at right back in their opening fixture against Blackpool. He had played in most matches up to the mid season point, but was strongly challenged and ultimately replaced in the right back role by club captain Herbert Rothwell.

Appearances: FL: 11 apps 0 gls FAC: 1 app 0 gls
Total: 12 apps 0 gls

LUMSDEN, Joseph 'Joe'

Outside or inside left
Born: Derby, 1875
Debut v Blackpool (h) 3.9.1898, won 4-1 (scored one)
Career: Burton Wanderers 1st November 1896. Liverpool 12th June 1897. Glossop North End 4th May 1898.

An excellent season with Burton Wanderers, in which he scored five goals in 29 appearances, earned Joe Lumsden an upward move to Liverpool. As deputy for Harry Bradshaw at Anfield he was restricted to six League outings and two goals, but he had two excellent seasons with Glossop. In particular, his pace and formidable shooting power in his first season saw him net 15 League goals, sharing goal scoring honours with Bob Donaldson, who scored 18, as North End sensationally won promotion to Division One at the first time of asking.

Appearances: FL: 53 apps 19 gls FAC: 5 apps 0 gls
Total: 58 apps 19 gls

LUPTON, John

Centre half
Born: Liverpool, October quarter 1878
Died: Newsham General Hospital, Liverpool, 17th March 1953
Debut v Sheffield United (h) 2.12.1899, drawn 2-2
Career: White Star Wanderers 16th July 1897. Glossop 17th November 1899.

Initially fielded at right half by Glossop, Lupton was quickly move to centre half, and an outstanding display against Aston Villa was praised by the *Athletic News* correspondent who considered that: "He was the shining light in the defence, always in the thick of the action." Following relegation from the top flight at the close of his first season, the signing of Scottish centre half Dave McCartney from Lugar Boswell in October 1900 restricted Lupton to occasional outings as cover for the wing half and full back berths.

Appearances: FL: 42 apps 0 gls FAC: 1 app 0 gls
Total: 43 apps 0 gls

McCARTNEY, David 'Dave'

Centre half
Born: Auckinleck, Ayrshire, 1874
Died: New South Wales, Australia, 8th December 1949
Debut v Gainsborough Trinity (h) 20.10.1900, won 3-0
Career: Cronberry. Dalbeattie. Lugar Boswell August 1900. Glossop 3rd October 1900. Watford May 1903. Chelsea 2nd May 1906. Northampton Town 3rd May 1907 to cs 1910.

Dave McCartney marshalled Glossop's defences in gallant, but ultimately unsuccessful, attempts to win back their place in the First Division, following relegation in 1899-1900. Fifth position in 1900-01 was the nearest they came to promotion, their challenge based on a sound defence that conceded just 33 goals in 34 League matches. He was later to win Southern League championships with both Watford, unbeaten throughout the season, and Northampton Town. His brother, John, had a lengthy career in management, including seven years in charge of Portsmouth. He lifted the Third Division South title in 1924, and promotion to the top flight in 1927.

Appearances: FL: 73 apps 5 gls FAC: 8 apps 0 gls
Total: 81 apps 5 gls
Honours: Watford: Southern League Division Two champions 1904. Northampton Town: Southern League First Division champions 1909.

McCOSH, Hunter

Inside left
Born: Tarbolton, Ayrshire, 1874
Debut v Walsall (h) 25.3.1899, won 2-0 (scored one)
Career: Annbank 26th January 1899. Glossop North End 8th March 1899. Annbank May 17th 1901.

A product of the famous Scottish nursery club, Annbank, Hunter McCosh made an immediate impact on arrival at North Road. In his second appearance he scored the only goal of the game against Barnsley, and in the final seven matches of the season, he was on the winning side on five occasions, with two matches drawn. His first outing in Division One was less enjoyable, Football League champions Aston Villa putting nine goals into the Glossop net, without a reply. McCosh played only twice more in the first team, and despite scoring one of the goals in a 3-3 draw at West Bromwich Albion in October, the *Football*

Post reported that he had been responsible for a few "shady tricks" and was cautioned by the referee on more than one occasion.

Appearances: FL: 10 apps 3 gls Total: 10 apps 3 gls

McDIARMID, George

Half back
5' 7½"   11st 10lbs
Born: Gartsherrie, 1880
Died: 1946 (unknown location)
Debut v Stockport County (a) 30.9.1905, lost 0-5
Career: Cambuslang. Nottingham Forest 8th May 1900. Airdrieonians 4th December 1901. Grimsby Town June 1903. Glossop 30th September 1905. Clyde July 1907. Grimsby Town 31st October 1907. Darlington 20th July 1908.

George McDiarmid's first League club was Nottingham Forest, but the young defender appeared in only four First Division matches before returning to Scotland to join Airdrieonians. He assisted the 'Onians' to promotion from Division Two in season 1902-03, but departed in the close season for the first of his two separate spells with Grimsby Town. Variously described as a successful sprinter and the best centre half in Division Two, a rather less complimentary and contradictory verdict was "A plodder all through", which was probably meant to indicate that he was more solid than showy. He gave good service in the heart of Glossop's defence until displaced by Patrick Galvin for the final two and a half months of his final season.

Appearances: FL: 50 apps 3 gls FAC: 3 apps 0 gls Total: 53 apps 3 gls

Honours: Airdrieonians: Scottish League Division Two champions 1903

MACDONALD, Edwin

Right half 5' 9"   11st 0lbs
Born: Arbroath
Debut v Lincoln City (h) 25.3.1911, won 2-0
Career: Dundee. Glenavon. Arbroath cs 1909. Glossop May 1910.

At the time of his transfer to Glossop, Edwin Macdonald was described as: "The finest junior in the North of Scotland." He was also said to have: "Great command of the ball, and a magnificent shot." Sadly, he failed to live up to his advance billing, having to wait to the final weeks of the season before earning a brief taste of League football. He did, however, do a little better than his Arbroath team mate, 20 year-old wingman George Willocks, who was signed along with Macdonald, but did not appear in the League side.

Appearances: FL: 5 apps 0 gls Total: 5 apps 0 gls

McEWAN, Robert 'Bob'

Left back 5' 10"   13st 3lbs
Born: Edinburgh, 1881
Debut v Chelsea (a) 1.9.1906, lost 2-9
Career: Edinburgh Roseberry *circa* 1895. St Bernard's 20th November 1901. Bury 1903. Rangers. Heart of Midlothian. Chelsea 25th May 1905. Glossop 31st August 1906. Queens Park Rangers 28th July 1908. Dundee May 1909.

Bob McEwan played with a number of junior clubs before entering into serious football. He took his first step on the ladder when he became associated with Edinburgh Roseberry- at the surprisingly early age of fourteen years. He played at left full back with them for six seasons, after which he migrated to St Bernard's of the same city, at that time playing in the Scottish League Second Division. For this club he played at left back for two seasons before crossing the Border and for the first time taking part in English football with Bury. In Scotland, McEwan took part in an inter-city match between selected teams representing Edinburgh & Glasgow, he also figured in the King Cup & Moir Cup Competitions, for which he was awarded winners' medals. With the Gigg-lane spectators McEwan soon became a decided favourite. They were impressed by his neat way of checking a rush, his confident kicking and tackling, and the clear-headed judgment with which he met situations that would often upset a more mature player. Certainly, McEwan made his mark with Bury, and after a brief flirtation with both the Rangers and Hearts in his native Scotland he migrated south to join Chelsea. Injury disrupted his season at Stamford Bridge after he had appeared in the first 19 League matches of the season. Glossop re-signed only one full back in the 1906 close season, but with the new season a matter of days away, protracted negotiations were completed and McEwan arrived at North Road. He might have wished that he had remained on the books at Stamford Bridge after meeting his former colleagues in the season's opener, the 9-2 defeat being Glossop's worst reverse for nearly four years. In the following week, the same eleven redeemed themselves with a 2-1 home win against the Wolves. McEwan missed only three matches in his first season, but lost his place midway through his second term after an injury sidelined him, Eddie Gettins taking over at left full back. Although offered terms by Jack Robertson, Glossop's player-manager and a former playing colleague at Chelsea, McEwan declined and was transferred to Queens Park Rangers, for whom he made just one Southern League appearance. His career wound up back in Scotland with Dundee (12 appearances).

Appearances: FL: 55 apps 1 gl FAC: 5 apps 0 gls Total: 60 apps 1 gl

McEWEN, James 'Jimmy' 'Punch'

Defender 5' 5"   11st 0lbs
Born: Kirkdale, Liverpool,
16th October 1872
Died: Barnes, SW London,
27th May 1942
Debut v Blackpool (h) 3.9.1899,
won 4-1
Career: Lansdowne. Bootle
1892. Liverpool South End.
Luton Town June 1894. Glossop
North End 4th May 1898, along with two other
players for a combined fee of £200. Bury 12th July
1900. Luton Town May 1903. Norwich City 1st May
1905, appointed manager July 1907. Fulham coach
May 1909. Glossop manager March 1911 to
February 1914. Arsenal assistant trainer May 1914,
trainer-coach to 1940.

"For his size, I don't think it is possible to find his
equal." Thus ran an appreciation by the *Athletic
News* in January 1899 after a particularly
impressive display by Glossop's left full back, who
was said to be "Here, there and everywhere –
kicking, tackling and breaking up combination."
Certainly he was a key figure in Glossop's elevation
to the top flight as they won promotion, at the first
time of asking, in the 1898-99 season. He went on
to achieve even greater renown with Bury of the
First Division, who won the FA Cup in 1903
without conceding a single goal, and by the record
margin of 6-0 against Derby County. A further two
trophies were contested within the next ten days.
Bury winning the Lancashire Senior Cup by
beating Everton 1-0 at Gigg Lane. Two days later
they drew 2-2 with Manchester City in the
Manchester Senior Cup Final and the teams held
the trophy for six months each. A second spell with
Luton Town followed, taking his overall record
with the Hatters to 129 Southern League
appearances and one goal. He became the first
Norwich City player to make 100 appearances for
the club, captaining and later managing the team.
Injury enforced his retirement as a player, but he
was later to turn out twice in an emergency during
his spell as Glossop's manager, he was 39 years old
at the time. Subsequently, he spent in excess of a
quarter of a century with Arsenal, for whom his
son, James, appeared briefly in London
Combination matches in 1919. Known throughout
as 'Mac' or 'Punch', the first nickname is easily
explained but the second one remains a mystery.
Appearances: FL: 56 apps 1 gl FAC: 3 apps 0 gls
Total: 59 apps 1 gl
Honours: Bury: FA Cup winners 1903

McGEACHAN, John

Inside left 5' 9"   11st 0lbs
Born: Neilston, 1892
Died: Glossop, January quarter 1953, age 61
Debut v Hull City (h) 22.4.1911, drawn 0-0
Career: Kilbirnie Ladeside. Glossop February
1911. Hurst June 1913.

A recruit from the First Division of the Scottish
Junior League, McGeachan showed enough
promise in late season to earn a contract for 1911-
12. The *Athletic News* reported: "Big and broad
shouldered, McGeachan dribbled skilfully and
knew how to shoot, but was a little on the slow
side." He was unable to capitalise on an
opportunity that was presented when leading
scorer Moore was injured in October. The first five
of McGeachan's seven appearances brought a
return of just one point, and one goal scored.
Appearances: FL: 7 apps 0 gls Total: 7 apps 0 gls

McGREGOR, James

Right half
5' 9"   11st 9lbs
Born: Scotland
Debut v Leeds City (a)
2.9.1907, lost 1-2
Career: Queen's Park
September 1901. Vale of
Leven January 1904.
Grimsby Town 21st
November 1904. Glossop
15th May 1907.

Originally a full back, McGregor developed into a
capable and consistent wing half with the famous
amateurs, Queen's Park, completing 80 League
and 13 other appearances, scoring just once. Briefly
with Vale of Leven before joining Grimsby Town,
he gave excellent service to the Mariners,
appearing in 93 League matches and scoring three
goals. He was similarly effective with Glossop,
being absent on only one occasion in his first
season, and four times in his second, but he played
in only the first six matches of 1909-10 before
suffering a serious injury that kept him out of
action until the following March. An unconfirmed
report suggested that he had joined Rochdale in
July 1910. If this was the case, he did not appear in
their Lancashire Combination winning side in
1910-11.
Appearances: FL: 77 apps 1 gl FAC: 9 apps 0 gls
Total: 86 apps 1 gl

MacKENZIE, Thomas A.

Centre forward
5' 9"   11st 12lbs
Born: Petershill, Glasgow
Debut v Leeds City (a)
2.9.1907, lost 1-2
Career: Petershill FC.
Third Lanark cs 1903.
Sunderland 19th October
1905. Plymouth Argyle
16th May 1906.
Portsmouth 12th February
1907. Glossop 15th May 1907. Queens Park Rangers
12th May 1908. Brentford. Dunfermline Athletic.
McKenzie could not have wished for a better start
to his professional career, with major trophies
collected in each of his first two seasons with Third
Lanark. Subsequently, however, he achieved little
in English football. Eight appearances and one goal
for Sunderland was not the best start, although he
did somewhat better with Plymouth Argyle and
Portsmouth of the Southern League; 20
appearances and ten goals being scored for each
club. One goal in six Division Two outings for
Glossop saw him replaced when George Elmore,
the ex-West Bromwich Albion and Bristol Rovers
centre forward was signed in late October.
Appearances: FL: 6 apps 1 gl Total: 6 apps 1 gl
Honours: Third Lanark: Scottish League
Champions 1904; Scottish Cup winners 1905.

McKIE, Daniel 'Danny'

Forward
5' 10½"   12st 0lbs
Born: Walton-le-Dale,
January quarter 1885
Died: Preston, April
quarter 1933, age 48
Debut v Leicester Fosse
(h) 3.3.1906, drawn 0-0
Career: Army football.
Preston North End
1904. Glossop 27th
February 1906. Bradford
Park Avenue 21st May
1907. Chorley October 1908. Queen's Park Rangers
May 1910 to 1913. Merthyr Town cs 1913 to 1914.
Danny McKie played in only three First Division
matches for Preston North End, but in one of
them, a 2-0 win against Middlesbrough on 11th
March 1905, he scored both goals. On arrival at
Glossop, an early match report described his play
as: "Clever football of the close passing order". He
notched his first goal for Glossop in the 5-0 home
win against Clapton Orient on 14th April 1906, and
appeared at inside right in all but four matches of
the following season in which he scored only five
goals, but laid on numerous scoring opportunities
for leading marksman Sam Napier. McKie's move
to Bradford Park Avenue coincided with the

formation of the club, and its first season as
members of the Southern League. McKie
appearing at inside right in the opening day 3-1
win against Reading, during the season he
appeared in 14 League matches, and scored one
goal. In his first season with Chorley, promotion to
Division One of the Lancashire Combination was
achieved. With Queens Park Rangers, McKie
scored 10 Southern League goals and two in the FA
Cup in his first season, and followed with 16
Southern League goals in 1911-12, 12 of his goals
coming within the space of the first 14 matches of
the campaign. A final season with Merthyr Town
ended in their relegation from the Southern
League First Division, McKie's figures being 16
League matches and three goals, three FA Cup-ties
and one goal.
Appearances: FL: 39 apps 6 gls FAC: 2 apps 1 gl
Total: 41 apps 7 gls

McMILLAN, John Stuart 'Johnny'

Forward
5' 6½"   11st 0lbs
Born: Port Glasgow,
16th February 1871
Died: Birkdale,
Lancashire,
3rd November 1941
Debut v Chelsea (a)
1.9.1906, lost 2-9
Career: Port Glasgow
Athletic. St Bernard's cs
1890. Derby County
November 1890.
Leicester Fosse May
1896. Small Heath
January 1901. Bradford
City May 1903. Glossop player-manager May to
December 1906, then trainer from 1907 to 1908.
Birmingham trainer August 1909. Gillingham
manager July 1920 to August 1922.
At either inside left or on the wing, Johnny
McMillan was a classy performer. He scored 50
goals for Derby County, including five in one
match, a 9-0 victory against Wolverhampton
Wanderers in his seventh League game. He
remained with Leicester Fosse long enough to be
awarded a benefit match against Notts County,
leaving to join Small Heath after 131 League and
Cup appearances in which he scored 48 goals. A
roller coaster ride with Small Heath featured a
successive sequence of promotion, relegation and
promotion, McMillan contributing 25 League and
Cup goals in 52 matches. His next move was to the
newly formed Bradford City club, where he was the
players' choice to captain the side for their
inaugural season in the Second Division. He was
leading scorer in their first season with 16 goals in
36 League and Cup matches, and although his
success as a marksman was not maintained, he

remained a regular first team player throughout, totalling 91 League and Cup appearances, scoring 27 goals. Despite his veteran status, McMillan was considered Glossop's outstanding capture in May 1906. His role as player-manager was over in a matter of months when the Scottish international Jack Robertson took over the position in mid season, but he continued as a player until late in the campaign before taking over as trainer, with two emergency appearances in 1907-08 his last in League football. It was reported that he was offered seven pounds per week plus bonuses when he took charge at Gillingham, but he was less successful in management than his son, Stuart, who guided Derby County to success in the FA Cup Final of 1946.

Appearances: FL: 27 apps 1 gl FAC: 1 app 0 gls
Total: 28 apps 1 gl

McNAB, Andrew

Centre half   5' 8½"   12st 6lbs.
Born: Dalziel, Lanarkshire, 1882
Debut v Gainsborough Trinity (h) 2.9.1905, won 1-0
Career: Dalziel Rovers. Motherwell May 1902. Glossop August 1905. St Bernard's 1909. Broxburn United June 1910.

In his first season at Fir Park, Andrew McNab assisted Motherwell to win the Qualifying Cup and promotion to the First Division of the Scottish League as runners-up to Airdrieonians. Sadly, they lasted for only two seasons in the top flight, and McNab left at the close of the relegation season, 1904-05, to join Glossop. A faltering start to the season saw him deposed at centre half by George McDiarmid, but he returned to the side in mid term for a run of fourteen consecutive matches. Glossop finished the season in sixteenth place in Division Two, only two points better off than Burton United, who had to seek re-election. Only McDiarmid and Mair of the season's half backs were re-engaged, and McNab's whereabouts for the next three years have proved elusive, but he was subsequently traced with St Bernard's and Broxburn. He was still on Glossop's list in February 1907, when he applied to the Football League for a reduction in his transfer fee. He was original listed at £100 and requested a free transfer, but the League ruled that his fee should be set at £25. Outside of the game, he was employed as an iron moulder.

Appearances: FL: 18 apps 0 gls Total: 18 apps 0 gls

MAGINNIS, Hugh 'Hughie'

Left half
Born: 5th September 1880
Debut v Liverpool (a) 3.9.1904, drawn 2-2
Career: Brookvale Swifts. Linfield. Glossop May 1904. Linfield. Distillery.

Hughie Maginnis starred in Irish football with Linfield, winning his first full cap in February 1900, at the age of nineteen. The final three of his eight caps were awarded in March 1904, and three months later he was signed by Glossop. A press comment at the time stated: "Maginnis is pre-eminently a gentleman and thoroughly good in head work. His tackling, placing and shooting were the qualities that Glossop admired." He began at right half, but was operating on the left flank when he lost his place in a reshuffle after appearing in the first thirteen League matches and four FA Cup-ties, of which only three resulted in wins.

Appearances: FL: 20 apps 0 gls FAC: 4 apps 0 gls
Total: 24 apps 0 gls
Honours: Ireland International, 8 caps, 1900-1904. Irish League Representative, 3 appearances, 1898-1904. Linfield: Irish Cup winners 1898, 1899, 1902 and 1904.

MAIR, David 'Davie'

Left half
5' 6½"   11st 7lbs
Born: Dumbarton, 1880
Debut v Gainsborough Trinity (h) 2.9.1905, won 1-0
Career: Dumbarton Corinthians (for two seasons). Renfrew Victoria. Glasgow Ashfield.
Glossop 20th May 1905. Bradford Park Avenue 12th June 1907. Dundee August 1908. Motherwell October 1911 to 1915.

Davie Mair served a blacksmith's apprenticeship before embarking on a professional football career. He gained Scotland Junior International honours and appeared in the Scottish Junior Cup Final for Renfrew Victoria, who lost to Glasgow Ashfield, the club he joined before his first trip over the border to sign for Glossop. A hard working wing half with considerable skill in tackling and combination, he was also extremely fit, no doubt due in part to his being a teetotaller and a very moderate smoker. After missing only two League matches in as many seasons, he moved on to the newly formed Bradford Park Avenue club, appearing in 35 Southern League matches in 1907-08. Returning to Scotland, he appeared in 51 League matches and scored three goals for Dundee, and wound up his career with Motherwell, making 91 League appearances, scoring three goals.

Appearances: FL: 74 apps 0 gls FAC: 3 apps 0 gls
Total: 77 apps 0 gls
Honours: Scotland Junior International.

MARTIN, Blakey

Wing half
5' 8"   11st 0lbs
Born: Bradford,
October quarter 1890
Died: Bradford,
30th September 1960
Debut v Leeds City (h)
25.12.1914, lost 0-3
Career: Castleford
Town 1913. Glossop
July 1914. Castleford
Town. Derby County
May 1919. Southend
United June 1920. Llanelly June 1922.
When Jim Montgomery left Glossop to join
Manchester United in March 1915, Blakey Martin
took over at right half for the remainder of the
season. During World War one he served with the
Royal Marines in France and Gallipoli and was
awarded the Military Medal and Bar. When normal
League football recommenced he spent a season
with Derby County, but made only six first team
appearances. He joined Southend United when
they became founder members of the Football
League Division Three South, and was rarely
absent for two seasons, making 75 League
appearances, scoring five goals. He was released
when re-election was sought at the close of the
1921-22 season.
Appearances: FL: 10 apps 0 gls Total: 10 apps 0 gls
Honours: Southern League Representative, 1 app.
Welsh League Representative, 2 apps.

MEADOWCROFT, Harold Chadwick
Outside-right   5' 7"   10st 5lbs
Born: Workington, January quarter 1889
Died: K.I.A. Mametz, Somme, 1st July 1916, while
serving as a Private with the 20th Battalion of the
Manchester Regiment.
Debut v Wolverhampton Wanderers (h) 26.4.13,
lost 1-3
Career: Whitworth F.C. Rochdale 31st October
1907. Macclesfield October 1909. Heywood United
cs 1912. Glossop March 1913. Bury May 1913.
Harold Meadowcroft caught the eye of Bury
officials when he gave a very fine exhibition of
wing play for Glossop Reserves at Gigg Lane. He
had made just one senior appearance during his
brief stay with Glossop, but was quickly given a run
in the Bury side, commencing on October 4th in a 1-
0 win at Woolwich Arsenal, a game that attracted
an attendance of 30,000 spectators. Meadowcroft
had made only five first team appearances when
Bury spent £300 to secure the signature of James
Smith from Belfast Distillery, and he retained the

outside right position for the remainder of the
season.
Appearances: FL: 1 app 0 gls Total: 1 app 0 gls

MERCER, William
Outside left
Born: Cowdenbeath, 8th November 1874
Died: Donibristle, Fife, 1932
Debut v Grimsby Town (h) 7.1.1899, won 4-2
(scored one)
Career: Cowdenbeath 2nd July 1896. Hibernian 4th
May 1898. Glossop North End 31st December 1898.
Cowdenbeath 27th March 1899.
One of a pair of Hibernian players signed by
Glossop in May 1898, William Miller being the
other recruit from Easter Road. Both players had
joined Hibernian on the same day, and they joined
Glossop together on New Years' Eve 1898.
Continuing the theme, both made their debuts in
the following week against Grimsby Town. Glossop
were welcomed back to North Road following their
brilliant 2-0 win at Manchester City on the
previous Monday. Unfortunately, both full backs,
McEwan and Rothwell had picked up knocks at
Hyde Road and were not recovered in time to face
Grimsby Town. In a re-shuffled line-up,
opportunities were given to Mercer at outside left
and Miller at centre half. From a centre by Colville,
Mercer scored the opening goal, but otherwise did
little of note in a patchy display by the home side
who nevertheless managed to rouse themselves by
scoring three goals in the final twenty minutes of
the match. Mercer retained his position on the left
wing for the following week's visit to Newton
Heath that resulted in a disappointing 3-0 defeat.
Within days, he was released and returned to
Scotland, rejoining his first love, Cowdenbeath.
Appearances: FL: 2 apps 1 gl Total: 2 apps 1 gl

MILLER, William
Centre half
Debut v Grimsby Town (h) 7.1.1899, won 4-2
Career: Cowdenbeath 14th June 1897. Hibernian
4th May 1898. Glossop North End 31st December
1898. Galston 8th March 1899. Cowdenbeath 28th
March 1899. Galston 31st January 1902. Carfin
Emmett 14th October 1902.
Along with his ex-Hibernian team mate, William
Mercer, centre half William Miller did not shine on
his debut against Grimsby Town. He was next tried
at outside left against New Brighton Tower, and
scored in the emphatic 5-0 win. He was at inside
left for the visit of Newcastle United in the first
round proper of the FA Cup, which the visitors won
by 1-0. Miller's final League outing came in the 2-0
win against Woolwich Arsenal on February 4th.
Appearances: FL: 3 apps 1 gl FAC: 1 app 0 gls
Total: 4 apps 1 gl

MILNE, William 'Bill'
Centre forward   5' 9½"   11st 7lbs
Born: Montrose, 1889
Debut v Huddersfield Town (h) 26.11.1910, won 5-2 (scored one)
Career: Montrose. Glossop May 1910. Blackpool cs 1911. Aberdeen May 1912. Third Lanark 1913. Dundee May 1914.

As reserve centre forward to Harry Stapley, Glossop's crack amateur international marksman, Bill Milne was afforded few opportunities, despite scoring on his debut. He had a great scoring record as a junior, was sturdily built, and shot well with either foot, but he did not always command a regular starting role with his other clubs. If there were deficiencies on his overall play, he lacked nothing as a goal scorer. With Blackpool he scored six goals in 21 appearances, following with nine in 18 appearances for Aberdeen. Eight in 16 appearances for Third Lanark preceded his final spell in senior football with Dundee, where he failed to score in a single appearance.
Appearances: FL: 4 apps 1 gl Total: 4 apps 1 gl

MONK, Frank Vivian

Centre half
5' 10"   11st 10lbs
Born: Salisbury, July quarter 1886
Died: Salisbury, 15th November 1962
Debut v Hull City (a) 9.9.1911, lost 0-2
Career: Queen's Road School (Wimbledon). St Mark's College. Chelsea 1908. Salisbury City. Southampton 1910. Glossop amateur August 1911. Fulham October 1911. Southampton March 1912. Salisbury City 1912. (In February 1913 his registration with the Fulham club was cancelled at the request of the player.)

One of a number of England amateur internationals to assist Glossop, Frank Monk was a schoolmaster and all round sports man. He won honours for swimming, cricket and athletics, and was Salisbury Marathon champion in 1909. Once described as being: "Tall, rather splendidly built, and gets about quickly." His scholastic studies limited his availability, and his best return in senior football was with Southampton, for whom he appeared in 20 Southern League matches and one FA Cup-tie.
Appearances: FL: 2 apps 0 gls Total: 2 apps 0 gls
Honours: England Amateur International, 6 caps.

MONKS, Albert
Forward   5' 6"   11st 3lbs
Born: Ashton-under-Lyne, 6th May 1875
Died: Ashton-under-Lyne, October quarter 1936
Debut v Burnley (h) 2.9.1899, won 2-0
Career: Hurst Ramblers June 1895. Hadfield 6th May 1896. Ashton North End 7th May 1897. Glossop 3rd May 1899. Stalybridge Rovers 1st March 1900. Bury 20th May 1901. Everton 3rd May 1902. Blackburn Rovers 18th November 1902. Nelson. Swindon Town 14th May 1905. Stalybridge Rovers 26th May 1906. Southport Central 8th November 1906. Hyde F.C. 10th October 1907. Hurst.

Albert Monks was not alone in his failure to shine with Glossop in season 1899-1900, as the team crashed out of the First Division, winning only four matches during the season. He was, however, unfortunate in the matter of injuries, spending some time in the Manchester Hydropathic establishment of Mr Allison for treatment to a troublesome ankle injury. A clever inside forward, if on the small side, his seven goals in 17 Division One matches for Bury attracted attention. Everton signed him without giving him an opportunity in the League side, and he quickly moved on to Blackburn Rovers. His first season at Ewood was his best, with four goals in 19 League matches and one in three FA Cup-ties. His tour around Lancashire continued with a spell with non-League Nelson, before he migrated south to Swindon Town. In 1911 he was employed as an assistant schoolmaster.
Appearances: FL: 13 apps 1 gl Total: 13 apps 1 gl

MONTGOMERY, James 'Jim'

Right half
5' 9"   12st 4lbs
Born: Newfield, Co. Durham, October quarter 1890
Died: Durham N.W., October quarter 1960, age 70
Debut v Birmingham (h) 1.3.1913, lost 0-2
Career: Bishop Auckland. Shildon July 1912. Craghead United. Glossop (trial) January, professional February 1913. Manchester United March 1915. (Wartime guest player with West Stanley February 1919, Durham City March 1919). Manchester United junior coach October 1921. Crewe Alexandra. Craghead United.

A hard defender of the never-say-die type, Jim Montgomery gave splendid service to Glossop. Ever present in his first full season, his run continued with a further 29 consecutive League appearances before he was transferred to Manchester United in March 1915. His influence in the final weeks of the season helped United escape relegation from Division One, and he then enlisted in the Royal Inniskilling Fusiliers and was awarded the Military Medal for bravery in action in the First World War. Returning to Old Trafford after the hostilities he gave an almost repeat performance, returning after injury in late season to assist in another similar escape from relegation. Although United finished in twelfth position in the First Division, they had only two points more than Notts County who were relegated, along with Sheffield Wednesday.
Appearances: FL: 66 apps 1 gl FAC: 3 apps 1 gl
Total: 69 apps 2 gls

MOORE, James 'Jim'

Forward
5' 7"   10st 10lbs
Born: Handsworth,
11th May 1889
Died: Chesterfield,
January quarter 1951
Debut v Barnsley (h)
16.9.1911, lost 0-2
Career: Quebec Albion. Cradley Heath. Glossop May 1911. Derby County October 1913, fee £1,500. (Wartime guest player with Arsenal, Chesterfield Town, Rotherham County and Birmingham). Chesterfield March 1926, fee £450. Mansfield Town November 1927. Worcester City January to May 1929.

A remarkably clever dribbler, and a brilliant shot, Jim Moore was a rare opportunist and a continual source of worry to opposing defences. He first came to the fore in Birmingham League football and enhanced his reputation by heading Glossop's scoring lists during his two seasons at North Road. In combination with Harry Stapley, the pair did much to keep Glossop in the Second Division, most markedly in 1911-12 when they netted between them 27 of the 42 goals scored during the course of the season. Derby County paid what was at that time a very significant fee to take Moore to the Rams, and at either side of the Great War he appeared in 218 League and Cup matches and scored 82 goals. His total included five goals in one match versus Crystal Palace on Christmas Day 1922. When the Rams won the championship of Division Two in 1914-15, Moore headed the scoring list with 22 League goals. In wartime season 1915-16, Derby County reported Arsenal for playing Moore, who was engaged in munitions work in Birmingham at that time. The player stated that

the excellent train service from the midlands to London meant that his war work was unaffected by his playing for the Arsenal. An *Athletic News* report of the time suggested that Moore had not obtained Derby's permission to assist the Gunners, which seemed to be the main reason for the complaint. The rules applying at that time were that every player had the unrestricted choice of playing (a) for his old club, or (b) for any other club more convenient by reason of work or residence. He was approaching 37 years of age when he joined Chesterfield in March 1926, but despite his veteran status he continued to find the net, scoring 21 goals in 41 matches. He wound up an excellent career by assisting Worcester City to win the championship of the Birmingham League in 1929.
Appearances: FL: 67 apps 35 gls FAC: 3 apps 2 gls
Total: 70 apps 37 gls
Honours: England International, 1 cap. Derby County: FL Division Two champions 1915

MORGAN-OWEN, Morgan Maddox

Half back
Born: Cardiff,
20th February 1877
Died: Willington Hall,
Derbyshire, 14th August 1950
Debut v Gainsborough Trinity (h) 23.4.1904, lost 0-2
Career: Colet School, Rhyl. Shrewsbury School 1891 to 1896. Oxford University (Oriel College). Corinthians. Nottingham Forest
April 1901. Corinthians. Casuals. Glossop amateur April 1904. Also assisted London Welsh, Rhyl and Oswestry.

For the vital final fixture of season 1904-05, the absence of Irvine Thornley and Frank Norgrave (transferred to Manchester City earlier in the month) was greatly felt, despite the assistance of schoolmaster Morgan-Owen, the well-known centre-half of Corinthian fame. Although it could be seen that Welsh international was a first-class player, Glossop failed to make the best use of their chances to escape the last three places in the table, the 'Peakites' being well beaten be a Gainsborough Trinity side who worked hard from start to finish. Morgan-Owen was considered to be one of the outstanding centre halves of the Edwardian period. He was a schoolmaster at Forest School, Walthamstow until 1909, and later at Repton School until retirement in 1937. During the First World War he served as a Captain in the Essex

Regiment, and was awarded the D.S.O. A life vice president of the F.A., he also served a magistrate and councillor until his death at the age of 73. A younger brother, Hugh, was also a Corinthian and won five Wales caps between 1901 and 1907.

Appearances: FL: 3 apps 0 gls Total: 3 apps 0 gls
Honours: Wales International, 12 caps, 1897-1907

MORRIS, George Richard

Left half 5' 8"   11st 7lbs
Born: Manchester, April quarter 1876
Died: Manchester, July quarter 1939, age 63
Debut v Stoke (h) 3.2.1900, lost 1-2
Career: Manchester St Augustine's. Lincoln City 11th October 1897. Glossop 1st February 1900. Barnsley 8th November 1900. Millwall Athletic 16th November 1901. Nelson 12th October 1905.

Rarely absent from the Lincoln City line-up for much of his two seasons with the Imps, George Morris joined Glossop in February 1900 and made his debut alongside another new signing, goalkeeper Herbert Birchenough. The pair were thrown straight into a desperate battle to avoid relegation from Division One, and although they brought some immediate improvement to the defensive problems, the side did not win any of their final eleven League matches, and the hard won promotion of the previous season was squandered. Twelve months later Morris moved on to Millwall of the Southern League, and in all matches recorded 83 appearances, scoring just one goal. One appraisal at this time was: " Energetic to a degree, and when on top form, a splendid tackler".

Appearances: FL: 14 apps 0 gls Total: 14 apps 0 gls

MORRISON, William 'Billy'

Centre half
5' 11"   13st 6lbs
Born: West Benhar, Lanarkshire, 25th June 1879
Died: Dalmarnock, 19th February 1937
Debut v Oldham Athletic (h) 26.9.1908, won 2-1
Career: East Lanarkshire. West Calder Swifts January 1900. St Bernard's May 1902. Fulham 3rd May 1904. Glossop 26th September 1908. Clyde May1910. Raith Rovers May 1912. St Bernard's (loan) August 1915. Morton August 1915 to 1918-19. Raith Rovers trainer.

Billy Morrison was a powerfully built centre half who enjoyed much success with Fulham, winning two Southern League championships, and reaching the quarter-final and semi-final of the FA Cup within his total of 179 League and Cup appearances for the Cottagers. He was a member of the Fulham side who were beaten 3-2 by Glossop on the

opening day of season 1908-09. Later in the same month he was signed by Glossop, where he took over the centre half role at the expense of Jimmy Comrie. Rarely absent throughout, he marshalled the defence in splendid fashion, and was an outstanding performer in two seasons when the side finished eighth and then sixth in Division Two. He departed North Road to return to Scotland and in 1913 played in the Scottish Cup Final at Celtic Park, Raith Rovers losing 2-0 to Falkirk.

Appearances: FL: 68 apps 2 gls FAC: 7 apps 0 gls Total: 75 apps 2 gls
Honours: Raith Rovers, Scottish Cup Finalists 1913. Fulham: Southern League Champions 1906 and 1907

MORTON, Arthur

Centre forward
Born: Mellor, Derbyshire, 7th May 1883
Died: Hayfield, Derbyshire, 19th December 1935
Debut v Chesterfield (h) 7.11.1903, lost 0-2
Career: Glossop amateur October 14th 1903

Arthur Morton was an all-round sportsman, best known for his prowess as a County cricketer with Derbyshire, for whom he appeared in 350 matches between 1903 and 1926. A right-hand batsman and right-hand off break bowler, he scored 10,957 career runs at an average of 19.32 and took 981 wickets at 22.78. After retiring as a player he became a first-class umpire and stood in several Test Matches. He was less successful as a footballer, instanced by one report that suggested that: "He was too slow, and unable to decide what to do with the ball."

Appearances: FL: 6 apps 0 gls Total: 6 apps 0 gls

MUIR, James 'Jimmy'

Outside left
Debut v Nottingham Forest (a) 13.1.1900, lost 0-5
Career: Beith 20th May 1897. Third Lanark 2nd May 1898. East Stirlingshire August 1899. Glossop 4th January 1900.

Jimmy Muir played in half of Third Lanark's Scottish Division One matches in 1898-99, scoring on his debut at Celtic in a 2-1 defeat. He also scored twice in the 5-1 Glasgow Cup victory against

Linthouse, but the Thirds were beaten 2-1 in the semi-final by Queen's Park. Half a season with East Stirlingshire preceded his arrival at Glossop. He was hardly afforded a fair opportunity, as in three consecutive games he was fielded in three different positions (outside left, inside right and inside left). In his second appearance, he scored both of Glossop's goals in the 2-3 home defeat by Wolverhampton Wanderers, but when his third outing also ended in defeat, 1-2 versus Stoke, his sojourn in the League side was terminated.

Appearances: FL: 3 apps 2 gls Total: 3 apps 2 gls

MURPHY, Edward 'Eddie'

Forward
5' 9" 11st 10lbs
Born: Tunstall, April quarter 1881
Died: Stoke-on-Trent, 25th May 1916, age 35
Debut v Manchester United (a) 27.9.1902, drawn 1-1
Career: Tunstall. Glossop amateur September, professional 29th October 1902. Bury 27th July 1905. Swindon Town 28th August 1906. Bristol Rovers 21st August 1907.

A young player who developed remarkably quickly, Eddie Murphy was first tried at inside left against Manchester United and kept his place in the team for much of the remainder of the season. At either inside or outside left he played in all matches in the following season, scoring eleven goals. Injury restricted him to 23 appearances in his final season, but his form earned him a move to Bury of the First Division. Mainly fielded at outside left, he made 27 League appearances and two in the FA Cup, scoring two goals. His senior career wound up in the Southern League with Bristol Rovers. He played only twice, but scored in his final appearance, a 2-2 draw against Norwich City on 12th October 1907.

Appearances: FL: 86 apps 18 gls FAC: 5 apps 5 gls Total: 91 apps 23 gls

NAPIER, Samuel 'Sam'

Centre forward
5' 10" 11st 7lbs
Born: Belfast, July quarter 1883
Debut v Chelsea (a) 1.9.1906, lost 2-9
Career: Glentoran. Bolton Wanderers 31st August 1905. Glossop 8th May 1906. Linfield June 1907. Glentoran.

Sam Napier spent much of his season with Bolton Wanderers in the Lancashire Combination team, leading the first team attack on only four occasions. He found more opportunities in a season with Glossop, his smartness and accuracy near to goal netting him 14 goals, making him leading scorer by a very wide margin, despite missing eleven League matches. He remained for only one season before returning to Irish football, where he enjoyed much success in the years leading up to the World War One period.

Appearances: FL: 27 apps 14 gls FAC: 1 app 0 gls Total: 28 apps 14 gls

Honours: Irish League Representative, five apps, all with Glentoran, debut 20.3.11, last match 18.11.14. Glentoran: Irish Cup winners v Linfield 1914.

NEEDHAM, Archibald 'Archie'

Forward
5' 8" 11st 9lbs
Born: Ecclesall Bierly, August 1881
Died: Brighton, 29th October 1950
Debut v Barnsley (h) 4.9.1909, won 3-0
Career: Sheffield Schoolboys. Sheffield United amateur May 1901, professional 18th November 1902. Crystal Palace 5th May 1905. Glossop May 1909. Wolverhampton Wanderers June 1910. Brighton & Hove Albion July 1911 to cs 1915.

Despite a lengthy stay with Sheffield United, and a very respectable goals-to-games ratio (six in 16 matches), Archie Needham had to move on to further his career. He made a good start to his four-year association with Crystal Palace, scoring 19 goals and helping them to win the Southern League Division Two championship at the first attempt. They lost only one match and conceded only 14 goals in 24 league matches. He had the experience of 104 Southern League appearances by the time that he joined Glossop for the 1909-10 season. When the side beat Oldham Athletic 6-2 on 27th December, Glossop had won 13 and drawn three of 19 League matches, and had failed to score only once. Sadly the team's form evaporated, winning only five matches after New Years' Day. At its best, the team was finest to wear Glossop's colours with Needham, Harry Stapley and Ivan Sharpe in outstanding form. Of the three, Needham was the one to move on in the close season, opting to join Wolverhampton Wanderers. Twelve months later he was on the move again, joining up again with Jack Robson, the ex-Crystal Palace manager, then in charge at Brighton & Hove Albion. In four seasons at the Goldstone he became the club's utility man, able to occupy any outfield position with equal faculty. He had completed 131 matches and scored 14 goals when army service with the Footballers' Battalion effectively ended his football career. After the war he had a haberdashery business in Hove.

Appearances: FL: 31 apps 12 gls Total: 31 apps 12 gls

Honours: Crystal Palace, Southern League Division Two Champions 1906.

NEWCOMBE, Charles Neil

Inside left
Born: Great Yarmouth, 16th March 1891
Died: K.I.A., Fleuraix, France, 27th December 1915, age 24
Debut v Leicester Fosse (a) 21.2.1914, won 3-1
Career: Chesterfield School. Sheepbridge Works. Creswell. Chesterfield Town amateur cs 1910. Rotherham Town August 1912. Manchester United amateur November 1913. Glossop February 1914. Tibshelf Colliery.

The former head boy at Chesterfield School was an all round sportsman who scored six goals in 24 amateur appearances for his local Football League club and played in one match for Derbyshire C.C.C. in 1910 as a slow left-arm bowler and lower-order right handed batsman. He additionally signed an amateur form with Manchester United before joining Glossop where he deputised in two consecutive matches for inside left Albert Barnett. His debut at Leicester Fosse resulted in Glossop's first away victory of the season, but in the following week, a 2-1 home defeat by Wolverhampton Wanderers proved to be his final appearance.

Appearances: FL: 2 apps 0 gls Total: 2 apps 0 gls

NORGROVE, Frank

Defender
5' 8½"   12st 4lbs
Born: Hyde, July quarter 1878
Died: Hyde, 20th August 1948, age 70
Debut v Middlesbrough (h) 21.9.1901, won 1-0
Career: Glossop October 1900. Manchester City April 1904 to May 1912.

A wholehearted, fast and resourceful defender, Frank Norgrave's consistent displays at left full back saw him accumulate 67 consecutive League appearances before his transfer to Manchester City, along with Irvine Thornley, as the 1903-04 season drew to its close. The joint transfer became the subject of a Football Association inquiry that saw Glossop fined £250 for alleged illegal payments, which rather took the shine off the monies received for the transfer of two of Glossop's best players. Norgrave enjoyed a lengthy spell with Manchester City, proving to be an excellent clubman. His best seasonal return was 27 First Division matches in 1906-07, but he appeared in some first team football in every season of his stay, including eight matches as City won the championship of Division Two in 1909-10. In his penultimate campaign, Norgrave netted his only goal in League football against Sunderland in a 3-3 draw at Hyde Road on 22nd October 1910. His career record with the City was 94 League matches and one goal, and four FA Cup-ties. Outside of the game, Frank Norgrave worked in the building trade.

Appearances: FL: 79 apps 0 gls FAC: 4 apps 1 gl Total: 83 apps 1 gl

ORR, William 'Willie'

Full back
5' 10"   12st 2lbs
Born: Ayr, 1875
Died: Glossop, 21st December 1912, age 37
Debut v Burslem Port Vale (h) 8.4.1899, drawn 0-0
Career: Ayr Parkhouse January 1897. Glossop North End 8th March 1899. Manchester City 13th July 1901. Fulham cs 1903. Glossop 9th May 1904. Watford 30th August 1906. Glossop 6th

September 1907.

With promotion in their sights, Glossop North End entered the transfer market in a big way in March 1899. Four new Scottish players included Willie Orr and Hunter McCosh. To strengthen reserve ranks, Gallacher of Galston and Millar of Beith were recruited. The one English recruit, Johnson, of Hyde, was also destined to remain at reserve level. Of the newcomers, Orr was by far the most successful, a typical appraisal being: "The best back on the field was Orr, who never made a mistake, and played a brilliant defensive game." His three separate spells with Glossop were interspersed with spells at Manchester City, Fulham and Watford. With the City, he appeared in 13 matches during the 1902-03 season when the Second Division title was secured. Remembered as the full back who liked to wear a cap when playing, he died after a long illness at the age of 37, leaving a wife and four orphaned children. Mr George Dale, as former secretary of the Glossop club, was instrumental in raising a fund in aid of his widow and family. One of the early supporters of the fund, the Manchester City club, readily gave consent for a collection to be taken at their second round FA Cup-tie against Sunderland at Hyde Road on 1st February 1913.

Appearances: FL: 99 apps 0 gls FAC: 6 apps 0 gls
Total: 105 apps 0 gls
Honours: Manchester City FL Division Two champions 1903

PARKER, Henry 'Harry'
Forward   5' 6"   10st 10lbs
Born: Herrington, 1874
Debut v Middlesbrough (h) 21.9.1901, won 1-0
Career: Castle Donnington 23rd September 1898. Loughborough 10th October 1898. Glossop 17th April 1901. Whitwick White Cross cs 1902. Lincoln City June 1903 to cs 1904.

In the season that Glossop North End won promotion from the Second Division, Harry Parker launched his League career with Loughborough Town. The 'Luffs' had a poor season, finishing next to the foot of Division Two, and they fared even worse in the following campaign, winning only one League match, against Burton Swifts, and suffering a record 12-0 defeat at Woolwich Arsenal. Parker departed the sinking ship a fortnight before Loughborough played their final League match against Gainsborough Trinity on 28th April 1900. He had completed 54 League appearances and scored four goals for the 'Luffs' who folded in 1900, having failed to gain re-election to Division Two. A keen and enthusiastic forward, adept at either inside berth or at centre forward, his only drawback was said to be the need of a little more steadiness in front of goal. After a season in Midland League football with Whitwick White Cross, Parker returned to League football with Lincoln City, scoring three goals in 30 appearances, taking his overall career record to 108 matches and 10 goals.

Appearances: FL: 24 apps 3 gls FAC: 1 app 1 gl
Total: 25 apps 4 gls

PATON, James
Centre half
Born: Auchterderran, Fife
Debut v Loughborough (a) 24.12.1898, won 3-1
Career: Cowdenbeath 6th November 1896. Glossop North End 3rd October 1898. Raith Rovers 2nd August 1899. Cowdenbeath 28th November 1901.

It seems reasonable to assume that James Paton's single appearance for Glossop North End was made whilst on trial, considering that in August 1898 *The Scottish Referee* reported that the same player had been transferred from Cowdenbeath to Raith Rovers. This suggests that Cowdenbeath had retained his registration while allowing the player to go out on loan. A number of Cowdenbeath players attracted attention in season 1898-99 as they won a string of trophies that included the Fifeshire Championship and Charity Cup; the Wemyss Challenge Cup and the Dunfermline Hospital Cup. Six years on, the popular 'Miners' were elected to the Second Division of the Scottish League.

Appearances: FL: 1 app 0 gls Total: 1 app 0 gls

PATTISON, Samuel
Left half
Born: Hazel Grove, April quarter 1881
Died: Glossop, 16th March 1963, age 81
Debut v Lincoln City (a) 26.12.1900, drawn 1-1
Career: Stalybridge Rovers. Glossop March 1899. Stalybridge Rovers.

Sam Pattison's occupation, as given in Census records, was a "Cloth Looker". A rather eye-watering occupation in the textile industry, examining woven cloth for any faults. It is possible that he played his football as an amateur, but unfortunately Glossop's registration records did not always make clear a player's status. Pattison played only once in season 1900-01, being pressed into action in the unfamiliar role of outside left at Lincoln City on Boxing Day 1900. He was more regularly employed in the second half of the following season in his preferred role of left half.

Appearances: FL: 18 apps 0 gls FAC: 1 app 0 gls
Total: 19 apps 0 gls

PELL, William Henry

Right half
5' 8"   12st 7lbs
Born: Pattishall, Northamptonshire, January quarter 1882
Died: K.I.A. Le Touret area, 1st May 1915, age 33
Debut v Burton United (a) 6.9.1902, lost 1-2
Career: Kettering Town. Northampton Town 14th May 1900. Glossop 10th May 1902.

William Pell spent two seasons with Northampton Town, one in the Midland League, and in 1901-02 in the Southern League. In the latter campaign their leading scorer was Herbert Chapman, who later managed Huddersfield Town and Arsenal with outstanding success. In two seasons with Glossop, Pell was a mainstay of the defence, being an untiring worker, said to: "Tackle well and feed beautifully". His name appears in the Football League's registrations for the Glossop club in September 1905, and he is listed as 'retained' for the 1908-09 season, but he did not appear for the first team beyond season 1903-04. William Pell was a casualty of the First World War, when serving as a private with the 1st Battalion, Northamptonshire Regiment.
Appearances: FL: 62 apps 0 gls FAC: 4 apps 0 gls
Total: 66 apps 0 gls

PHILLIPS, Thomas

Wing half
5' 9½"   11st 0lbs
Born: Castleford, January quarter 1881
Debut v Burslem Port Vale (h) 10.9.1904, drawn 0-0
Career: Alloa Vale of Firth. Alloa Athletic. Glossop 9th May 1904.
The son of a glass blower, Tom Phillips moved with his family from Castleford to Alloa at an early age. A wing half with a robust style, and in the parlance of the

day: "A great breaker up." Phillips was one of the best of the numerous signings made by new manager Archie Goodall for the 1904-05 season. During his first campaign the well-built recruit from Alloa appeared in all three half back positions and at right full back. He appeared in 30 League matches and four FA Cup-ties, but he played less first team football in 1905-06 following the departure of manager Goodall.
Appearances: FL: 41 apps 1 gl FAC: 5 apps 0 gls
Total: 46 apps 1 gl

PORTER, Thomas Christopher 'Chris'
Inside forward   5' 6½"   11st 6lbs
Born: Broughton, Lancashire, 25th October 1885
Died: Killed in Action, Gallipoli, 4th June 1915, age 29
Debut v Gainsborough Trinity (a) 3.9.1910, lost 0-3
Career: Manchester Grammar School. Broughton F.C. (Manchester Amateur League). Northern Nomads. Stockport County amateur 1905. Old Mancunians (Easter tour to Belgium March 1907). Glossop amateur August 1909. Northern Nomads.
A clever and enthusiastic England amateur international, Chris Porter made his debut in League football with Stockport County in April 1906, and was immediately impressive. He scored the only goal of the game in County's 1-0 win at Bradford City in his second appearance, and followed with two goals in a 3-1 win against Burnley in the season's final match. Two years later he scored a hat trick against Clapton Orient in a 6-1 win that rounded off the 1907-08 season. He left Edgeley Park having scored 23 goals in 66 League matches. He joined Glossop's growing band of crack amateur players, being one of three internationals signed in the summer of 1909. The other two were T.T. Fitchie, last with Woolwich Arsenal, and A.K. Campbell from Southampton. With the likes of H. Stapley, J.E. Raine and I.G. Sharpe already on the books, there was only room for one professional – usually Archie Needham – in the Glossop forward line that season. Chris Porter's work for a private gas company took up increasing amounts of his time, but his final Glossop appearance, against the Wolves in October 1911, took his overall League record to exactly one hundred appearances. In summer months, he was a keen cricketer, initially with the Broughton Club, he was one of their best batsmen and on several occasions played for Lancashire C.C.C. Second XI. Securing an appointment at the L & Y Carriage works at Horwich, he joined Horwich C.C. of the South Lancashire League. He later joined Swinton C.C. of the same league.
Appearances: FL: 44 apps 11 gls FAC: 2 apps 0 gls
Total: 46 apps 2 gls
Honours: England Amateur International, 5 caps

PRENTICE, William
Outside right
Debut v Bolton Wanderers (a) 28.1.1905, lost 0-4
Career: Linthouse 1st November 1895. Armadale Volunteers 11th December 1895. Airdrieonians 7th July 1897. Shettleston. Glossop January1905. Bo'ness by January 1906.
One of two Scottish forward recruited by Glossop in January 1905, their arrival announced briefly in the local press as follows: "Prentice and Simpson, both on the big side, come with good reputations." In a season when Glossop promised much but achieved little, they finished in twelfth place in the Second Division. Prentice began brightly, in a run of four matches spanning February and March, he scored twice in the 3-2 win against Lincoln City, and once in the next home League match, a 5-0 win against Barnsley. In form typical of the season, after taking seven points from four matches, Glossop then suffered five straight defeats. It was another late-season signing from Scotland, Tom Callaghan, who finally solved the troublesome outside right position, dominating the position for the next two years.
Appearances: FL: 9 apps 3 gls Total: 9 apps 3 gls

PRYCE, John 'Jack'

Inside forward
5' 9" 11st 10lbs
Born: Cardross, Dumbarton, 25th January 1874
Died: Dumbarton, December 1905
Debut v Lincoln City (h) 1.10.1898, won 2-0
Career: Renton amateur 1893, professional 4th April 1895. Hibernian 22nd May 1896. Glossop North End 23rd September 1898. Sheffield Wednesday 25th February 1899, fee £155. Queens Park Rangers 29th June 1901. Brighton & Hove Albion October 1903 to May 1905.
Injury robbed Jack Pryce of a Scottish cap in 1897 when he had been selected to represent his country against Wales. The lightly built inside forward settled immediately on joining Glossop, a highlight being his hat trick in 4-2 win at Gainsborough Trinity on his fourth appearance. First Division side Sheffield Wednesday paid £155 for his services in late February, but he was unable to save them from relegation. In the following season they bounced straight back as champions of Division Two, with a 100% home record, in their first season at their new ground at Owlerton, Pryce missing only three matches during the successful campaign. Spells in Southern League football with Queens Park Rangers, and a two-year spell with Brighton & Hove Albion wound up his career.
Appearances: FL: 20 apps 6 gls FAC: 3 apps 2 gls
Total: 23 apps 8 gls

Honours: Renton, Scottish Cup finalist 1895. Sheffield Wednesday, FL Division Two champions 1900.

PRICE-WILLIAMS, Price
Left half 5' 7½" 11st 4lbs
Born: Wrexham, October quarter 1886
Died: Wrexham, January quarter 1919
Debut v Clapton Orient (h) 13.11.1909, won 3-1
Career: Wrexham 1907 to 1909. Glossop May 1909, registered for Football League matches September 24th 1909 to July 1910. Wrexham 1910 to 1915.
In two separate spells with Wrexham Pryce-Williams made 265 first team appearances and scored 17 goals. Between times he assisted Glossop for a season but made only five first team appearances as deputy to Clare Wilson, who dominated the left half back position. Pryce-Williams did, however, feature in two convincing victories over the Christmas period. On Christmas Day, Birmingham were beaten 4-1 and, two days later, Oldham Athletic were defeated 6-2, Harry Stapley scoring four of Glossop's goals. In 1912, Pryce-Williams appeared in an international trial match for a team of Welsh Professionals against a Welsh Amateur X1. Aside from football, he worked as a blacksmith.
Appearances: FL: 5 apps 0 gls Total: 5 apps 0 gls

RAE, William
Centre forward
Debut v West Bromwich Albion (a) 2.9.1901, won 1-0
Career: Falkirk Amateurs. Falkirk 9th January 1897. Douglas Wanderers 30th August 1900. Glossop 27th May 1901. Douglas Wanderers 25th April 1902. Linfield September 1905.
Only Gainsborough Trinity, with 30 Division Two goals, had an inferior scoring record to Glossop in season 1901-02. The fact that Glossop finished in a respectable eighth place in the table after scoring only 36 goals in 34 matches was thanks to a fairly settled defence that conceded only 40 goals. In attack, William Rae did not come up to expectations despite a fair amount of first team football. He played little in the second half of the season after Irvine Thornley, after only four reserve team matches, was promoted to the League side and showed immediate promise.
Appearances: FL: 13 apps 2 gls FAC: 2 apps 0 gls
Total: 15 apps 2 gls

RAINE, James Edmundson 'Jim'

Outside-right
5' 11"   12st 8lbs
Born: Winlaton Mill, 3rd March 1886
Died: Davos, Switzerland, 4th September 1928
Debut v Bradford Park Avenue (h) 12.9.1908, drawn 1-1

Career: An amateur throughout with Trinity College, Harrogate. Sheffield University. Rydal Mount (Colwyn Bay). Scotswood 1903. Sheffield United August 1904. Newcastle United 1905. The Pilgrims 1905. Sunderland December 1906. Bohemians (Newcastle) March 1908. Reading March 1908. Glossop September 1908. Stalybridge Rovers March 1911. South Shields April 1913. Also played rugby for Percy Park.

Educated at Trinity College, Harrogate, and Sheffield University, Jim Raine played in good-class non-League football at an early age, and owed much to instruction from Sheffield United's famous international winger, Walter "Cocky" Bennett. A well built, unflurried and confident forward, Raine made four Football League appearances for Newcastle United (one goal), one with Sheffield United and 52 (four goals) for Glossop. He served as a commissioned officer with the Durham Light Infantry during World War One, attaining the rank of major. Outside football he had a successful business career, becoming managing director of an iron and steel firm.

Appearances: FL: 52 apps 4 gls FAC: 7 apps 1 gl
Total: 59 apps 5 gls

Honours: England Amateur International, 10 caps. FL Representative v Irish League 1908. FA Tour to South Africa May/June/July 1910

REDFERN, James William
Outside-left
Born: New Mills, April quarter 1883
Died: Ashton-under-Lyne, 15th April 1911, age 27
Debut v Nottingham Forest (a) 17.11.1906, lost 0-2
Career: New Mills. Hyde. Glossop amateur August 1904. Stalybridge Rovers early 1908.

Amateur wingman and schoolmaster James Redfern had a lengthy association with the Glossop club, but it was not until two years after signing his first amateur form that he appeared in the League side. His three appearances were made consecutively as deputy for William Ross. Although on the losing side on his debut, maximum points were taken from his next two matches, 2-1 wins against Lincoln City at home, and at Burton Albion one week later. His final senior outing was in the 2-1 win against Newhall Swifts in the fifth qualifying round of the FA Cup on December 8th.

Appearances: FL: 3 apps 0 gls FAC: 1 app 0 gls
Total: 4 apps 0 gls

RIDGEWAY, William Henry
Forward
Born: Glossop, October quarter 1883
Died: Macclesfield, January quarter 1940, age 56
Debut v Chesterfield (h) 20.9.1902, lost 0-3
Career: Glossop Central. Glossop 26th August 1902. Glossop Central. Glossop again 15th December 1904. Was re-instated as an amateur by the FA in 1905, and noted with Glossop Central again in January 1907.

A labourer in a paper works and a promising forward in local junior football, Ridgeway had two separate spells with Glossop but struggled to make an impact in isolated first team appearances. His only goal came in a 2-3 defeat at Leicester Fosse on 14th March 1903. When resigned in December 1904, he played in two first team matches during the month both of which ended in draws, 0-0 at Gainsborough Trinity and 1-1 against Burton United at North Road. Reporting on the latter game, the *Athletic News* considered that: "If Glossop intend to get out of the last three (in the table) some new forwards will have to be found." Apparently, on one occasion the three inside men completely missed the ball with the goal at their mercy with Bromley, the Burton goalkeeper, lying injured in the goalmouth.

Appearances: FL: 7 apps 1 gl Total: 7 apps 1 gl

ROBERTS, William
Forward
Born: Crowden, Cheshire, January quarter 1883
Debut v Bristol City (h) 13.9.1902, lost 0-2
Career: Glossop St James. Glossop amateur 29th August 1902. Hadfield Star August 1907.

Within the space of two seasons and five first team appearances, Roberts proved to be handily versatile, appearing initially at outside left, followed by one appearance at inside left and three at inside right. It was from the latter position that he scored his only League goal in one of the 1903-04 season's best victories, 6-2 against Burnley at North Road on 21st November.

Appearances: FL: 5 apps 1 gl Total: 5 apps 1 gl

ROBERTSON, James 'Jimmy'

Inside right
Born: Glasgow, 1880
Debut v Leeds City (a) 2.9.1907, lost 1-2 (scored)
Career: Glasgow United. Crewe Alexandra 8th June 1901. Small Heath 13th April 1903, fee £25. Chelsea 28th April 1905, fee £50. Glossop 27th August 1907. Leyton F.C. May 1909. Ayr United November 1911. Leeds City June 1912. Gateshead August 1913 to 1915.

Jimmy Robertson left Small Heath – who changed their name to Birmingham in the following month – after just six First Division matches and two goals. He joined Chelsea for the Pensioners first Football League season, and scored 14 goals in 18 League and Cup matches. In the following campaign, eight goals in 13 League matches assisted Chelsea to promotion (in the season that they defeated Glossop 9-2 in the opening fixture) from Division Two as runners-up to Nottingham Forest. In the following season, despite being offered a re-engagement, he moved on to Glossop, following his Chelsea manager and namesake, J.T. Robertson, to North Road. A forceful inside forward with a good shot in either foot, he top scored with 17 goals in his first season, including four goals in the 5-1 defeat of Hull City on November 9th. Missing only five matches in the following term, he scored 10 League goals in 33 matches and one in six FA Cup-ties. He subsequently had spells in the Southern League, the Scottish League, and a season with Leeds City of the Second Division, for whom he scored seven goals in 27 League appearances. Two seasons of non-League football with Gateshead rounded off his career.

Appearances: FL: 68 apps 27 gls FAC: 8 apps 1 gl Total: 76 apps 28 gls

ROBERTSON, John Tait 'Jackie'

Left half
5' 8"   11st 6lbs
Born: Dumbarton, 25th February 1877
Died: Milton, Hants, 24th January 1935
Debut v Wolverhampton Wanderers (a) 5.1.1907, lost 0-4
Career: Poinfield. Sinclair Swifts. Greenock Morton. Everton October 1895. Southampton 19th May 1898.

Rangers 16th August 1899, fee £300. Chelsea player-manager 4th September 1905. Glossop player-manager 29th December 1906. Manchester United Reserve team manager-coach June 1909. Subsequently coached on the Continent with MTK Budapest and Rapid Vienna.

Capped by Scotland whilst on the books of Everton, Southampton and the Rangers, Jackie Robertson won all of his caps at left half, but he was equally effective in the forward line. Powerful in the tackle and with a tendency to run with the ball from midfield, he excelled in headwork and was a fine shot, and was probably without equal in his position at the turn of the century. He was captain of his country in 1900, when Scotland, wearing Lord Roseberry's racing colours of pink and primrose hoops, beat England 4-1 at Parkhead, R.S. McColl, the Queen's Park amateur the scorer of a hat trick. Robertson had taken a circuitous route to the Rangers, via Morton, Everton and Southampton, but then settled at Ibrox for six seasons, winning three consecutive League titles, following up by appearing in three successive Scottish Cup finals. He was appointed player-manager to Chelsea in 1905, and took them to third place in Division Two in his first season. Appointed in a similar capacity by Glossop in December 1906, he scored the winning goal against Grimsby Town in his second appearance, and six goals in 14 matches, despite appearing in four different forward positions and at left half. Generally from inside left, he played in most matches in 1907-08, when his role became that of a provider of openings, the main beneficiary being his former Chelsea colleague, Jimmy Robertson, who scored 17 League goals. In the bruising FA Cup-tie against Manchester City at Hyde road on 11th January, Robertson was ordered off the field for a 'studs up' challenge on City's captain, Irvine Thornley. In the FA inquiry that followed, Glossop's player-manager was suspended for fourteen days. Rather unusually, the referee, Mr R.J. Pitchford, was suspended for the remainder of the season as the committee considered that the match had not been properly controlled. In his final season, Jackie Robertson virtually retired from playing to concentrate on managerial duties, and in June 1909 he accepted the post of coach and manager to Manchester United's Reserve team, and later continued his coaching career on the Continent.

Appearances: FL: 46 apps 10 gls FAC: 4 apps 0 gls Total: 50 apps 10 gls

Honours: Scotland International, 16 caps, 1898-1905. Scottish League Representative, 6 apps. Southampton: Southern League Champions 1899 Rangers: Scottish League Champions 1900, 1901, 1902. Scottish Cup winners 1903; finalists 1904, 1905.

ROBOTHAM, Horace Osborne 'Harry'

Right half
5' 10½"   11st 0lbs
Born: Heath Town, near Wolverhampton, July 1879
Died: K.I.A., Somme, 12th September 1916, age 37
Debut v Chelsea (a) 1.9.1906, lost 2-9
Career: Wolverhampton Post Office. Redshaw Albion (Leeds). Ossett 1899. Hunslet amateur December 1899. Wolverhampton Wanderers 13th August 1901. Fulham cs 1903. Brentford 9th December 1905. Glossop 27th June 1906. New Brompton 27th July 1907. Wellington Town 15th October 1908.

Harry Robotham's football career did not lack variety and he obviously liked a change in outside employments, at different times working as a window cleaner and a grocer. He spent the greater part of his football career in the Southern League after making his bow in the Football League with the Wolves, for whom he made seven appearances and scored one goal. He next assisted Fulham (34 League matches) before moving to Brentford (21 appearances). His season with Glossop was spent in competition with Tom Kelly for the right half position. Kelly was considered a better defensive half, while Robotham was a spirited forager, keen to get forward in support of his attack. He left to join New Brompton, his last senior club, his 34 appearances taking him beyond a century of matches in League and Southern League football. In 1915 he enlisted with the Footballers 23rd Battalion of the Middlesex Regiment, and lost his life at the Somme, his body was never found.

Appearances: FL: 23 apps 4 gls FAC: 1 app 0 gls
Total: 24 apps 4 gls

ROSS, William

Centre forward
5' 11½"   12st 0lbs
Born: Kiveton Park, near Sheffield, January quarter 1874
Died: Sheffield, January quarter 1949, age 75
Debut v Gainsborough Trinity (h) 2.9.1905, won 1-0
Career: Chesterfield Town August 1894. Sheffield United 29th May 1895. (Gainsborough Trinity, loan, 25th May 1897). Lincoln City 2nd November 1897. Gravesend United 11th May 1898. Reading May 1899. Notts County 4th May 1900. Grimsby Town 11th June 1904, fee £25. Glossop 11th May 1905 to 1907. (Signed again October 1911 but did not appear in the League side).

William Ross began with Chesterfield Town and 15 goals in 23 matches saw him quickly snapped up by Sheffield United. He found limited opportunities at Bramall Lane and a broken ankle proved troublesome. In terms of goal scoring – 12 in 23 matches – a season with Reading was a success, but he was pleased to return north and spent the next four seasons with Notts County. Ross scored 12 of his total of 28 League goals in his first season, but his value as a team player was never in doubt and he completed 110 League appearances before moving on to Grimsby Town for whom he scored eight goals in 33 appearances. On arrival at Glossop, he was described as: "An unassuming, gentlemanly, and intelligent fellow." He was also a tall, strongly built, centre forward, with a thorough knowledge of his role, being cool under all conditions, and able to keep both wings on the move. As well as football, Ross was a talented cricketer, good enough to have spent time on the ground staff of Nottinghamshire C.C.C. In April 1907 he was reinstated as an amateur and registered to play cricket for Glossop. Having made the decision, the Central Lancashire League committee then decided to hold a special meeting to further consider whether or not a professional footballer should be allowed to take up cricket as an amateur. A brother, Philip, was a centre half with Chesterfield Town in 1893-94 and a nephew, Bernard, signed an amateur form with Glossop on 9th December 1911, but he did not reach first team level. On retiring from the game William became a Derbyshire licensee, and in January 1915 attempted to join the board of the Glossop club, but the Football Association would not allow it. Former professionals were invariably refused permission to become club directors at this time.

Appearances: FL: 52 apps 21 gls FAC: 4 apps 0 gls
Total: 56 apps 21 gls

ROTHWELL, Herbert

Full back
Born: Newton Heath, Manchester, 28th February 1877
Died: Morecambe, Lancashire, 28th February 1955, age 78
Debut v Blackpool (h) 3.8.1898, won 4-1
Career: Newton Heath Athletic. Glossop North End amateur September 1897, registered for FL matches June 1898. Manchester United

amateur October 1902. Crewe Alexandra amateur October 1903. Manchester City amateur December 1903. Newton Heath Athletic. Chorlton-cum-Hardy April 1904. Failsworth FC November 1904.

The son of a Manchester Alderman, Herbert Rothwell, who played as an amateur throughout his career, was a trained engineer and a director in the family brewing business at Newton Heath, Manchester. He captained Glossop North End to promotion from the Second Division in season 1898-99, playing in all but four League matches during the successful campaign; he also netted two goals, both scored against Lincoln City in home and away matches. He eventually lost his first team place at right back to Herbert Burgess (q.v.) and joined up with Manchester United. He played in most of the League and Cup matches in 1902-03, when United finished fifth in Division Two and enjoyed a lengthy run in the FA Cup. Rothwell then moved across from Clayton to Hyde Road but did not feature in Manchester City's first team. In the following year, 1904, he joined the amateur Chorlton-cum-Hardy F.C. party for their three-match Easter tour to Germany. They lost the opening fixture 2-0 to the Berlin Britannia Club, the hosts' two goals scored by a player named Perry who hailed from London. The Balspiel Club of Leipzig were the next opponents and they were beaten 2-1, Herbert Rothwell failing to add to the score when he missed from a penalty kick in the last minute of the game. The tour wound up with a match against the Germania Club, (Hamburg), that resulted in a 1-0 victory for the tourists. Two of Herbert Rothwell's brothers were footballers. Charles played odd matches for Newton Heath over a three-year period as an amateur inside forward, scoring one League goal in two appearances, and two FA Cup goals in one appearance. Brother Gerard played in Glossop's "A" Team in 1902. Herbert Rothwell lived in retirement at Bare, Morecambe, and died in Morecambe Hospital on his 78th Birthday.

Appearances: FL: 71 apps 3 gls FAC: 8 apps 0 gls Total: 79 Apps 3 gls

ROUND, Henry

Outside right

Born: Mansfield, *circa* 1891

Debut v Leeds City (h) 27.12.1913, drawn 1-1

Career: Clowne White Star. Glossop (trial) December 1913.

When Glossop opened the 1913-14 season by fielding five different players on the right wing in as many matches, it was obvious that they were having extreme difficulty in finding a worthy successor to Edward Cooper, who had been transferred to Newcastle United in the previous season. In two trial matches during December, the second a 1-5 defeat at Clapton Orient, Henry Round failed to impress. He was just one of eleven

players who occupied the problem position, with Ralph Toward the most successful, appearing in eighteen matches.

Appearances: FL: 2 apps 0 gls Total: 2 apps 0 gls

SAUNDERS, James E

Goalkeeper

5' 9"   11st 6lbs

Born: Birmingham

Debut v Sheffield United (a) 7.4.1900, lost 0-4

Career: Glossop 20th March 1900. Middlesbrough 4th February 1901. Newton Heath 20th August 1901. Nelson 18th May 1906. Lincoln City 12th October 1906. Chelsea May 1909. Watford May 1910, fee £50. Lincoln Liberal Club 1911.

James Saunders' League career got off to the worst possible start when his Glossop contract was cancelled in January 1901, after he had appeared in just one League match. He was briefly with Middlesbrough without reaching first team level, but had a lengthy stay with Newton Heath, his stay spanning the demise of the Heathens and the birth of Manchester United in April 1902. Aside from 11 outings in 1901-02 he was cast in a reserve role, his best spell coming with Lincoln City (65 appearances). He followed his Lincoln City manager, David Calderhead, to Chelsea, but played in only two League matches, and wound up with four Southern League outings for Watford.

Appearances: FL: 1 app 0 gls Total: 1 app 0 gls

SCARRATT, William Henry

Centre forward

Born: Wellington, Shropshire, January quarter 1878

Died: Wellington, Shropshire, January quarter 1950

Debut v Bury (h) 17.3.1900, drawn 0-0

Career: Glossop 11th August 1899. Wellington Town 17th June 1900. The Imperial Yeomanry January 1902. Wellington Town 12th February 1902. Glossop 29th November 1902. Shrewsbury Town 21st May 1906 to 1908.

In seven matches for Glossop in the First Division, Scarratt failed to find the net, but he was not alone in his failure in front of goal, the team as a whole scored only 31 goals in 34 League engagements and finished at the foot of the table with only 18 points. Glossop were without their captain, Herbert Rothwell, for the visit of Bury, and Scarratt, described as "a second teamer", made his League debut on the left wing. When the teams were ready for the kick-off, the referee had failed to appear and linesman Mr. A. Briggs of Blackburn officiated. Still short of one official, the correspondent of the

Athletic News was pressed into service to run the line! Snow fell throughout the game, and a dull encounter ended goalless. In the following week, Bury contested the semi-final of the FA Cup and progressed at the expense of Nottingham Forest They met Southampton in the final at Crystal Palace and won 4-0. On 22nd October 1897, Glossop North End signed from South Shore F.C. a player named James Scarratt, but it is not known whether he was related to William Henry.

Appearances: FL: 7 apps 0 gls Total: 7 apps 0 gls

SHARPE, Harry

Inside right
5' 10½" 11st 12lbs
Born: Bury,
July quarter 1894
Debut v Arsenal (a)
1.9.1914, lost 0-3
Career: Bury 1913. Tonge F.C. Glossop June 1914.(Wartime guest player with Bury). Harry Sharpe, who worked as a drawer in a woollen mill, joined his local team, Bury, as a teenager. He had not appeared in the League side when he left to join Tonge, but he was subsequently offered another opportunity in League football by Glossop. Although operating in a side that struggled from the outset, his wholehearted and keen displays ensured that he held his place in the side. Although lacking something as a goal getter, he was a continual source of anxiety to the opposition, with a neat touch and plenty of tricks when approaching goal. Service in the Great War with the 133rd Heavy Battery Brigade put an abrupt halt to his promising career, and it is not known where he played after the hostilities, but he had not been fixed up with another League club in August 1919.

Appearances: FL: 30 apps 6 gls FAC: 1 app 0 gls
Total: 31 apps 6 gls

SHARPE, Ivan Gordon A

Outside left
5' 10" 11st 4lbs
Born: St Albans,
15th June 1889
Died: Southport,
9th February 1968
Debut v Burnley (a)
5.9.1908, lost 2-3
Career: Watford Grammar School. St Albans Abbey. Watford amateur October 1907. Glossop amateur August 1908. Stockport County amateur cs 1909. Brighton & Hove Albion amateur February 1911. Derby County October 1911. Leeds City amateur June 1913. Glossop. Leeds United amateur 1920.Yorkshire Amateurs.

Ivan Sharpe was a dangerous outside left, endowed with splendid speed and fine ball control. He was said to dribble in the old Corinthian style, and had more than one way of beating a full back. He was working as a journalist on the *Glossop Chronicle* when he first joined Glossop F.C. and he subsequently became president of the Football Writers' Association, editor of the *Athletic News*, and sports commentator for the *Sunday Chronicle*. He was a member of the highly successful FA Party tour party to South Africa in 1910, when the tourists won all of their 23 matches with a goal average of 143 scored, 16 conceded. In League football he scored 44 goals in 202 matches for his four clubs, including 29 appearances and six goals in Derby County's Division Two championship side in season 1911-12. As an amateur player throughout he additionally made odd appearances for English Wanderers, and the reserve sides of Nottingham Forest and Luton Town.

Appearances: FL: 86 apps 16 gls FAC: 1 app 0 gls
Total: 87 apps 16 gls

Honours: England Amateur International, 11 caps. Gold Medal winner with Great Britain in the Stockholm Olympics in 1912. Derby County FL Division Two Champions 1912. FA Tour to South Africa 1910.

SIDEBOTTOM, James

Outside left
Born: Mottram, April quarter 1881
Debut v Darwen (a) 25.2.1899, won 2-0
Career: Glossop North End amateur (trial) January 1899.

From a list of the playing staff in season 1898-99, Sidebottom was described as a forward from local football who was given a trial at Darwen on 25th February and was then quickly released. The Glossop eleven that played at Barley Bank had a number of changes, necessitated by the transfer of Jack Pryce to Sheffield Wednesday earlier in the week. Before an attendance of about 1,000 – said to be a fair number for the Darwen club – Glossop took the lead twenty minutes from time through Donaldson. The youthful wingman Sidebottom was then said to have made a very commendable effort to add to his side's score, but it was Killean who next netted to give Glossop the points. The result proved to be the first win in a sequence of ten matches to the end of the season that included eight wins and two draws, form that clinched promotion to the First Division. Sidebottom, employed in the local textile industry as a cotton waste bleacher, did not feature again in senior football.

Appearances: FL: 1 app 0 gl Total: 1 app 0 gls

SIMPSON, Hugh
Inside right
Born: Shettleston, 1885
Debut v Bradford City (a) 11.2.1905, drawn 1-1
Career: Shettleston. Bo'ness. Glossop 26th January 1905. Raith Rovers 1905. Bo'ness January 1906. Leith Athletic July 1912. Abercorn (loan) 1913-14. Cowdenbeath August 1913.
A mid season recruit from Bo'ness, one of the foremost provincial teams in the East of Scotland. Simpson's introduction, at the expense of the rather lightweight Tom Cairns, brought about an immediate improvement in the side's form. Following the creditable draw at Bradford City on his debut, three impressive home wins followed, Simpson scoring in the 5-0 defeat of Barnsley, and followed by netting the winner in the 2-1 win against West Bromwich Albion. Sadly, a startling loss of form in the next five matches saw the side without a win and only one goal scored. In general terms the Glossop forwards were much less productive than in the previous season, with only 37 goals scored, compared with 57 in the previous campaign. Simpson was one of several forward released in the close season, when he returned to Scotland to play his football, and continue in his employment as a joiner.
Appearances: FL: 10 apps 2 gls Total: 10 apps 2 gls

SMITH, Sydney Ernest

Inside left
5' 8½"   11st 8lbs
Debut v Gainsborough Trinity (a) 28.12.1908, lost 1-3
Career: Glossop amateur December 1908. Partick Thistle September 1909 to cs 1910.
Ernest Smith made only two League appearances for Glossop, but joined Partick Thistle in the season that they moved from the Burgh of Partick to their new home in Maryhill. He played in the first Scottish League match contested at Firhill, a 1-1 draw against Clyde on 2nd October 1909. He played in half of the League matches during the season, scoring six goals in 17 matches
Appearances: FL: 2 apps 0 gls Total: 2 apps 0 gls

SPARKES, Harold
Centre forward
Born: Glossop, January quarter 1896
Died: K.I.A. in the Arras area, 3rd June 1917, age 21
Debut v Bury (a) 20.2.1915, lost 0-5
Career: Glossop amateur 20th February 1915.
It was probably unrealistic to expect local amateur centre forward Harold Sparkes to succeed where other more experienced players had failed to lift the fortunes of the Glossop club, for whom a re-election application seemed inevitable. Predictably, his introduction did nothing to improve results, as following the 5-0 defeat at Bury, the side went down in the next two engagements, 1-0 against both Preston North End and Nottingham Forest. Some two years on, he lost his life in the Great War when serving as a private with the 16th Battalion of the Royal Scots. In his tragically short life, Harold Sparkes had served a plumbing apprenticeship. At the time of his death, his home was in Hadfield.
Appearances: FL: 3 apps 0 gl Total: 3 apps 0 gls

SPIBY, Samuel 'Sam'
Inside left
Born: Ashton-under-Lyne, July quarter 1877
Died: Ashton-under-Lyne, January quarter 1953, age 75.
Debut v Walsall (h) 2.3.1901, won 2-0
Career: Glossop amateur January 1901.
Glossop made two changes for the visit of Walsall. Spiby was introduced for his League debut in place of Barlow, and new signing Brooks, described as the 'Ashton cyclist', supplanted Brodie at left back. The weather was of the worst possible description, and considerably affected the attendance, estimated at 2,000. The swamped condition of the ground also had a detrimental effect on the standard of the play, which was below average throughout. The visitors had the advantage of a gale of wind in the first half, but their efforts in front of goal were poor in the extreme. There was no score in the first half, but when Glossop had the advantage of the hurricane, they peppered the Walsall goal. The two goals of the match being scored by Arthur Goddard, both being netted from a difficult angle. Sadly, Spiby was deemed a failure with a perpetual habit of being off-side, and being too individualistic, with disastrous results.
Appearances: FL: 1 app 0 gls Total: 1 app 0 gls

SPIKSLEY, Frederick 'Fred'

Outside left
5' 7"   11st 4lbs
Born: Gainsborough, Lincolnshire, 25th January 1870
Died: Goodwood Racecourse, Sussex, 28th July 1948
Debut v Liverpool (a) 3.9.1904, drawn 2-2
Career: Gainsborough Jubilee Swifts. Gainsborough Trinity. Sheffield Wednesday January 1891. Glossop 9th June 1904. Gainsborough Trinity January 1905. Leeds City 3rd February 1905. Southern United Secretary. Watford 9th February-

May 1906. Coaching appointments in Sweden (1911), Denmark and Nuremberg, Germany until August 1914. Barcelona coach 1918. Real Club Espana O.D., Mexico. Reforma Club, Mexico, coach 1923. Fulham coach 1924-26. F.C. Nuremberg 1926. Lausanne Sports, Switzerland to 1929.

Fred Spiksley's extraordinary life began at the Crown and Anchor Inn, Gainsborough, where he was born in 1870. Aside from reaching the very highest level as a footballer, he was multi-lingual, a musician, and a prize-winning athlete over 440 yards, a skater and a rower. At one time a printer and later a bookmaker, he suffered internment during World War One when he was coaching at FC Nuremberg, but managed to escape. In early days he was capped by Lincolnshire when a Gainsborough Trinity player. He won a Midland League championship and the Lincolnshire Senior Cup before joining Sheffield Wednesday, at that time operating in the Football Alliance. In May 1892 they were elected to the Football League. They narrowly avoided relegation in their first season, despite outstanding performances from Fred Spiksley, who was leading scorer with 18 goals in 31 League and Cup matches. He scored both goals as Wednesday beat the Wolves in the 1896 FA Cup Final, by 2-1 at Crystal Palace, and in eleven seasons scored 100 League goals in 293 matches, and a further 16 goals in 31 FA Cup-ties. In seven International matches for England, he began by scoring twice on his debut in a 6-0 victory against Wales on 13th March 1893, and twice again in his second appearance, a 5-2 win against Scotland on 1st April 1899. In 1899 his benefit with the Wednesday amounted to nearly £300. Finally released with a free transfer, Spiksley joined Glossop, but he had played no first team football in season 1903-04, and it was quickly evident that his best days were behind him. When his playing career wound up with 11 appearances for Watford, he turned successfully to coaching on the Continent and in Mexico. Given his life long love of horse racing, his death at a meeting at the Goodwood course seemed strange but sadly appropriate.

Note: On June 20th 1998, two of Fred Spiksley's medals were sold at auction by Christie's, Glasgow. His 15ct gold Division One championship medal, 1902-03, realised £5,750. His medal for the English League v the Scottish League, April 21st 1894, realised £632.

Appearances: FL: 4 apps 0 gls FAC: 1 app 0 gls
Total: 5 apps 0 gls

Honours: England International, 7 caps, 1893-98. FL Representative, 2 apps, 1894-1903. Sheffield Wednesday: FA Cup winners 1896. FL Division Two Champions 1900; FL League Champions 1903 and 1904.

SPITTLE, Thomas
Right back   5' 8"   10st 10lbs
Born: Whitechapel, July quarter 1888
Debut v Clapton Orient (a) 28.9.1912, lost 0-1
Career: Glossop May 1911. Newport County.

Glossop commenced season 1911-12 with five full backs on their books, and with only two positions to fill, Tom Spittle spent his first season at North Road in the Reserves, with Hampton and Cuffe the favoured pairing in the League side. Opportunity knocked early in his second season, when a faltering start to the campaign saw him introduced at right back at the expense of George Hampton. Displays described as "Fearless" earned him an extended run in the side, but by mid season and with the club again dropping like a stone he lost his first team place in a re-shuffle, and never regained it. He was not retained, and in August 1913 had not found another club as the new season opened, but was later noted with Newport County.

Appearances: FL: 15 apps 0 gls FAC: 1 app 0 gls
Total: 16 apps 0 gls

STANFORD, James
Inside forward   5' 10"   12st 10lbs
Born: Ancoats, Manchester, October quarter, 1884
Debut v Bristol City (a) 3.9.1913, lost 1-4
Career: Eccles Borough August 1907. Manchester United May 1910. Rochdale December 1911. Macclesfield September 1912. Glossop August 1913. Eccles Borough October 1914. Hardman & Holden, Manchester, amateur May 1923.

For the 1913-14 season, Glossop commenced with their finances in good order. Substantial transfer fees, totalling £3,575, had been banked from the sale of four of the previous season's players. Sadly, the replacements signed were all quite new to League football and collectively failed to reach the required standard. Stanford, recruited from Macclesfield, had a good turn of speed but was lacking in the finer points of the game. After appearing in the first three matches of the season, all of which ended in defeat, he lost his place in the side, reappearing only once more in a 1-2 defeat at Fulham on 17th January 1914.

Appearances: FL: 4 apps 0 gls Total: 4 apps 0 gls
Honours: Rochdale: Lancashire Combination champions, 1912.

STAPLEY, Henry S 'Harry'

Forward
5' 9½"   11st 0lbs
Born: Southborough,
Kent, 29th April 1883
Died: Glossop,
29th April 1937
Debut v Fulham (a)
2.9.1908, won 3-2
(scored two)
Career: King Charles
School. Bromley. Ilford
Alliance. Harleston.
Horwich Church. Reading
Collegiate School.
Reading 'A' Team. Woodford Town. West Ham
United. Glossop amateur August 1908. Leyton FC
cs 1909.

Of sallow complexion and frail build, Harry Stapley
looked nothing like a centre forward, and charging
an opponent would not have entered into his
modus operandi. Said to be hardly able to
despatch a heavy ball from the centre to the wing,
his method was timing and placing. Seeming
always to be in the right place at the right moment,
most of his goals came from close range and were
placed with unerring accuracy a few inches inside
the goalpost. Often described as: "the gentle centre
forward" he dribbled with great skill and made the
game look easy. He joined Glossop from West Ham
United, having obtained a scholastic appointment
in the town. Season after season he was among the
leading goal scorers in the Second Division.
Certainly amongst the best amateur centre
forwards of his era, he headed Glossop's scoring
lists for three seasons from 1908 to 1911 and again
in 1913-14. Outside of the game, he later worked as
an estate agent for the Hill-Wood family.
Appearances: FL: 187 apps 93 gls FAC: 14 apps 1 gl
Total: 201 apps 94 gls
Honours: England Amateur International, 13
caps. Represented the United Kingdom in the1908
Olympic Games.

STAPLEY, William John 'Will'

Centre half
5' 10½"   12st 0lbs
Born:
Southborough,
Kent, January
quarter 1887
Died: Brixham,
Devon,
19th January 1964
Debut v
Gainsborough
Trinity (h)
23.2.1909,
drawn 2-2

Career: Dulwich Hamlet. West Ham United.
Glossop amateur February 1909. The Pilgrims.
The younger brother of Harry, the siblings first
played together when Will deputised for Morrison
at centre half in the match against Gainsborough
Trinity on 23rd February 1909. Brother Harry
opened the scoring in the match that ended in a
draw of two goals each. It was not until September
1910 that Will took over the role of centre half in
the League side, and although there was talk of
him retiring in 1912, he did in fact continue to the
bitter end, as he missed only one match in
Glossop's final season in the Second Division,
scoring his only senior goal from centre half in the
1-0 win against Nottingham Forest on 31st October
1914. In January 1916 he enlisted in the Royal
Horse Artillery. Outside of the game, William was a
clerical worker, and as an amateur player
throughout he played in odd matches for the
Pilgrims, and in 1921 for Ashton Brothers (of
Hyde) in 1921, at the age of 34.
Appearances: FL: 120 apps 1 gl FAC: 6 apps 0 gls
Total: 126 apps 1 gl
Honours: England Amateur International

STOODLEY, Henry Claude

Inside forward
Born: Plumstead, October
quarter 1889
Died: South Essex, January
quarter 1963, age 73
Debut v Huddersfield Town (h)
2.11.1912, won 1-0
Career: Walthamstow
Grange. Glossop amateur
March 1912. Leicester Fosse
August 1913. Merthyr Town
May 1914. Norwich City November 1920.
Claude Stoodley had to wait patiently for his
League debut, but an indifferent start to season
1912-13 led to his introduction in early November.
He scored from centre forward in a 2-0 win against
Grimsby Town on his third appearance, and scored
three goals in two Qualifying FA Cup-ties against
Ripley Town & Athletic and Southall. With his next
club, Leicester Fosse, he scored a hat trick against
Tottenham Hotspur in the FA Cup, but only
another three goals in 25 League appearances.
Before football shut down for the duration,
Stoodley spent the 1914-15 season with Merthyr
Town. The 'Red & Greens' were in the running for
promotion from the Second Division of the
Southern League for most of the season, but
faltered in the final month of the season, finishing
third in the table, two points adrift of the runners-
up, Stalybridge Celtic, and three behind the
champions, Stoke. In post war football, he did not
appear in Norwich City's League side.
Appearances: FL: 12 apps 2 gls FAC: 2 apps 3 gls
Total: 14 apps 5 gls

SUNTER, John
Centre forward
Debut v Bristol City (a) 10.10.1914, lost 1-3
Career: Glossop amateur October 1914.
John Sunter's first appearance in Glossop's colours was in the August pre-season trial match, when he was described as: "A dangerous player, quick and keen." He was destined, however, to spend a season in reserve, apart from his one senior outing at Bristol City. The game was attended by many wounded soldiers, among a crowd of about 10,000 spectators. Ernie Gadsby, Glossop's inside left, formerly played for Bristol City, and was up against some of his former colleagues. With the score at 2-1 in favour of the home side, Sunter was denied an equalising goal when his shot was acrobatically saved by Howling, the Bristol City goalkeeper. Bristol then scored from a penalty kick in the last minute. In the second half, Sunter was spoken to by the referee, Mr H. Smith, for an over vigorous charge on Bristol's international centre half, Billy Wedlock, who had frustrated almost all of Sunter's efforts throughout the ninety minutes.
Appearances: FL: 1 app 0 gls Total: 1 app 0 gls

SUTCLIFFE, Joseph Robert

Left half
Born: Moortown, Lincolnshire, April quarter 1875
Died: Registered in the Amounderness district, June 1935.
Debut v New Brighton Tower (a) 24.9.1898, drawn 2-2
Career: Glossop North End amateur 11th September 1897, registered for Football League matches June 1898. Glossop St. James cs 1899.
In addition to his intermittent appearances during the 1898-99 promotion season, Bob Sutcliffe also assisted the club with clerical and administrative duties. The locally produced centre or wing half back had been retained at the close of the 1897-98 season, but after failing to establish himself in Glossop's first Football League campaign, he was released and returned to local amateur football with St James. He subsequently served the Glossop club as honorary secretary for a period of ten years, but resigned in October 1912. At the time he was reported to be "Devoting himself to aviation". His position was covered by the appointment of manager J. McEwan to the dual capacity of secretary-manager. Bob Sutcliffe later returned to the fold, leaving for the last time in February 1916 on taking up a business appointment in Nottingham.
Appearances: FL: 7 apps 0 gls Total: 7 apps 0 gls

SWINDELLS, James S
Winger
Born: Hayfield, October quarter 1884
Died: Hayfield, 23rd June 1955, age 70.
Debut v Preston North End (a) 6.12.1902, drawn 0-0
Career: Glossop St. James. Glossop amateur 6th November 1902.
Local amateur outside right James Swindells made his first four appearances consecutively in December 1902, and had the selection committee opted to retain a winning line-up he would have been given further opportunities. Following the creditable draw at Preston North End on his debut, his next three matches resulted in victories against Burslem Port Vale, Barnsley and Stockport County. Four years on, again in the month of December, he made three appearances on the left wing, and in one of them, scored the only goal of the match in the 1-0 win against Burnley on December 22nd 1906.
Appearances: FL: 7 apps 1 gl Total: 7 apps 1 gl

SYNOTT, William James

Right back
5 9½"   11st 4lbs
Born: Derry, Ireland, April quarter 1880
Debut v Liverpool (a) 3.9.1904, drawn 2-2
Career: Shelbourne. Belfast Celtic. Glossop 9th May 1904 to December 1905. Belfast Celtic (there September 1906). Glentoran November 1906.
William Synott enjoyed a good first season with Glossop, it was felt that he would enhance his reputation on moving to England, and this he did, appearing for much of the season at right full back in partnership with Willie Orr. Eleven 'clean sheets' in League matches kept the side out of the bottom reaches of the table, as the attack managed only 37 goals in 34 League matches. In April 1905, he was selected to play for Ireland against Wales, but in view of the perilous position occupied by his club, he declined and turned out instead against Doncaster Rovers. Injury restricted him to only one League appearance in his second season, when Eastham, Keir and Cuffe all contested the first team right full back position. For reasons undisclosed, Synott was suspended *sine die* by the club in December 1905. At the same time, the directors suspended Phillips and Whitehouse for one month and placed them on the transfer list, and Brown and McNab were substantially fined.
Appearances: FL: 27 apps 0 gls FAC: 3 apps 0 gls Total: 30 apps 0 gls

THOMPSON, Alfred Alexander

Inside forward
Born: Liverpool, 28th April 1891
Died: Leytonstone, 19th April 1969
Debut v Stockport County (a) 27.9.13, drawn 1-1
Career: Crewe College. Liverpool amateur 1910. Glossop amateur October 1913. Arsenal amateur May 1914. Brentford July 1919. Guildford United May 1921. Queens Park Rangers June 1922. Gillingham (trial) August 1923. Sheppey United (trial) October 1923. Chatham Town. Sittingborne May 1926. Chatham Town June 1927. Sheppey United. Tunbridge Wells Rangers August 1928. Ashford Town June 1930. Canterbury Waverley. Canterbury Amateurs August 1933. Eton Manor committee member April 1948.

Said to have netted 110 goals in schools football, Thompson's brief association with Glossop included a glimpse of his abilities as a goal scorer when he netted both goals in a 2-1 win against Bury on 15th November 1913. An elementary schoolteacher by profession, he was next with Arsenal, without appearing at League level. At about this time he was described as being: "Nicely built, fairly fast, and dribbled admirably." Post war he assisted Brentford in season 1919-20, when they were a Southern League team, and in the following season, when they were founder members of the Football League's Third Division. His combined figures for the Bees being 44 matches and 10 goals. His lengthy career continued in Southern League circles, and he was still turning out for Canterbury Amateurs in his 42nd year.
Appearances: FL: 7 apps 2 gls Total: 7 apps 2 gls

THOMPSON, Robert 'Bob'

Forward
5' 11½"   12st 0lbs
Born: Coundon Grange
Debut v Fulham (h) 2.1.1913, won 2-0
Career: Wingate Albion. Preston North End (debut) April 1911. Glossop December 1912 (And re-signed 26th September 1913). Centre forward Bob Thompson made his debut for Preston North End in the final fixture of season 1910-11, a 2-0 win against Bradford City. In the following term, when North End were relegated from the top flight, Thompson scored two goals in eleven League appearances. Despite a poor start to the following season, in the course of which he lost has place after five matches, Preston won promotion, suffering only four defeats to take the championship. Thompson, meanwhile, had left

Deepdale in mid term, but he was slow to settle at North Road, but then scored four goals against Barnsley in a 5-1 win in March 1914. In the final season before League football was suspended, his seven goals in 27 matches, plus one in the FA Cup, made him the season's leading goal scorer.
Appearances: FL: 45 apps 14 gls FAC: 3 apps 1 gl
Total: 48 apps 15 gls

THORNLEY, Hartley

Left half
Born: Glossop, April quarter 1884
Died: Glossop, October quarter 1959
Debut v Blackpool (a) 1.2.1902, drawn 1-1
Career: Glossop amateur January 1902. Glossop Central (In late 1902) and noted with them again in January 1907. Stalybridge Rovers early 1908.

One of three Glossop butchering brothers, Hartley Thornley was said to play "A harassing game" in the half back line. His energetic displays were a feature of Glossop's Lancashire Combination side, but he played only once in the League eleven. He made his debut at Blackpool along with his elder brother, Irvine, who with an unstoppable shot gave Glossop the lead. A strong east wind spoilt much of the play, Blackpool being penned in their own half of the field, and in the second forty-five minutes Glossop scarcely progressed over the halfway line. Meanwhile, back at North Road, Glossop Reserves, with Shanks in Hartley Thornley's usual left half position, lost 3-1 to Accrington Stanley, Pattison scoring Glossop's goal.
Appearances: FL: 1 app 0 gls Total: 1 app 0 gls

THORNLEY, Irvine

Forward
5' 8½"   11st 0lbs
Born: Glossop, October quarter 1883
Died: South Shields, 24th April 1955
Debut v Blackpool (a) 1.2.1902, drawn 1-1 (scored)
Career: Glossop Villa. Glossop St James. Glossop January 1902. Manchester City 2nd May 1904, fee £750 South Shields Adelaide. August 1912. Clydebank 1917. Hamilton Academical cs 1919. Houghton F.C. (North Eastern League).
Irvine Thornley commenced his football career at the age of seventeen with Glossop Villa, who were operating in the Glossop and District Junior League. During the season that he spent with the club he figured at centre forward, and assisted them very materially in winning the league championship by scoring no fewer than forty goals. The following season he joined St James', who

were operating in the Glossop and District Senior League, but he had only been with them for about five months when he was invited to join Glossop FC. He had played in only four reserve team games when he was promoted to the League eleven. He promptly scored on his debut and netted five goals in fifteen appearances. In the following season his record was sixteen goals from 34 appearances, and he led the scoring lists again in 1903-04 with twenty-one goals in just thirty-two matches, his total including three hat tricks scored against Lincoln City, Barnsley and Bolton Wanderers. His transfer to Manchester City resulted in an FA inquiry in which City were found guilty of having used undue influence to secure the player's signature. The suggestion being that illicit cash payments had been made to both the young man and his father, Thomas Thornley, who was warned off all clubs and grounds. Immensely popular during his eight-year stay at Hyde Road, he became the first City player to receive a benefit cheque with a value in excess of £1,000. In 204 League and FA Cup appearances he netted 93 goals, and with his last senior club, Hamilton Academical, he scored 16 goals in 27 matches.

Appearances: FL: 79 apps 42 gls FAC: 5 apps 5 gls Total: 84 apps 47 gls

Honours: England International, 1 cap v Wales 18.3.1907. FL Representative, 2 apps. Manchester City: FL Division 2 champions, 1910.

THORNLEY, Jonathan 'Jack'

Forward
Born: Glossop, April quarter 1886
Died: K.I.A. 31st March 1918
Debut v Blackpool (h) 17.2.1903, won 1-0
Career: Glossop December 1902. (Signed again August 1906)

Glossop's Football League registration documents failed to indicate whether Jack Thornley played as an amateur or as a professional, but the former is most likely to be the case. Like most of the Thornley clan, John's occupation was listed as a "Tripe dresser" although he later worked in the cotton industry as a mule spinner's 'piecer'. Said to play "A good bustling, sound game", he made two League appearances at outside right in season 1902-03, and after a lengthy interval, three appearances at centre forward, as deputy for Sam Napier, in season 1906-07. In the latter season, he had a good match against Failsworth for the Reserves, scoring all of his team's goals in the 4-2 win on 29th December, and a hat trick against Oswaldtwistle Rovers in a 6-1 win on 1st April 1907. Jack Thornley lost his life while serving with the Cheshire Regiment. He is buried in the communal cemetery in Wimereux.

Appearances: FL: 5 apps 0 gls FAC: 1 app 0 gls Total: 6 apps 0gls

TINTO, Richard

Inside right
Born: Easington, October quarter 1875
Died: Woodside, Coatbridge, Lanarkshire, 9th August 1944, age 68
Debut v Blackpool (h) 3.9.1898, won 4-1 (scored one)
Career: Glasgow Rangers 10th March 1897. Glossop North End trial January 1898, professional 20th April 1898; released 24th December 1898. Linthouse 18th November 1899. Albion Rovers 14th August 1900.

Richard Tinto's place in Glossop's history came when he scored North End's first-ever goal in the Football League. He was associated with the Rangers without breaking into their first team, and initially came to Glossop on trial in the season prior to their entry into the Football League. He scored twice in the first three matches of the season, and after a spell in reserve scored twice against Burton Swifts in a 5-0 win on 3rd December 1898. A goal in the FA Cup against Stockport County followed, but he played only once more prior to being released on Christmas Eve. He was probably unfortunate to be around when Glossop North End had a strong attack, with Donaldson leading the list with 18, followed by Lumsden on 15, and Gallacher with 11. Tinto returned to Scotland, resuming his work as a coalminer.

Appearances: FL: 6 apps 4 gl FAC: 1 app 1 gl Total: 7 apps 5 gls

TOMKINSON, Alfred

Inside left 5' 10" 11st 4lb
Born: Burslem, 1st May 1887
Died: Newcastle-under-Lyme, 15th October 1973, age 86
Debut v Bradford Park Avenue (a) 26.12.1910, lost 0-6
Career: Smallthorne United. Tunstall Park (for two years). Stoke (trial). Leek United. Glossop May 1910. Doncaster Rovers August 1911. Exeter City (trial) January/February 1912. Leek United.

Alf Tomkinson, a potter from Burslem, won a number of junior honours with the Tunstall Park club including two league championships, a Maybank Cup winners' medal and a runners-up medal in the Burslem Park Cup. His progress continued apace, as he was reported to have scored 56 goals for Leek United in the season prior to his arrival at Glossop. He did not feature in the League side until Boxing Day 1910, and saw little of the ball as Bradford Park Avenue scored six goals without a reply. In his second appearance he netted Glossop's goal in the 1-1 draw against Burnley on 2nd January. In subsequent appearances he scored against Lincoln City, Barnsley and West Bromwich Albion, but despite his very respectable ratio as a goal scorer, his all-

round game was lacking in the qualities needed in the vital role of attack leader. After a spell with Doncaster Rovers, he was offered a trial by Exeter City, and in one first team appearance at New Brompton he scored the Grecians' goal in a 4-1 defeat, but was not offered a permanent engagement.
Appearances: FL: 9 apps 4 gls Total: 9 apps 4 gls

TOWARD, Ralph William

Outside right
5' 9"   11st 6lbs
Born: Lanchester, April quarter 1889
Died: Langley Park, 15th December 1963, age 74
Debut v Leicester Fosse (h) 21.3.1913, won 3-0
Career: Leadgate Park. Craghead United. Glossop (trial) January, professional February 1913. Durham City.

A clever and direct dribbler on the right touchline, Ralph Toward was quickly offered terms after impressive displays during a one-month trial. Once introduced into the League side, he dominated the outside right position, his first 37 League appearances being made consecutively. A provider of openings rather than a goal scorer on his own account, his modest total of four League goals was boosted by two goals scored in FA Cup-ties against Coventry City and Queens Park Rangers in 1914-15. After leaving Glossop he joined Durham City and returned to his trade as a colliery blacksmith.
Appearances: FL: 66 apps 4 gls FAC: 2 apps 2 gls Total: 68 apps 6 gls

TUFNELL, Ernest 'Ernie'

Inside left 5' 9"   11st 3lbs
Born: Burton-on-Trent, July quarter 1884
Died: Birmingham, March 1949, age 64
Debut v Oldham Athletic (a) 28.12.1907, drawn 0-0
Career: Long Eaton. Worcester City 19th January 1906. Glossop 15th May 1907. Kidderminster Harriers 7th August 1908. Stourbridge.
Ernie Tufnell joined Glossop from Worcester City of the Birmingham League. He had scored three goals in just four appearances in his brief stay, and had joined them along with his brother, Harry, who netted the Worcester club's first transfer fee - £20 – when transferred to Bury. Harry later made over 200 appearances for Barnsley and scored the winning goal in the 1912 FA Cup Final. Ernie, by comparison, was less successful. The highlight of his season with Glossop was his scoring the only goal of the game against Gainsborough Trinity at

North Road on 3rd March 1908. Five months later he was back in the Birmingham League with Kidderminster Harriers.
Appearances: FL: 7 apps 1 gl FAC: 1 app 0 gls Total: 8 apps 1 gl

TURNELL, Reginald Leaf 'Reg'

Outside right
5' 9"   11st 6lbs
Born: Aberystwyth, April quarter 1891
Died: K.I.A., in the Cambrai area, 23rd November 1917, age 26
Debut v Leeds City (a) 6.9.1913, lost 0-3
Career: Southport Central. Glossop May 1913.
Despite the finances of the Glossop club being well in credit - £3,575 having been received for the transfers of Butler, Williams, Hodkinson and Cooper – the only close season signings in 1913 were players who were new to League football. Assistant schoolmaster Reg Turnell, from Southport Central, was billed as "A very speedy outside right", but found himself underemployed during the season, afforded only four League outings and infrequent appearances in friendly matches with the reserve team who had failed to be readmitted to the Central League. In August 1915, a *Liverpool Echo* report of a cricket match 'Somewhere in France' mentioned Corporal Reg Turnell of the 7th Liverpool Brigade, who went into bat fourth wicket down for his team and carried his bat for 16 to win a low scoring match against the Fifth Field Ambulance Brigade, who had scored just 40 all out.
Appearances: FL: 4 apps 0 gls FAC: 1 app 0 gls Total: 5 apps 0 gls

TUSTIN, William Arthur

Goalkeeper
5' 11½"   11st 5lbs
Born: Aston, April quarter 1879
Died: Birmingham, April quarter 1943, age 63
Debut v Bradford City (h) 27.10.1906, lost 1-2
Career: Bournbrook. Soho Villa. Kidderminster Harriers. Stafford Rangers. Glossop amateur June 1906. Brighton & Hove Albion May 1908 to June 1909.
Goalkeeper Bill Tustin graduated from Birmingham junior football, and first hit the headlines when his team, Stafford Rangers, reached the sixth qualifying round of the FA Cup. They drew 2-2 with Blackpool at Bloomfield Road

but were beaten 3-0 in the replay. Obviously a robust outfit, the Rangers conceded five penalties over the two meetings, but Blackpool only managed to score from one of them, Tustin saving the other four. Initially in reserve to Joe Frail, who commenced as first choice and survived the opening day 2-9 thrashing at Chelsea, Tustin was introduced after the first eight matches of the season in which 28 goals were conceded. He held his place in the side for the remainder of the season, but found stiff competition in his second season from Mick Byrne, and later Joe Butler. His season with Brighton saw him cast in a reserve role, as he lost his place after appearing in the first three matches of the season. Outside of the game, he worked variously as a general labourer and a brass-dresser.
Appearances: FL: 48 apps 0 gls FAC: 5 apps 0 gls
Total: 53 apps 0 gls

UNDERWOOD, Alexander 'Tosher'

Outside left
5' 6½"   11st 5lbs
Born: Street, January quarter 1878
Died: Chiswick, 28th November 1960, age 82
Debut v Fulham (a) 2.9.1908, won 3-2
Career: Fulham amateur 1898. Bristol St. George. Bristol Rovers 16th February 1899. Grays United 2nd July 1901. Fulham (loan) October 1901. Brentford 4th January 1902. Glossop 5th May 1908. Clapton Orient cs 1909 to 1910.
Heralded as "The fastest wingman in the Southern League" on his arrival at Glossop, Underwood made his debut against the club where his career commenced, and for whom he made his debut

some seven years earlier. The best spell of his career came in a six-year association with Brentford, for whom he completed 175 League appearances and scored 24 goals. He was never able to hold down the outside left position with Glossop, with strong competition from Billy Grimes in early season, and from amateur international Ivan Sharpe, who became first choice from February onwards. Underwood's final season in senior football was spent with Clapton Orient, for whom he made 37 League appearances and scored one goal. He later settled in Middlesex and ran a boot and shoe repairing business in Brentford.
Appearances: FL: 18 apps 0 gls FAC: 6 apps 0 gls
Total: 24 apps 0 gls

WADDELL, Dr. Thomas Mayne Reid
Centre forward
Born: In Japan, 21st March 1882
Died: Warrington, 19th May 1926
Debut v Blackpool (h) 23.2.1907, drawn 0-0
Career: Cliftonville. Glossop amateur February 1907. Cliftonville June 1907. Glossop amateur December 1907.
One of Glossop's more colourful amateur footballers, Dr. Waddell was working as a physician and surgeon in Glossop at the time of his signing. A dashing and enthusiastic attack leader, he had lead the Irish attack against Scotland at Dublin in March 1906 when playing his club football for Cliftonville of the Irish League. In his first season at Glossop, he deputised for Irishman Sam Napier in February and March, initially for a run of five matches, in the last of which he scored the winning goal in a 2-1 victory against Barnsley. On the subject of the Doctor's birthplace, doubtless there are several current footballers hailing from Japan, but it was something of a novelty in pre-World War One days!
Appearances: FL: 7 apps 1 gl FAC: 1 app 0 gls
Total: 8 apps 1 gl
Honours: Ireland International, 1 cap 1906.

WALL, Leonard John 'Len'
Inside forward   6' 0"   12st 8lbs
Born: Ditherington, Shropshire, April quarter 1889
Died: Ditherington, Shropshire, January quarter 1951, age 61
Debut v Birmingham (a) 13.9.1909, drawn 2-2
Career: Ditherington Athletic. Shrewsbury All Saints. Welshpool. Shrewsbury Town. Glossop May 1909. Manchester City October 1910, fee £500. Dundee November 1913. Crystal Palace June 1914. Wellington Town. Shrewsbury Town June 1919. Walsall May 1921. Bloxwich Strollers January 1922. Bargoed August 1922. West Cannock Colliery January 1927.
A youthful reserve player of sturdy build whose potential was fully realised following his £500

transfer from Glossop to Manchester City. A clever player, if not gifted with a great amount of pace, he scored on his second appearance, from centre forward, at Aston Villa, but was more successfully switched to the middle line, operating at either centre or left half with equal faculty. After 42 appearances he joined Dundee, but returned after 17 appearances to join Crystal Palace of the Southern League. At about this time he was described as: "A great breaker up of attacks, who believes in the maxim that keeping the ball on the ground is the best way to assist his forward." He enlisted in the 4th King's Shropshire Regiment in February 1915 and in a distinguished spell of active service was awarded the Military Medal. Len Wall's final League club, Walsall, were contesting their first season in the Third Division North, and he appeared at centre half in their first Football League fixture, a 1-0 defeat at Lincoln City, but made only two more first team appearances before dropping into non-League football in mid season.
Appearances: FL: 10 apps 1 gl Total: 10 apps 1 gl

WALLACE, William
Outside left
Debut v Leicester Fosse (h) 7.12.1901, drawn 1-1
Career: Glossop amateur September 1901.
Thought to be a local, as he was reported to be "Ex-Glossop 'A' Team" at the time of his debut against Leicester Fosse, although his name is reminiscent of the hero of Scotland (1274-1305) who drove the English garrisons out of Scotland, but was then defeated at Falkirk in 1298. Speculation aside, Wallace was dubbed "A real trier, with plenty of speed." In eighteen consecutive appearances in the second half of the campaign he solved the problem outside left position, following the release of the former Manchester City wingman, George Douglas.
Appearances: FL: 18 apps 1 gl FAC: 1 app 0 gls Total: 19 apps 1 gl

WARD, George
Full back
Born: Burton-on-Trent, July quarter 1883.
Debut v Grimsby Town (a) 20.4.1901, lost 0-1
Career: Gresley Rovers. Glossop April 1901.
Introduced for the final two fixtures of the 1900-01 season, George Ward's displays did not impress one observer who reported – rather unkindly – as follows: "Beyond a few smart touches in the earlier stages, his kicking was both unsafe and feeble, which did not make him a reliable defender." Ward remained on the club's books for the following season, but made only one further first team appearance in a 1-2 defeat at Gainsborough Trinity on 14th September 1901.
Appearances: FL: 3 apps 0 gls Total: 3 apps 0 gls

WARD, William

Left back
5' 11½"
12st 11lbs
Born: Sheffield, January quarter 1890
Debut v Arsenal (a) 8.9.1914, lost 0-4
Career: Sheffield United. Castleford Town. Glossop 26th August 1914.
Strapping full back William Ward was one of a pair of players signed from Castleford Town club, the other being Blakey Martin, said to be a promising left half. Without managing to command a regular spot in the League side, the powerfully built defender played in exactly half of the season's fixtures, deputising on both flanks for the more experienced pairing of John Cuffe and Robert Dearnaley. In earlier days, Ward commenced with Sheffield United but did not reach first team level. In August 1919, when League football returned to normal following the Great War, Ward was reported to be 'unattached', and he did not reappear in senior football.
Appearances: 20 apps 0 gls FAC: 1 app 0 gls Total: 21 apps 0 gls

WEIR, Alexander 'Alec'

Left half   5' 8"   11st 0lbs
Born: Probably in Scotland, *circa* 1882
Debut v Leeds City (a) 2.9.1907, lost 1-2
Career: Stenhousemuir. Celtic. Reading 18th May 1906. Glossop 9th May 1907. Stockport County May 1909.
Tenacious wing half Alex Weir was a 'regular' during two seasons spent with Glossop, missing only one match in his first season and six in his second. He arrived at North Road from Reading, along with two other players from Elm Park, centre half Jock Comrie and full back Eddie Gettings. Weir left to join Stockport County in May 1909, but made only one first team appearance.
Appearances: FL: 69 apps 0 gls FAC: 3 apps 0 gls Total: 72 apps 0 gls

WHITEHOUSE, Frank 'Tinker'
Forward 5' 6"   11st 6lbs
Born: Newcastle-under-Lyme,
January quarter 1879
Debut v Gainsborough Trinity (h) 2.9.1905,
won 1-0
Career: Bucknall. Burslem Port Vale June 1899. Stoke May 1900. Glossop July 1905. Stoke November 1906. Stafford Rangers. Dresden Queen's Park.
Frank Whitehouse commenced in Division Two with Burslem Port Vale. He scored once in 19 League appearances and moved up a Division when he joined Stoke in May 1900. He spent five seasons at the Victoria Ground, scoring 24 goals in 95 League and Cup matches. He was one of four new forwards signed by Glossop for the 1905-06 season, arriving along with England international Edgar Chadwick, from Blackpool; Ross from Grimsby Town and Carr from Renton. After appearing in the opening ten matches of the season, in which only five points were collected, Whitehouse lost his place in the side. He returned after a lengthy absence and scored against Manchester United and Grimsby Town in January, but ended his season in the Reserves, his final senior appearance coming in a 1-3 defeat at Chesterfield on March 24th. He appeared in just two first team games in his second spell with Stoke.
Appearances: FL: 20 apps 4 gls Total: 20 apps 4 gls

WILLIAMS, David H 'Dai'
Centre forward   5' 8"   11st 10lbs
Born: Liverpool
Debut v Blackpool (h) 21.9.1912, won 2-0
Career: St Helens Recreation. Stafford Rangers. Glossop September 1912. Notts County November 1912, fee £750. Belfast Celtic August 1914. Cliftonville November 1914. Liverpool April 1915. (Wartime guest player with Arsenal September 1916) Luton Town July 1919. Brighton & Hove Albion February 1920, fee £200. Maidstone United May 1921.
Despite having played on only six first team matches for Glossop, Dai Williams commanded a useful fee when transferred to Notts County after the briefest of stays at North Road. The *Nottingham Post Annual* for 1913-14, commenting on his first season with the Magpies, stated that: "Williams came from Glossop with the reputation as a thrusting centre forward and a fine shot, and if he did not quite come up to expectations, he was always a genuine trier." Notts lost their place in the First Division, scoring only 28 goals in 38 matches, and in the promotion season that followed, Williams scored twice in seven early season matches. After Army service during the First World War, Williams assisted both Luton Town and Brighton & Hove Albion, costing the Goldstone club their then record transfer fee of £200.
Appearances: FL: 6 apps 2 gls Total: 6 apps 2 gls

WILLIAMS, Richard William

Goalkeeper
Born: Birkenhead, January quarter 1870
Died: Eastham, Wirral, 9th December 1939
Debut v Blackpool (h) 3.9.1898, won 4-1
Career: Bromborough Pool. Everton May 1891. Luton Town 6th April 1897. Glossop North End 5th May 1898 to May 1900.
Said to stand over six feet tall and with a build to match, Richard Williams provided a formidable barrier for an onrushing forward. He commenced with Everton in season 1891-92, appearing in nine First Division matches and one FA Cup-tie. In the following season he made 11 League appearances and seven in FA Cup-ties, including an appearance in the Final against Wolverhampton Wanderers, played at the Manchester Athletic Grounds at Fallowfield, the Wolves winning by 1-0. He was established as first choice in the following term, missing only four matches, and had accumulated a total of 70 League and Cup appearances when he was transferred to Luton Town, who had been elected to the Second Division, taking the place of Burton Wanderers. Williams appeared in Luton's first match, a 1-1 draw at Leicester Fosse, and held his place throughout the season. Although an eighth place finish was considered a creditable performance, the season's attendance figures had proved disappointing in the extreme. The upshot being that many of the club's players were released in the close season. The Glossop club, themselves embarking on life in the Second Division, were quick to profit from Luton's problems, signing no fewer than four of their best players, Williams, McEwan, Gallacher and Donaldson. In Glossop's first season, Williams guarded his goal to such effect that he was undefeated in 13 matches and conceded just 38 goals in 34 League matches. Sadly, elevation to the First Division proved much more exacting, the overworked goalkeeper shipping 47 goals in his 18 League appearances. His replacement, Herbert Birchenough from Burslem Port Vale, certainly tightened the defensive lines, but could not prevent Glossop's relegation, after just one season in the top flight.
Appearances: FL: 52 apps 0 gls FAC: 6 apps 0 gls Total: 58 apps 0 gls
Honours: Everton, FA Cup finalists, 1893

WILSON, Clare

Wing half
5' 9"   12st 0lbs
Born: Boroughbridge, Yorkshire, April quarter 1886
Died: Bilston, October quarter 1953
Debut v West Bromwich Albion (h) 12.12.1908, lost 1-3
Career: Gateshead Town. Wallsend Park Villa. Bradford City February 1907. Glossop December 1908, in exchange for W.T. Grimes. Oldham Athletic December 1911, fee £50. Gateshead September 1913.
Clare Wilson had appeared in only two first team matches for Bradford City when he was transferred to Glossop in exchange for Billy Grimes, one inside left being exchanged for another. In his second season at North Road, Wilson was switched to left half back, and he missed only a handful of matches before returning to the First Division with Oldham Athletic. Said to be a little lacking in pace but nothing in effort, he could be relied upon to provide a workmanlike display in all three half back positions, but his appearances at Boundary Park were restricted to 21 by the presence of Athletic's all-international middle line.
Appearances: FL: 109 apps 6 gls FAC: 8 apps 0 gls
Total: 117 apps 6 gls

WOODALL, Llywellyn Charles

Goalkeeper
Born: Romiley, Cheshire, January quarter 1880
Died: See below
Debut v Burslem Port Vale (h) 26.4.1902, lost 0-1
Career: Romiley F.C. Glossop April 1902.
Skilful displays for the Reserves earned Woodall a trial in the League side in the final fixture of the 1901-02 season, against Burslem Port Vale at North Road. Played in bright, pleasant weather, and attended by a fair crowd, Glossop kicked off towards the station goal. In the early stages, smart work and an inviting centre delivered by Wallace was netted by Kennedy but the point was disallowed for offside. The visitors took the lead following a tussle in the goalmouth, and lead 1-0 at the interval. Lusty cries of "Play up Glossop" failed to infuse much dash into the home team, the visitors being much the superior side. Woodall was kept busy in the Glossop goal, and invariably showed sound judgment, but the Peakites were outplayed at every point of the game, and were unable to obtain an equalising goal. **Note**: At some stage, Woodall emigrated to Australia, and his name appears on Australian Electoral Rolls up to and including 1958, when he was living in Watson, New South Wales. He does not appear in the next E.R., in 1961, suggesting that he died between these dates.
Appearances: FL: 1 app 0 gls Total: 1 app 0 gls

SEASON BY SEASON GRIDS 1898-99 to 1914-15

Some attendances are missing from the pages that follow. Newspaper reports of the time sometimes did not give an estimate of the attendance, or might use words such as "small" or "moderate".

Also, please note that the line-ups of some of Glossop's games in the qualifying rounds of the F.A. Cup are incomplete. Glossop are one of four Division One clubs in the history of the competition that have been obliged to play in qualifying rounds; the others are Stoke, Notts County and Bolton Wanderers. The publisher will be pleased to hear from anyone who can help fill in any of the gaps.

Goal scorers differ in some reports. Shirt numbers were not used at the time. Reporters sometimes had to sit out in the open in all weathers. It is not surprising if they made the odd mistake!

1898/99

North Road

#		Date	Opponent	Score	Scorers	Att	Bartley T	Clifford T	Colville G	Colvin R	Connachan J	Donaldson R	Evenson I	Gallacher W	Killean E	Lomax H	Lumsden J	McCosh H	McEwen J	Mercer W	Millar W	Orr W	Paton J	Pryce J	Rothwell H	Sidebottom J	Sutcliffe JR	Tinto R	Williams R
1	Sep	3	BLACKPOOL	4-1	Tinto, Lumsden, Gallacher, Donaldson	2500	11	5	4			9		10	2		7		3						6			8	1
2		10	Grimsby Town	1-1	Bartley	6000	8	5	4			9		7	2		11		3						6			10	1
3		17	NEWTON HEATH	1-2	Tinto	6000	8	5	4			9		7	2		11		3						6			10	1
4		24	New Brighton Tower	2-2	Donaldson 2	600	7	5	4	10		9		8			11		3					2			6		1
5	Oct	1	LINCOLN CITY	2-0	Bartley, Rothwell	2500	11	5	4			8		7			10		3					9	2			6	1
6		15	LUTON TOWN	5-0	Gallacher, Donaldson, Lumsden 2, Sharpe (og)	3000	7		4			9		8	2		11		3					10	6			5	1
7		22	Leicester Fosse	2-4	Gallacher 2	3000	7		4			9		8	2		11		3					10	6			5	1
8	Nov	5	Gainsborough Trinity	4-2	Gallacher, Pryce 3	6000			4	7		9	5	8	2		11		3					10	6				1
9		12	MANCHESTER CITY	1-2	Colvin	2000			4	7		9	5	8	2		11		3					10	6				1
10		26	Walsall	0-2		2000			4	7		9		8	6	2	11		3					10	5				1
11	Dec	3	BURTON SWIFTS	5-0	Gallacher, Tinto 2, Pryce, Lumsden	2000	5		4	9				7	6	2	11		3					10				8	1
12		17	SMALL HEATH	1-2	Colvin	1900		5	4	7				8	6	2	11		3					10				9	1
13		24	Loughborough	3-1	Gallacher 2, Lumsden				4	7		9		8	6		11		3					10	5		2		1
14		26	Lincoln City	2-2	McEwen, Rothwell	6000		5	4	7		9		8	6		11		3					10	2				1
15		27	Barnsley	1-1	Porteous (og)	3000		5	4	7		9		8	6		11		3					10	2				1
16		31	Blackpool	2-1	Donaldson 2	12000		5	4	10		9		7	6		11		3					8	2				1
17	Jan	2	Manchester City	2-0	Donaldson, Killean	12000		5	4	10		9		7	6		11		3					8	2				1
18		7	GRIMSBY TOWN	4-2	Mercer, Donaldson, Pryce, Lumsden	2000	3	4				9		7	6	2	10			11	5			8					1
19		14	Newton Heath	0-3		12000		5	4			9		7	6		10		3		11			8	2				1
20		21	NEW BRIGHTON TOWER	5-0	Donaldson 2, Lumsden, Millar, Pryce	1500		5	4			9		7	6		10		3		11			8	2				1
21	Feb	4	WOOLWICH ARSENAL	2-0	Donaldson 2	2000		5	4			9		7	6		10		3		11			8	2				1
22		11	Luton Town	2-0	Donaldson 2	4000		5	4	11		9		7	6		10		3					8	2				1
23		13	Woolwich Arsenal	0-3		3000		5	4	11		9		7	6		10		3					8	2				1
24		18	LEICESTER FOSSE	1-3	Lumsden	1000		5	4	11		9		7	6		10		3					8	2				1
25		25	Darwen	2-0	Donaldson, Killean	1000		5	4			9		8	7		10		3					2		11	6		1
26	Mar	4	GAINSBOROUGH TRIN.	5-1	Lumsden 2, Donaldson, Connachan 2	5000			4	7	11	9		8	5		10		3					2			6		1
27		7	DARWEN	5-0	Lumsden 2, Colville, Connachan, Gallacher	1000			4	9	10	8		7	5		11		3					2			6		1
28		25	WALSALL	2-0	McCosh, Gallacher	1000		5	4			9		8	7	6	11	10	3					2					1
29		31	BARNSLEY	1-0	McCosh	2000		5	4			9		8	7	6	11	10	3					2					1
30	Apr	1	Burton Swifts	2-1	Connachan, Clifford	4000		5	4		6	9		8	7		11	10	3					2					1
31		3	Burslem Port Vale	2-1	Lumsden, Donaldson	3500		5	4			9		8	7	6	11	10	3					2					1
32		8	BURSLEM PORT VALE	0-0		6000		5	4			9		8	7	6	11	10	3			2							1
33		15	Small Heath	1-1	Lumsden	6000		5	4			9		8	7	6	11	10	3					2					1
34		22	LOUGHBOROUGH	4-0	Lumsden, Gallacher, Killean, Donaldson	3000		5	4			9		8	7	6	11	10	3					2					1
					Apps		7	25	33	16	11	32	2	32	24	11	34	7	33	2	3	1	1	20	32	1	7	6	34
					Goals		2	1	1	2	4	18		11	3		15	2	1	1	1			6	2			4	

Two own goals

F.A. Cup

		Date	Opponent	Score	Scorers	Att	Bartley T	Clifford T	Colville G	Colvin R	Connachan J	Donaldson R	Evenson I	Gallacher W	Killean E	Lomax H	Lumsden J	McCosh H	McEwen J	Mercer W	Millar W	Orr W	Paton J	Pryce J	Rothwell H	Sidebottom J	Sutcliffe JR	Tinto R	Williams R
Q3	Oct	29	NEW BRIGHTON TOWER	4-2	Donaldson, Gallacher, Pryce, Colvin	3000				7		9		8			11							10	2				1
Q4	Nov	19	CREWE ALEXANDRA	1-0	Bartley		9		4								11								2				1
Q5	Dec	10	Stockport County	2-0	Tinto, Pryce	5000		5		9				7	2		11		3					8				9	1
R1	Jan	28	NEWCASTLE UNITED	0-1		8000		5	4			9		7	6		11		3	10				8	2				1

Three qualifying round line-ups not known in full

1899/1900

18th in Division One: Relegated

North Road

#	Date	Opponent	Res	Scorers	Att	Armstrong A	Birchenough H	Burgess H	Carlin JC	Clifford T	Colville G	Connachan J	Davidson AL	Evans L	Gallacher W	Goddard AM	Jackson TJ	Jones R	Killean E	Lumsden J	Lupton FJ	McCosh H	McEwen J	Monks A	Morris GR	Muir J	Orr W	Rothwell H	Saunders JE	Scarratt W	Williams R
1	Sep 2	BURNLEY	2-0	Gallacher, Lumsden	6000					5	4	8		11	7				6	10			3	9			2				1
2	4	Aston Villa	0-9		15000					5	4	8			7				6	11		10	3	9			2				1
3	9	Preston North End	0-1		5000					5	4	8		11	7				6	10			3	9			2				1
4	16	NOTTM. FOREST	3-0	Gallacher 2, Monks	6000					5	4	8		11	7				6	10			3	9			2				1
5	23	Wolverhampton Wan.	0-4		3000						4			11	5		7	9	6	10			3	8			2				1
6	30	Stoke	0-1		5000						4	10		11			9	7	6				3	8			2				1
7	Oct 7	SUNDERLAND	0-2		5000					5	4				7		9	11	6	10			3	8			2				1
8	14	West Bromwich Albion	3-3	Evans, Connachan, McCosh	6000					5	4	9			7				11	6		10	3	8			2				1
9	21	EVERTON	1-1	Connachan	3000					5	4	9			7	8			11	6		10	3				2				1
10	Nov 11	Bury	1-2	Connachan	2500	1				5	4	9			7	8			11	6		10					2	3			
11	18	NOTTS COUNTY	0-0		4000					5	4	8		9	7				11	6		10					2	3			1
12	25	Manchester City	1-4	Lumsden	14000					5	4	10	9	11					6	8			3	7			2				1
13	Dec 2	SHEFFIELD UNITED	2-2	Gallacher 2	5000				10	6	4			9	7	8				11	5		3				2				1
14	16	ASTON VILLA	1-0	Davidson	6000				10		4		9	11	7	8			6		5		3				2				1
15	23	Liverpool	2-5	Evans 2	5000				10		4	7		9	11	8			6		5		3				2				1
16	26	Derby County	1-4	Gallacher	12000				10	6	4	9		11	7	8					5		3				2				1
17	30	Burnley	1-3	Goddard	3000					5	4	9		11	7	8			6				3		10		2				1
18	Jan 6	PRESTON NORTH END	0-2		2000	1			11	5	4	8		9	7				6	10							2	3			
19	13	Nottingham Forest	0-5		4000				10		4	9			7	8			6		5					11	2	3			1
20	20	WOLVERHAMPTON W.	2-3	Miur 2	4000				10		4	9			7	8			6		5					11	2	3			1
21	Feb 3	STOKE	1-2	Carlin	3000		1		8		4	9			7	11			6	10	5						2	3			
22	24	Sunderland	0-0		6000		1				4	9			7	8			11	10	5		3				6	2			
23	27	BLACKBURN ROVERS	4-2	Connachan, Goddard 2, Lumsden	4000		1				4	8			7	10			11	9	5		3				6	2			
24	Mar 3	Blackburn Rovers	2-2	Gallacher, Lumsden	6000		1				4	9			7	8			10	11	5						6	2		3	
25	14	Newcastle United	0-1		6000		1				4	9			7	8			10	11	5						6	2		3	
26	17	BURY	0-0		2000		1				4	9			7	8			6		5		3				2	3	11		
27	24	Notts County	0-0		5000		1				4				7	8			10	11	5			6			2	3		9	
28	31	MANCHESTER CITY	0-2		10000		1				4	9			7	8			10		5			6			2	3		9	
29	Apr 7	Sheffield United	0-4		5000						4			11	7	8			10		5		3	6	9		2				1
30	13	DERBY COUNTY	1-3	Goddard	2800		1				4	9		11	7	8			10		5			6			2	3			
31	14	NEWCASTLE UNITED	0-0		2000		1				4	10		9	7				6		5						2	7		8	
32	16	Everton	1-4	Rothwell	7000		1				4			11	7				10		5		3	6			2	8		9	
33	24	WEST BROMWICH ALB.	1-1	Killean	2025		1				4								11	10	5		3		6		2	8		9	
34	28	LIVERPOOL	1-2	Colville	2000		1				4	9							11	10	5			6				3		8	
	Apps					2	13	1	8	15	32	17	13	19	22	22	3	7	30	19	21	3	21	13	14	3	21	29	1	7	18
	Goals								1		1	4	1	3	7	4			1	4		1		1		2		1			

F.A. Cup

#	Date	Opponent	Res	Scorers	Att	Armstrong A	Birchenough H	Burgess H	Carlin JC	Clifford T	Colville G	Connachan J	Davidson AL	Evans L	Gallacher W	Goddard AM	Jackson TJ	Jones R	Killean E	Lumsden J	Lupton FJ	McCosh H	McEwen J	Monks A	Morris GR	Muir J	Orr W	Rothwell H	Saunders JE	Scarratt W	Williams R
Q3	Oct 28	STOCKPORT COUNTY	2-2	Connachan 2	3000					5	4	9																			1
rep	Nov 1	Stockport County	0-3							5	4	9		8		7			11	6		10					3				2	1

1900/01

North Road

#		Date	Match	Score	Scorers	Att	Barlow A	Bell T	Birchenough H	Brodie D	Brooks J	Burgess H	Chesworth F	Colville G	Crump F	Goddard AM	Goodall J	Hall T	Hyde W	Jones J	Kennedy J	Kent WE	King R	Lupton FJ	McCartney D	Orr W	Pattison S	Rothwell H	Spiby S	Ward G
1	Sep	1	NEWTON HEATH	1-0	Kennedy	4000			1				10	4	9	7		6			8	3	11	5		2				
2		8	Chesterfield	1-0	Crump	5500			1				10	4	9	7		6			8	3	11	5		2				
3		15	Middlesbrough	2-2	Chesworth 2	11000			1				10	4	9	7		6			8	3	11	5		2				
4		22	BURNLEY	0-1		2500			1			4	10		9	7		6			8	3	11	5		2				
5		29	Burslem Port Vale	0-0		2000			1			4	10		9	7		6			8	3	11	5				2		
6	Oct	6	LEICESTER FOSSE	3-1	Goddard 2, King	2000			1			4			9	7		6		10	8	3	11	5						
7		13	New Brighton Tower	0-1		4000			1			4			9	7		6		10	8	3	11	5		2				
8		20	GAINSBOROUGH TRIN.	3-1	Goddard 3	1500	9		1						10	7		6			8	3	11	4	5	2				
9		27	Walsall	1-2	Goddard	3000	9		1						10	7		6			8	3	11	4	5	2				
10	Nov	17	WOOLWICH ARSENAL	0-1		3000	9		1					4	10	7					8	3	11	6	5	2				
11		24	Blackpool	0-0		1500			1				10	4	9	7					8	3	11	6	5			2		
12	Dec	1	STOCKPORT COUNTY	6-0	Goddard, King, Chesworth 2, Crump 2	4000			1				10	4	9	7		6			8	3	11	5				2		
13		8	Small Heath	0-1		8000			1			2	10	4	9	7		6			8	3	11	5						
14		15	GRIMSBY TOWN	0-0		3000			1				10	4	9	7		6			8	3	11	5				2		
15		25	CHESTERFIELD	1-1	Crump	4000	11		1			3	10	4	9	7		6			8			5	2					
16		26	Lincoln City	1-1	McCartney	6000			1			3	10	4	9	7		6			8		11	5	2					
17		29	Newton Heath	0-3		5000			1			3	10	4	9	7		6			8		11			2				
18	Jan	12	MIDDLESBROUGH	2-0	Hall, Crump	4000			1			3	9	4	10	7		11			8			6	5	2				
19		19	Burnley	1-5	Goddard	2000			1			2	9	4	10	7		6			8	3	11	5						
20	Feb	9	BURSLEM PORT VALE	1-2	Crump	4000			1			3	10	4	9	7	11	6			8			5		2				
21		16	NEW BRIGHTON TOWER	0-1		3000			1	2		3	11	4	10	7	9		6		8			5						
22		21	Leicester Fosse	2-1	Kennedy, Crump	1000	10		1	2		3	11	4	9	7					8			5		6				
23		23	Gainsborough Trinity	1-1	Goddard		10		1		3		11	4	9	7		2			8			5		6				
24	Mar	2	WALSALL	2-0	Goddard 2	2000			1		3	2	11	4	9	7		6			8			5						10
25		9	Burton Swifts	3-1	Crump, Goddard, Barlow		11		1			2	10	4	9	7		3			8			5		6				
26		16	BARNSLEY	2-1	Goddard, Barlow	2000	11		1			3	10	4	9	7		2			8			5		6				
27		23	Woolwich Arsenal	0-2		5000	11		1			2	3	10	4	9	7		6		8			5						
28		30	BLACKPOOL	6-0	Crump 2, Barlow 2, Kennedy, Chesworth	2000	11		1			3	10	4	9	7		6			8			5		2				
29	Apr	5	BURTON SWIFTS	3-0	Barlow, Crump, Kennedy	4000	11		1			3		4	10	7	9	6			8			5		2				
30		6	Stockport County	3-1	Chesworth, Crump, Kennedy	3000	11		1			3	10	4	9	7		6			8			5		2				
31		8	Barnsley	2-2	Crump, Kennedy	3000	11		1			3	10	4	9	7					8	6		5		2				
32		13	SMALL HEATH	2-0	Crump 2	2000	11		1			3	10	4	9	7		6			8			5		2				
33		20	Grimsby Town	0-1		6000	11		1				10	4	9	7					8	6		5		2				3
34		27	LINCOLN CITY	2-0	Goddard, Hall	1500	10		1			3	11	4	9	7		6			8			5						2
			Apps				12	4	34	3	4	21	28	28	34	34	2	29	1	2	34	14	16	21	27	16	1	6	1	2
			Goals				5						6		15	14		2			6		2		1					

F.A. Cup

		Date	Match	Score	Att	Barlow A	Bell T	Birchenough H	Brodie D	Brooks J	Burgess H	Chesworth F	Colville G	Crump F	Goddard AM	Goodall J	Hall T	Hyde W	Jones J	Kennedy J	Kent WE	King R	Lupton FJ	McCartney D	Orr W	Pattison S	Rothwell H	Spiby S	Ward G
IR	Jan	5	Stoke	0-1	5000			1				10	4	9	7		11			8			6	5	3		2		

1901/02

8th in Division Two

North Road

League (Division Two)

No		Date	Opponent	Score	Scorers	Att	Badenoch GH	Birchenough H	Burgess H	Coates F	Colville G	Crump F	Dougal G	Durber P	Farrington GS	Goddard AM	Goodall J	Hall T	Kennedy D	McCartney D	Norgrove F	Parker H	Pattison S	Rae W	Rothwell H	Thornley H	Thornley I	Wallace W	Ward G	Woodall LC
1	Sep	2	West Bromwich Albion	1-0	Crump	5000		1	2		4	9	11	3		7	8	6		5				10						
2		7	CHESTERFIELD	3-1	Crump, Goodall 2	5000		1	2		4	10	11	3		7	8	6		5				9						
3		14	Gainsborough Trinity	1-2	Crump	3000		1	2			10	11	3		7	8	6		5				9					4	
4		21	MIDDLESBROUGH	1-0	Crump	2000		1	2			8	11	3		7		6		5	4	10		9						
5		28	Bristol City	0-2		6000		1	2			8	11	3		7		6		5	4	10		9						
6	Oct	5	BLACKPOOL	3-1	Goodall, Parker, Crump	1000		1	2			9	11	3		7	8	6		5		10	4							
7		12	Stockport County	0-0		4500		1	2		4	9	11	3		7	8	6		5		10								
8		19	NEWTON HEATH	0-0		7000	7	1	2		4	10		3		9	8	6		5		11								
9		26	Burton United	1-1	Goddard	4000	7	1	2		4	8		3		9		6		5		10		11						
10	Nov	9	LINCOLN CITY	1-1	Goodall	2000	7	1	2		4	10	11	3			8	6		5		9								
11		23	WOOLWICH ARSENAL	0-1		3000	7	1	2		4	10	11	3		8		6		5		9								
12	Dec	7	LEICESTER FOSSE	1-1	Goodall	1000	7	1	2		4	9		3		8	10	6		5							11			
13		21	BURNLEY	0-0		1000	7	1	2		4			3		11	8	6		5				9			10			
14		26	Barnsley	4-1	McCartney, Rae, Goddard, Badenoch		7	1	2			10		3		11	4	6		5		8		9						
15		28	Burslem Port Vale	0-1			8	1	2		4	10				7		6	3	5		11		9						
16	Jan	4	Chesterfield	0-1		1000	7	1	2		4	10		3		11		6		5		9		8						
17		11	GAINSBOROUGH TRIN.	0-0		1000	8	1	2		4	10		3		7		6		5		11		9						
18		18	Middlesbrough	0-5		9000	8	1	2			9		3		7	10			5		11	6	4						
19	Feb	1	Blackpool	1-1	I Thornley	2000	4	1	2			8		3		7				5		11			6		9	10		
20		8	STOCKPORT COUNTY	2-1	Crump 2 (1p)	600	8	1	2			10		3		7				5	4	6					9	11		
21		15	Newton Heath	0-1		6000	8	1	2					3		7				5	4	10	6				9	11		
22		22	BURTON UNITED	2-1	Crump 2	1000	8	1				10		3		7				5	4	6	2				9	11		
23	Mar	1	DONCASTER ROVERS	3-1	Badenoch, Parker, Rae	1000	7	1				8		3						5	4	10	6	9	2			11		
24		4	BRISTOL CITY	1-2	Parker	2500	7	1				8		3						5	4	10	6	9	2			11		
25		8	Lincoln City	0-1			7	1	2			8		3						5	4	10	6				9	11		
26		15	WEST BROMWICH ALB.	1-2	McCartney	2000	7	1	2			8		3				6		5		10	4				9	11		
27		22	Woolwich Arsenal	0-4		6000	7	1	2			8		3						5	6	10	4				9	11		
28		28	Preston North End	2-2	I Thornley 2	4000	7	1	2			8		3					4	5		10	6				9	11		
29		29	BARNSLEY	1-1	Wallace	2000	7	1	2			8		3					4	5		10	6				9	11		
30		31	Doncaster Rovers	2-1	Thornley, Crump	3000	7	1	2			8		3						5	4	10	6				9	11		
31	Apr	1	Leicester Fosse	1-1	Crump	2500	7	1	2	5		8		3				6	4			10					9	11		
32		12	PRESTON NORTH END	3-1	I Thornley, Kennedy, Badenoch		7	1	2	5		8		3					4			10	6				9	11		
33		19	Burnley	1-1	Badenoch	1000	7	1	2			8		3				5	4			10	6				9	11		
34		26	BURSLEM PORT VALE	0-1		1500	7		2			8		3	9			5	4			10	6					11		1
			Apps				27	33	31	2	12	32	9	33	1	21	14	24	3	29	12	24	16	13	4	1	13	18	1	1
			Goals				4					11				2	5			1	2		3	2			5	1		

One own goal

F.A. Cup

		Date	Opponent	Score	Scorers	Att	Badenoch GH	Birchenough H	Burgess H	Coates F	Colville G	Crump F	Dougal G	Durber P	Farrington GS	Goddard AM	Goodall J	Hall T	Kennedy D	McCartney D	Norgrove F	Parker H	Pattison S	Rae W	Rothwell H	Thornley H	Thornley I	Wallace W	Ward G	Woodall LC
Q3	Nov	2	ST HELENS	5-2	Parker, Dougal, Hall, Crump 2	400		1	2			9	11			7	8	6		5		10			4					
Q4		16	Nantwich	3-1	Badenoch, Astbury (og), Goddard		7	1				10				8	9						11							
Q5		30	STOCKPORT COUNTY	2-0	Goodall, Crump	3000	7	1	2		4	10				8	9	6		5			11							
IR	Dec	14	Leicester Fosse	1-0	Goodall	3000	7	1	3		6	10		2		9	4			5		8						11		
R1	Jan	25	NOTTM. FOREST	1-3	Goddard	2500	8	1	2			10		3		7	11	6		5				4			9			

Barber played at 3 in Q3

99

1902/03

North Road

#	Mon	Date	Opponent	Result	Scorers	Att	Badenoch GH	Birchenough H	Boden JA	Burgess H	Carr RS	Clark DC	Coates F	Dyke J	Fielding P	Freeman J	Goodall J	Hancock J	Harrison T	Hunt H	Jack R	Kennedy D	McCartney D	Murphy EJ	Norgrove F	Pell W	Ridgway WH	Roberts W	Swindells J	Thornley I	Thornley J
1	Sep	6	Burton United	1-2	I Thornley	2000	8			2	7	1	6				11					10	5		3	4				9	
2		13	BRISTOL CITY	0-2		1000	8			2	7	1	6				10						5		3	4		11		9	
3		20	CHESTERFIELD	0-3		1000	8	1		2	7		6				11						5		3	4	10			9	
4		27	Manchester United	1-1	og (Read)	12000	7			2		1	5				6			11			9	10	3	4				8	
5	Oct	11	Blackpool	2-2	McCartney, Goodall	2000	7			2		1	5				6			11			9	10	3	4				8	
6		18	WOOLWICH ARSENAL	1-2	I Thornley	1000	4			2	7	1	5				6			11			9	10	3					8	
7		25	Doncaster Rovers	1-4	McCartney	2500	7			2		1	5				6			11			9	10	3	4				8	
8	Nov	8	Small Heath	1-3	Badenoch	5000	7			2		1	6				8			11			9	10	3	4				9	
9		22	Manchester City	2-5	Jack 2	10000	7			2		1	6								11	9	5	10	3	4				8	
10	Dec	2	BURNLEY	2-0	Hunt, I Thornley		7		5	2		1	6							9	11			10	3	4				8	
11		6	Preston North End	0-0		3000			5	2		1	6							9	11			10	3	4			7	8	
12		9	BURSLEM PORT VALE	2-1	Hunt, I Thornley	3000			5	2		1	6							9	11			10	3	4			7	8	
13		20	Barnsley	1-0	I Thornley	2000				2		1	6							9	11		5	10	3	4			7	8	
14		25	STOCKPORT COUNTY	3-0	I Thornley 2, Murphy	4000			5	2		1	6				9				11			10	3	4			7	8	
15		26	Lincoln City	0-1		3000			4	2		1	6							9	11		5	10	3		7			8	
16		27	GAINSBOROUGH TRIN.	4-2	Jack, Goodall 2, Hunt	1200			4	2		1	6				7			9	11		5	10	3					8	
17	Jan	3	BURTON UNITED	3-0	Hunt 2, I Thornley	1200			5	2		1	6				7			9	11			10	3	4				8	
18		10	Bristol City	1-1	Badenoch	6000	7		5	2		1	6							9	11			10	3	4				8	
19		17	Chesterfield	0-10		4000	7		5			1	6				10			9	11		2		3	4				8	
20		24	MANCHESTER UNITED	1-3	Hunt	5000	7		5	2		1	6				10			9	11				3	4				8	
21		31	Stockport County	3-2	Jack 2, I Thornley	4000	7		5	2		1	6							9	11			10	3	4				8	
22	Feb	14	Woolwich Arsenal	0-0		10000			5	2		1	6				7			9	11			10	3	4				8	
23		17	BLACKPOOL	1-0	I Thornley	2000			5	2		1	6				10			9				11	3	4				8	7
24		24	DONCASTER ROVERS	3-0	Murphy 2, Hunt	3000			5	2		1	6			7				9	11			10	3	4				8	
25		28	LINCOLN CITY	2-0	I Thornley 2	2000			5	2		1	6							9	11			10	3	4				8	
26	Mar	7	SMALL HEATH	0-1		2000	7			2		1	6				9				11		5	10	3	4				8	
27		14	Leicester Fosse	2-3	Ridgway, I Thornley	1500	7		5	2		1	6								11			10	3	4	9			8	
28		21	MANCHESTER CITY	0-1		7000	7		5	2		1	6							9	11			10	3	4				8	
29		28	Burnley	1-2	Jack	500	7		6	2		1									11		5	10	3	4	9			8	
30	Apr	4	PRESTON NORTH END	1-2			7		5	2		1									11			10	3	4	9			8	
31		10	LEICESTER FOSSE	1-2	Coates	4000	7		5			1	9		7	2					11		6	10	3	4				8	
32		11	Burslem Port Vale	0-1		2000	6		2			1									11		7	10	3	4	9			8	
33		18	BARNSLEY	2-2	Dyke, I Thornley	1000			5	2		1	6	7		9					11			10	3	4				8	
34		25	Gainsborough Trinity	1-1	I Thornley	4000			5			1	9					2	6		11			10	3	4				8	7
			Apps				21	1	25	28	4	33	32	1	1	2	18	1	1	16	30	2	17	29	34	32	5	1	4	34	2
			Goals				2						1	1			3			7	6		2	3			1			16	

One own goal

F.A. Cup

	Mon	Date	Opponent	Result	Scorers	Att	Badenoch GH	Birchenough H	Boden JA	Burgess H	Carr RS	Clark DC	Coates F	Dyke J	Fielding P	Freeman J	Goodall J	Hancock J	Harrison T	Hunt H	Jack R	Kennedy D	McCartney D	Murphy EJ	Norgrove F	Pell W	Ridgway WH	Roberts W	Swindells J	Thornley I	Thornley J
Q3	Nov	1	Crewe Alexandra	3-0	Murphy, 2 ano							1					9							10							
Q4		15	WREXHAM	4-0	Murphy 3, Coates		7			2		1	6				9				11		5	10	3	4				8	
Q5		29	ST HELENS RECREATION	5-0	I Thornley, 4 ano		7			2		1	6							11	9			10	3	4				8	5
IR	Dec	13	NEW BROMPTON	2-1	Norgrove, I Thornley		7			2		1	6				9				11		5	10	3	4				8	
R1	Feb	7	STOKE	2-3	Badenoch, Burgess	2000	7			2		1	6							9	11		5	10	3	4				8	

1903/04

North Road

#		Date	Opponent	Score	Scorers	Att	Bainbridge JR	Bardsley E	Barnes G	Boden IA	Clark DC	Coates F	Earnshaw J	Fisher J	Galley W	Goodall AL	Green W	Hancock J	Hewitt J	Jones S	Morgan-Owen MM	Murphy EJ	Norgrove F	Morton A	Pell W	Roberts W	Thornley I
1	Sep	5	BURTON UNITED	0-1		2000	7		11	5	1				6		2			9		10	3		4		8
2		12	Bristol City	0-5		8000	7		11	5	1				6		2			9		10	3		4		8
3		19	MANCHESTER UNITED	0-5		3000	7		11	5	1				6		2			9		10	3		4		8
4		26	Burslem Port Vale	1-1	Thornley	3000	7		11	5	1				6		2			9		10	3		4		8
5	Oct	10	WOOLWICH ARSENAL	1-3	Thornley	1000	7			5	1	10			6		2			9		11	3		4		8
6		17	Barnsley	0-4		3000	7				1	5			6		2			9		11	3		4	10	8
7		24	LINCOLN CITY	5-0	Thornley 3, Boden, Bainbridge	1200	7		11	5	1	9			6		2					10	3		4		8
8	Nov	7	CHESTERFIELD	0-2		1000	7			5	1	10			6		2					11	3	9	4		8
9		14	Bolton Wanderers	1-0	Murphy	5000	7			5	1	6				10	2					11	3		4	8	9
10		21	BURNLEY	6-2	Bainbridge, Murphy 2, Thornley, Roberts, Coates		7			5	1	6				10	2					11	3		4	8	9
11		28	Preston North End	0-3		3000	7			5	1	6		8		10	2					11	3		4		9
12	Dec	5	GRIMSBY TOWN	1-1	Murphy	1000	7			5	1	6		9		10	2					11	3		4		9
13		12	Leicester Fosse	2-4	Green, Murphy	6000	7			5	1	6		8		10	2					11	3		4		9
14		19	BLACKPOOL	0-1			7			5	1	6				10	2					11	3		4		9
15		25	Blackpool	2-3	Murphy, Green	5000	7			5	1	6			4	10	2					11	3	8			9
16		26	Gainsborough Trinity	1-0	Murphy	2500	7			5	1	6				10	2					11	3	9	4		8
17	Jan	2	Burton United	0-2		2000	7			5	1	6				10	2					11	3	9	4		8
18		9	BRISTOL CITY	1-1	Thornley	800	7			5	1	6				10	2					11	3	9	4		8
19		16	Manchester United	1-3	Thornley	8000	7			4	1	10			6	5	2					11	3	9			8
20		23	BURSLEM PORT VALE	4-1	Coates, Bainbridge, Thornley 2	1000	7			6	1	9				5	10	2				11	3		4		8
21	Feb	6	Bradford City	1-2	Thornley	5000	7			6	1	9				5	10	2				11	3		4		8
22		13	BARNSLEY	7-0	Murphy 2, Goodall, Thornley 3, Boden		7	11		6	1	5				9		2				10	3		4		8
23		20	Lincoln City	1-3	Murphy	2000	7	11		5	1	6				9		2				10	3		4		8
24		27	STOCKPORT COUNTY	5-1	Thornley 2, Murphy, Goodall, Bardsley	2000	7	11		5	1	6				9		2	4			10	3				8
25	Mar	1	BRADFORD CITY	2-0	Goodall, Thornley	1000	7	11		5	1	6	2			9			4			10	3				8
26		5	Chesterfield	0-0			7	11		5	1	6	2			9						10	3		4		8
27		12	BOLTON WANDERERS	3-3	Thornley 3		7	11		5	1	9	2		6							10	3		4		8
28		19	Burnley	4-2	Goodall 3, Bainbridge	3000	7	11		5	1	6	2			9						10	3		4		8
29		26	PRESTON NORTH END	2-2	Thornley, Goodall		7	11		5	1	6	2			9						10	3		4		8
30	Apr	1	Stockport County	0-3		6000	7	11		5	1	6	2			9						10	3		4		8
31		2	Grimsby Town	0-2		4000	7	11		5	1	6	2			9						10	3		4		8
32		4	Woolwich Arsenal	1-2	Goodall	17000	7			5	1	6	2			9	10					11	3		4		8
33		9	LEICESTER FOSSE	5-0	Green, Goodall 3, Boden	3000	7			5	1	6				9	10	2	8			11	3		4		8
34		23	GAINSBOROUGH TRIN.	0-2			7			3	1	6	2			9	10			8	4	11			5		

	Bainbridge JR	Bardsley E	Barnes G	Boden IA	Clark DC	Coates F	Earnshaw J	Fisher J	Galley W	Goodall AL	Green W	Hancock J	Hewitt J	Jones S	Morgan-Owen MM	Murphy EJ	Norgrove F	Morton A	Pell W	Roberts W	Thornley I
Apps	34	10	5	33	34	30	9	3	11	15	15	25	1	3	6	1	34	33	6	30	4	32
Goals	4	1		3		2				11	3					11				1	21

F.A. Cup

Scratched after drawn to play Heywood in Q3

1904/05

12th in Division Two

North Road

#	Date		Opponent	Score	Scorers	Att	Bell A	Boden JA	Brown J	Cairns T	Callaghan T	Cameron WS	Clough JW	Davies F	Gall L	Goodall AL	Green W	Irvine J	Keir C	Lawrence ET	Maginnis H	Morgan-Owen MM	Murphy EJ	Orr W	Phillips T	Prentice W	Ridgway WH	Simpson H	Spiksley F	Synott WJ
1	Sep	3	Liverpool	2-2	Gall, Cairns	13000		5	6	8				1	7	9							4	10	3				11	2
2		10	BURSLEM PORT VALE	0-0		4000		5	9	8				1	7					11	4		6	10	3					2
3		17	Bristol City	0-2		6000		5		8				1	7	9				11	4		6	10	3					2
4		24	MANCHESTER UNITED	1-2	Lawrence	4000		5		8				1	7	9				11	4		6	10	3					2
5	Oct	1	BOLTON WANDERERS	1-2	Lawrence	2500		5		8				1	7	9	10			11	4		6		3					2
6		8	Chesterfield	2-1	Murphy, Gall			5	9	8				1	7						4		6	10	3				11	2
7		15	BRADFORD CITY	3-1	Lawrence 2, Brown	2000		5	9	8				1	7					11	4		6	10	3					2
8		22	Lincoln City	0-3		4000			9	8				1	7	5					4		6	10	3				11	2
9	Nov	5	Barnsley	0-0				5	9	8				1	7					11	4		6	10	3					2
10		19	Burnley	1-3	Irvine	2000	9	5	4	8				1	7	11		10					6		3					2
11	Dec	3	Blackpool	1-4	Boden	3000	11	5	9	8				1	7			10			4		6		3					2
12		17	Gainsborough Trinity	0-0		3000		5	9	8				1	7			11			4		6		3			10		2
13		24	BURTON UNITED	1-1	Irvine	1000		5		8				1	7			10		11	4		6		3			9		2
14		26	Leicester Fosse	2-0	Goodall 2	3000		5	4	8				1	7	9		10		11			6		3					2
15		27	BRISTOL CITY	0-1		3000		5	6	8	11		10	1	7	9					4				3					2
16		31	LIVERPOOL	0-2		1500		5	4	8	9			1	7			10		11			6		3					2
17	Jan	7	Burslem Port Vale	1-0	Irvine	1000		5	6	8		10		1	7	9		11			4				3					2
18		14	DONCASTER ROVERS	2-0	Cameron 2	1000		5	6	8		9		1	7			11			4			10	3					2
19		21	Manchester United	1-4	Cameron	15000		5		8		9		1	7			10			4		6	11	3					2
20		28	Bolton Wanderers	0-4		5000		5		8		9		1						11	4		6	10	3		7			2
21	Feb	4	CHESTERFIELD	0-1		1500		5		8		9		1						11	4		6	10	3		7			2
22		11	Bradford City	1-1	Murphy	10000		5				9		1						11	4		6	10	3		7	8		2
23		18	LINCOLN CITY	3-2	Cameron, Prentice 2	1000		3	4			9		1						11			6	10	5		7	8		2
24	Mar	4	BARNSLEY	5-0	Cameron 2, Irvine, Simpson, Prentice	1200		6	4			9		1				11						10	3	5		8	7	2
25		7	WEST BROMWICH ALB.	2-1	Irvine, Simpson	2765		6	4			9		1				11						10	3	5		8	7	2
26		11	West Bromwich Albion	0-1		2000		6	4			9		1				11	2		4			10	3	5		8	7	
27		18	BURNLEY	0-0		2000		6	4			9		1				11	2		4			10	3	5		8	7	
28		25	Grimsby Town	0-3		4000		6	4			9		1				11	2		4			10	3	5		8	7	
29	Apr	1	BLACKPOOL	0-0		1500		6	4			9		1				11						10	3	5		8	7	2
30		8	Doncaster Rovers	1-2	Cairns	2000		5	4	7		9		1				11					6	10	3			8		2
31		15	GAINSBOROUGH TRIN.	3-1	Cameron 2, Murphy	2000		2	6	8	7	9		1				11			4	5		10	3					
32		21	LEICESTER FOSSE	0-0		3000		5		8	7	9		1				11	2		4		6	10	3					
33		22	Burton United	2-2	Murphy, Cameron	1000		6			7	9		1				11	2		4			10	3	5		8		
34		29	GRIMSBY TOWN	2-0	Brown, Cameron	1000		6	4		7	9		1				11	2					10	3	5		8		
			Apps				2	33	28	22	4	19	1	34	19	11	1	25	6	11	20	1	23	33	30	9	2	10	4	26
			Goals					1	2	2		10			2	2		5		4			4			3		2		

F.A. Cup

	Date		Opponent	Score	Scorers	Att	Bell A	Boden JA	Brown J	Cairns T	Callaghan T	Cameron WS	Clough JW	Davies F	Gall L	Goodall AL	Green W	Irvine J	Keir C	Lawrence ET	Maginnis H	Morgan-Owen MM	Murphy EJ	Orr W	Phillips T	Prentice W	Ridgway WH	Simpson H	Spiksley F	Synott WJ
Q3	Oct	29	Nantwich	2-1	Goodall, Cairns			5	9	8				1	7	10					4		6		3				11	2
Q4	Nov	12	STOCKPORT COUNTY	1-1	Brown	2500		5	9	8				1	7	10				11	4		6		3					2
rep		16	Stockport County	0-0				5	9	8				1	7	10				11	4		6		3					2
rep2		23	Stockport County	0-1				5	9	8				1	7	10				11			6		3	2				

The first replay was abandoned in extra time because of fog

A second replay (at Glossop) on Nov 21 was abandoned at half time because of snow.

Pattison played at 4 in replay 2

1905/06

16th in Division Two

North Road

#		Date	Opponent	Result	Scorers	Att	Brown J	Callaghan T	Cameron WS	Carr L	Chadwick WE	Cuffe JA	Dargue J	Davies F	Eastham JB	Frail JM	Hodson RJ	Irvine J	Keir C	Lindsay A	Mair D	McDiarmid G	McKie D	McNab A	Morgan-Owen MM	Orr W	Phillips T	Ross W	Synott WJ	Whitehouse F
1	Sep	2	GAINSBOROUGH TRIN.	1-0	Chadwick	2000		7	9		10			1							6					3	4	11		8
2		9	Bristol City	1-2	Ross	4000		7	9		10			1							6					3	4	11		8
3		11	Clapton Orient	0-2		2500	5	7	9		10			1							6					3	4	11		8
4		16	MANCHESTER UNITED	1-2	Cameron	10285			9		8			1			10	2			6	5				3	4	11		7
5		23	Grimsby Town	1-1	Whitehouse	4000	4		9		8			1	2		10				6	5				3		11		7
6		30	Stockport County	0-5		6000	4		9		8			1	2		10				6	5				3		11		7
7	Oct	2	Burton United	0-1		2000	4		9		8			1			10	2			6	5				3		11		7
8		7	BLACKPOOL	4-1	Callaghan, Ross, Chadwick, Cameron	700	4	7	9		10			1	2						6	5				3		11		8
9		14	Bradford City	0-2		12000	6	11	9		8			1	2						4	5				3		7		10
10		21	WEST BROMWICH ALB.	1-3	Callaghan	5000	4	7	11		10			1	2						6	5				3		9		8
11		28	Leicester Fosse	1-2	Ross	4000	4	7	8	11	9			1	3			2			6	5				3		10		
12	Nov	4	HULL CITY	3-1	Phillips, Chadwick, Carr	1500	9	7		10	8			1			11	2			6	5				3	4			
13		11	Lincoln City	1-4	Brown	2000	9	7		10	8			1	3			11			6	5				3	4		2	
14		18	CHESTERFIELD	2-0	Brown 2	1200	9	7		10	8			1	2			11			6	5				3	4			
15		25	Burslem Port Vale	3-3	Chadwick, Brown 2	3000	9	7		10	8			1	2			11			6	5				3	4			
16	Dec	2	BARNSLEY	2-2	McDiarmid, Brown	3000	9	7		10	8			1	2			11			6	5				3	4			
17		16	BURNLEY	1-1	Cameron	2000		7	9		8	2	10	1				11			6	5		4		3				
18		23	Leeds City	0-1		9000	4	7	9		10	2	8	1							6	5				3		11		
19		26	CHELSEA	2-4	Cuffe, Cameron	4000	4	7	9		10	2	8	1							6	5				3		11		
20		30	Gainsborough Trinity	0-2		2000	4	7	9		8	2	10	1				11			6	5				3				
21	Jan	1	BURTON UNITED	2-0	Callaghan, Irvine	2000	4	7	9		8	2	10	1				11			6	5				3				
22		6	BRISTOL CITY	1-5		1000	4	7	9		8	2	10	1				11			6	5				3				
23		20	Manchester United	2-5	Whitehouse, Cameron	10000			9		10			1	2			11			6	8		5		3	4			7
24		27	GRIMSBY TOWN	2-0	Whitehouse, Cameron	1000			9	10	8	2		1	3			11			6	4		5						7
25	Feb	3	STOCKPORT COUNTY	1-0	Cameron	2000		7	9		10			1	2			11			4			5		3	6			8
26		10	Blackpool	0-1		2000		7	9		10			1	2			11			6	4		5		3				8
27		17	BRADFORD CITY	2-3	Cameron 2	1500		7	9		10			1	2			11			6	4		5		3				8
28		24	West Bromwich Albion	0-6		5000			9		10			1	3		8	11	2		6	4		5						7
29	Mar	3	LEICESTER FOSSE	0-0		2000		7	11						2	1	10				6	4	9	5		3				8
30		10	Hull City	2-1	Chadwick, Ross	7000		7	11						2	1					6	5	4			3		11		8
31		17	LINCOLN CITY	2-2	Cameron, Whitehouse	1200		7	9		10				2	1		11			6	5	4			3				8
32		24	Chesterfield	1-3	Ross	2000		7	9		10				2	1					6	5	10	4		3		11		8
33		31	BURSLEM PORT VALE	3-2	Ross 2, Cameron	2000	4	7	9		10	3			2	1					6	5		8				11		
34	Apr	7	Barnsley	1-1		2000	4	7	9		10	3			2	1					6	5		8				11		
35		14	CLAPTON ORIENT	5-0	McKie, Callaghan, Ross 3	3000	4	7	9		10	3			2	1					6	5		8				11		
36		16	Chelsea	0-0		10000	4	7	9		10	3			2	1	8				6	5						11		
37		21	Burnley	0-1		2000	4	7	9		10	3			2	1	8				6	5						11		
38		28	LEEDS CITY	1-2	Ross	1500	4	7	9		10	3			2	1	8				6	5						11		
			Apps				24	31	32	7	35	13	7	27	27	8	3	23	8	2	37	29	5	18	1	28	11	21	1	20
			Goals				6	4	13	1	5	1						1			1	1					1	11		4

F.A. Cup

#		Date	Opponent	Result	Att	Brown J	Callaghan T	Cameron WS	Carr L	Chadwick WE	Cuffe JA	Dargue J	Davies F	Eastham JB	Frail JM	Hodson RJ	Irvine J	Keir C	Lindsay A	Mair D	McDiarmid G	McKie D	McNab A	Morgan-Owen MM	Orr W	Phillips T	Ross W	Synott WJ	Whitehouse F
Q4	Dec	9	BRIGHTON & HOVE ALB.	0-1	1500	9	7			8			1			10	2			6	5				3	4	11		

#		Date	Opponent	Score	Scorers	Att	Bell G	Callaghan T	Cuffe JA	Frail JM	Fyfe J	Galvin P	Goodwin R	Kelly T	Mair D	McDiarmid G	McEwan R	McKie D	McMillan JS	Napier S	Redfern TW	Robertson JT	Robotham H	Ross W	Swindells J	Thornley J	Tustin WA	Waddell TMR
1	Sep	1	Chelsea	2-9	Ross 2	8000		7	2	1					6	5	3	8	10	9			4	11				
2		8	WOLVERHAMPTON W.	2-1	Napier, Ross	2000		7	2	1					6	5	3	8	10	9			4	11				
3		15	Clapton Orient	0-3		6500		7	2	1					6	5	3	8	10	9			4	11				
4		22	GAINSBOROUGH TRIN.	3-1	Ross, Napier 2	2000		7	3	1	10				6	5	2	8		9			4	11				
5		29	Stockport County	0-5		5000		7	2	1	10				6	5	3	8		9			4	11				
6	Oct	6	HULL CITY	2-4	Fyfe, Napier	3000		7	2	1	10				6	5	3	8		9			4	11				
7		13	CHESTERFIELD	3-1	Fyfe 2, Galvin	2000		7		1	10	11	2		6	5	3	8		9			4					
8		20	Blackpool	1-4	Robotham	3000		7		1	10	6	2			5	3	8		9			4	11				
9		27	BRADFORD CITY	1-2	Robotham	3000		7			11		2		6	5	3	8	10	9			4				1	
10	Nov	3	West Bromwich Albion	1-5	Fyfe	13000		7			10		2	5	6	8	3			9			4	11			1	
11		10	LEICESTER FOSSE	2-2	Napier 2	3000		7			10		2	5	6	8	3	4		9				11			1	
12		17	Nottingham Forest	0-2		8000		7			10		2	5	6	8	3			9	11		4				1	
13		24	LINCOLN CITY	2-1	Callaghan, Napier	2000		7			9		2	4	6	5	3	10		8	11						1	
14	Dec	1	Burton United	2-1	McDiarmid, McKie	2000		7					2	4	6	5	3	8	10	9	11						1	
15		15	Burslem Port Vale	1-4	McDiarmid	3000		7			9		2	4	6	5	3	8	10							11	1	
16		22	BURNLEY	1-0	Swindells	1000		7					2	5	6		3	8	10	9			4		11		1	
17		25	Barnsley	0-3		5000		7					2	5	6		3	8	10	9			4			11	1	
18		29	CHELSEA	0-1		4000		7					2	5	6	3		8	10	9			4	11			1	
19	Jan	1	LEEDS CITY	2-0	Napier 2	5000		7	3				2	4	6	5		8	10	9						11	1	
20		5	Wolverhampton Wan.	0-4		5000		7	3				2	4	6	5		8	10		9						1	
21		19	CLAPTON ORIENT	3-0	McKie, Ross, Napier	990		7	2						6	5	3	8	10	9			4	11			1	
22		26	Gainsborough Trinity	1-2	Napier	2000		7	2						6	5	3	8	10	9			4	11			1	
23	Feb	2	STOCKPORT COUNTY	2-3	Napier, Ross	4000		7	2						6	5	3	8	10	9			4	11			1	
24		9	Hull City	0-5		7000		7	2						5		3	8	10			6	4	11		9	1	
25		12	GRIMSBY TOWN	1-0	Robertson	500		7	2				5		4	6		3	8	10		11				9	1	
26		16	Chesterfield	3-1	McMillan, Callaghan 2	2000		7	2				5		4	6		3	8	10		11				9	1	
27		23	BLACKPOOL	0-0		3000		7	2				5		4	6		3	8	10		11					1	9
28	Mar	2	Bradford City	1-2	McKie	13000		7	2				5		4	6		3	8	10		11					1	9
29		16	Leicester Fosse	2-2	Kelly, Robertson	7000		7	2				5		4	6		3	8	10		11					1	9
30		23	NOTTM. FOREST	0-2		4000		7	2				5		4	6		3	8	10						11	1	9
31		29	BARNSLEY	2-1	McKie, Waddell	4000		7	2				5		4	6		3	8	10		11					1	9
32		30	Lincoln City	1-2	McKie	3000		7	2				5		4	6		3	8	10	9						1	
33	Apr	1	Leeds City	4-1	Galvin, Ross, Robotham, Robertson	8000		7	2				5		4	6		3		10	9	8		11			1	
34		6	BURTON UNITED	2-2	Robertson, Galvin	2000		7	2				5		4	6		3			9	8	11	10			1	
35		13	Grimsby Town	1-2	Robotham	1000		7	2					5	6		3	8			9	10	4	11			1	
36		16	WEST BROMWICH ALB.	0-0		1000		7	2					5	6		3	8				10	4	11			1	9
37		20	BURSLEM PORT VALE	4-0	Napier 2, Robertson 2	2000		7	2					5	6		3	8		9		10	4	11			1	
38		27	Burnley	1-1	Callaghan	2500	10	7	2					5	6		3	8		9			4	11			1	
					Apps		1	38	26	8	11	14	14	23	37	21	35	34	24	27	3	14	23	23	3	3	30	6
					Goals			4			4	3		1		2		5	1	14		6	4	7	1			1

F.A. Cup

		Date	Opponent	Score	Scorers	Att	Bell G	Callaghan T	Cuffe JA	Frail JM	Fyfe J	Galvin P	Goodwin R	Kelly T	Mair D	McDiarmid G	McEwan R	McKie D	McMillan JS	Napier S	Redfern TW	Robertson JT	Robotham H	Ross W	Swindells J	Thornley J	Tustin WA	Waddell TMR
Q5	Dec	8	Newhall Swifts	2-1	Fyfe, Callaghan			7			9		2	4	6	5	3	8	10		11						1	
R1	Jan	12	Brentford	1-2	McKie	12500		11	3		8			4	5	2		10		9			6	7			1	

1907/08

17th in Division Two

North Road

#	Mon	Date	Opponent	Score	Scorers	Att	Butler JH	Byrne MTG	Comrie J	Copeland DC	Cuffe JA	Elmore GV	Galvin P	Gettins E	Gould W	Greechan J	Grimes WJ	Hofton LB	McEwan R	McGregor J	McKenzie T	McMillan JS	Pattison S	Robertson J	Robertson JT	Ross W	Tufnell E	Tustin WA	Waddell TMR	Weir A
1	Sep	2	Leeds City	1-2	J.Robertson	5000			5		2			7	11				3	4	9			8	10					6
2		7	WOLVERHAMPTON W.	1-1	J.Robertson	3000	1		5		2			7	11				3	4	9			8	10					6
3		14	Gainsborough Trinity	0-1		4000	1		5		2			7	11				3	4	9			8	10					6
4		21	STOCKPORT COUNTY	1-1	McEwan	4000	1		5		2			7	11				3	4	9			8	10					6
5		28	Grimsby Town	0-4		5000	1		5	10	2			7	11	9			3	4				8						6
6	Oct	5	Leicester Fosse	1-3	McKenzie	9000	1		5	10	2			7	11				3	4	9			8						6
7		12	BLACKPOOL	2-2	Grimes, Gould	1500	1		5		2			7	9		11		3	4				8	10					6
8		19	Stoke	0-4		7000	1		5		2	9		7	3		11			4				8	10					6
9		26	WEST BROMWICH ALB.	2-1	J.Robertson, Elmore	2000	1		5		2	9		7	3		11			4				8	10					6
10	Nov	2	Bradford City	1-2	Gould	12000	1		5		2			7	9		11		3	4				8	10					6
11		9	HULL CITY	5-1	Grimes, J.Robertson 4	2000			5		2	9		7	3		11			4				8	10			1		6
12		16	Derby County	0-2		8000			5		2	9		7	3		11			4				8	10			1		6
13		30	Fulham	1-6	J.Robertson	13000			5		2	9		7			11		3	4				8	10			1		6
14	Dec	14	Chesterfield	7-3	J.Robertson 2,Elmore,Ross,Grimes 2,Ewing (og)	2000			5		2	9		7			11		3	4				8		10		1		6
15		21	BURNLEY	3-1	Gould 2, Elmore	1000			5		2	9		7	3		11			4				8	10			1		6
16		25	CLAPTON ORIENT	2-1	Ross, Grimes	3000			5		2	9		7			11		3	4				8		10		1		6
17		28	Oldham Athletic	0-0		10000			5		2	9		7			11		3	4				8	10			1		6
18	Jan	1	LEEDS CITY	0-2		2000			5		2	9		7			11		3	4				8	10			1		6
19		4	Wolverhampton Wan.	0-5		6000		6	5					7	3		11		2	4				8	9			1		
20		18	Stockport County	2-3	J.Robertson, McGregor	8000			5		2		9	7			11		3	4				8		10		1		6
21		25	GRIMSBY TOWN	1-2	Grimes	1500			5		2			7	3		11			4				8		10		1	9	6
22	Feb	1	LINCOLN CITY	3-1	Elmore, Grimes, Ross	2000			5		2	9		7	3		11			4				8		10		1		6
23		8	Blackpool	0-4		3000	1		5		2	9		7	3		11			4				8	10					6
24		15	STOKE	2-0	Elmore, Grimes	1000	1		5		2	9		7	3		11			4				8	10					6
25		22	West Bromwich Albion	1-1	J.Robertson	4140			5		2	9		7	3		11			4				8	10			1		6
26		29	BRADFORD CITY	2-2	JT.Robertson 2	2000			5		2	9		7	3					4				8	10		11	1		6
27	Mar	3	GAINSBOROUGH TRIN.	1-0	Tufnell	1500			5		2	9		7	3					4				8	10		11	1		6
28		7	Hull City	2-3	Elmore, J.Robertson	8000			5			9		7	3				2	4				8	10		11	1		6
29		14	DERBY COUNTY	2-3	Grimes, J.Robertson	3000			5		2			7	3		11			4	9			8	10			1		6
30		21	Lincoln City	1-0	Gould	3000	1		5			9		7	3		11		2	4				8	10					6
31		24	LEICESTER FOSSE	2-3	Galvin, JT.Robertson	2500	1		5				9	7	3		11		2	4				8	10					6
32	Apr	9	Clapton Orient	0-0		3000	1		5		2	9		7	3		11			4				8	10					6
33		11	CHESTERFIELD	3-2	J.Robertson, JT.Robertson, Comrie	2000	1		5		2	9		7	3					4				8	10		11			6
34		17	BARNSLEY	3-1	Elmore, J.Robertson 2	3000	1		5		2	9		7	3					4				8	10		11			6
35		18	Burnley	0-1		6000	1		5		2	9		7	3					4		10		8			11			6
36		21	Barnsley	1-4	Elmore	5000	1		5			9		7	3				2	4		10		8			11			6
37		25	OLDHAM ATHLETIC	0-0		6000	1		5					7	3		11		2	4		10	9	8					6
38		29	FULHAM	1-2	Hofton	500	1		5			9			3	10	11	7	2	4				8						6
			Apps				9	11	35	2	30	24	6	32	31	2	33	1	20	37	6	3	1	35	29	8	7	18	1	37
			Goals						1			8	1		5		9	1	1		1			17	4	3	1			

One own goal

F.A. Cup

	Mon	Date	Opponent	Score	Scorers	Att	Butler JH	Byrne MTG	Comrie J	Copeland DC	Cuffe JA	Elmore GV	Galvin P	Gettins E	Gould W	Greechan J	Grimes WJ	Hofton LB	McEwan R	McGregor J	McKenzie T	McMillan JS	Pattison S	Robertson J	Robertson JT	Ross W	Tufnell E	Tustin WA	Waddell TMR	Weir A
Q5	Dec	7	West Stanley	3-0	Gould 3	6500			5	2				7	9		11		3	4				8	10			1		6
R1	Jan	11	MANCHESTER CITY	0-0		6500			5	2				7			11		3	4				8	10		9	1		6
rep		15	Manchester City	0-6		20000			5					7	3		11		2	4				8	10		9	1		6

1908/09

8th in Division Two

North Road

#		Date	Opponent	Res	Scorers	Att	Blackburn G	Butler JH	Comrie J	Cuffe JA	Dearnaley I	Elmore GV	Gettins E	Gould W	Greechan J	Grimes WJ	Harvey EA	Hofton LB	McGregor J	Morrison W	Raine JE	Robertson J	Robertson JT	Sharpe IGA	Smith SE	Stapley HS	Stapley WJ	Underwood AT	Weir A	Wilson C
1	Sep	2	Fulham	3-2	H.Stapley 2, Greechan	10000		1	5	3					10		7	2	4			8				9		11	6	
2		5	Burnley	2-3	H.Stapley, J.Robertson	8000		1	5	3					10			2	4			8		7		9		11	6	
3		12	BRADFORD PARK AVE.	1-1	Gould	5000		1	5	3				11	10		7	2	4			8				9			6	
4		19	Wolverhampton Wan.	0-0		3000		1		3					10		7	2	4	5		8				9		11	6	
5		26	OLDHAM ATHLETIC	2-1	J.Robertson 2	5000		1		3					10		7	2	4	5		8				9		11	6	
6	Oct	3	Clapton Orient	2-0	H.Stapley 2	8000		1		3					10		7	2	4	5		8				9		11	6	
7		10	LEEDS CITY	0-0		4000		1		3					10		7	2	4	5		8				9		11	6	
8		17	Barnsley	3-1	Greechan, J.Robertson, H.Stapley	3000		1		3					10		7	2	4	5		8				9		11	6	
9		24	TOTTENHAM HOTSPUR	1-1	Elmore	6000		1		3		9			10		7	2	4	5		8						11	6	
10		31	Hull City	0-0		8000		1		3					10		7	2	4	5		8				9		11	6	
11	Nov	7	DERBY COUNTY	3-1	H.Stapley, Blackburn 2	4000	7	1		3					10			2	4	5		8				9		11	6	
12		14	Blackpool	1-2	Blackburn	6000	7	1		3					10			2	4	5		8				9		11	6	
13		21	CHESTERFIELD	2-0	J.Robertson, Grimes	3000	7	1		3						10		2	4	5		8				9		11	6	
14		28	BOLTON WANDERERS	0-2		3000	7	1		3						10		2	4	5		8				9		11	6	
15	Dec	5	Stockport County	2-4	Hofton 2	12000	7	1		3								9	4	5	2	8						11	6	10
16		12	WEST BROMWICH ALB.	1-3	H.Stapley	3074		1		3			7					2	4	5		8		11		9			6	10
17		19	Birmingham	2-1	H.Stapley, J.Robertson	6000		1		3			7					2	4	5		8	6	11		9				10
18		26	Bradford Park Avenue	0-1		20000		1		3			7					2	4	5		8				9		11	6	10
19		28	Gainsborough Trinity	1-3	Ward (og)	4000		1		3	5		7					2	4			8				9		11	6	10
20	Jan	2	BURNLEY	1-2	H.Stapley	3000		1		3			7					2	4	5		8				9		11	6	10
21		23	WOLVERHAMPTON W.	3-2	Raine, Hofton, J.Robertson	5000		1		3			7					2	4		5	8				9		11	6	10
22		30	Oldham Athletic	1-2	H.Stapley	9000		1		3			7					2	4	5		8				9		11	6	10
23	Feb	13	Leeds City	1-3	Hofton	10000		1		3			7					9	4	5	2	8		11					6	10
24		23	GAINSBOROUGH TRIN.	2-2	H.Stapley, Wilson			1		3			7					2	4			8		11		9	5		6	10
25		27	Tottenham Hotspur	3-3	Sharpe, Raine 2	12000		1		3			7					2	4		5	8		11		9			6	10
26	Mar	16	GRIMSBY TOWN	1-0	H.Stapley			1		3			7					2	4	5		8				9		11	6	10
27		20	BLACKPOOL	3-0	Sharpe, J.Robertson, Elmore	4000		1		3		7						2	4	5		8		11		9			6	10
28		23	HULL CITY	2-1	Browell (og), H.Stapley	1200		1		3		7						2	4	5		8		11		9			6	10
29		27	Chesterfield	1-2	J.Robertson	3000		1		3		7						2	4	5		8		11		9			6	10
30		30	BARNSLEY	3-0	Sharpe, H.Stapley, J.Robertson			1		3		7						2	4	5		8		11		9			6	10
31	Apr	3	Bolton Wanderers	0-2		15400		1		3			7					2	4	5		8		11		9			6	10
32		9	FULHAM	0-0		5000		1		3		9						2	4	5		8		7				11	6	10
33		10	STOCKPORT COUNTY	2-0	Greechan, Elmore 2	5000		1		3		9			8			2	4	5				7				11	6	10
34		12	Grimsby Town	0-2		7000		1		3		9			8			2	4	5				7				11	6	10
35		17	West Bromwich Albion	0-1		15000		1		3								2	4	5		8		11	7	9			6	10
36		20	CLAPTON ORIENT	4-0	Elmore 2, J.Robertson, H.Stapley	1000		1		3		7						2	4	5		8		11		9			6	10
37		21	Derby County	0-4		3000		1		3		9			8			2	4		5				7			11	6	10
38		24	BIRMINGHAM	3-1	H.Stapley 3	1000		1		3			7					2	4	5		8				9			6	10
			Apps				5	38	3	35	1	11	9	1	17	12	5	34	34	32	21	33	3	17	2	31	1	18	32	23
			Goals				3					6		1	3	1		5			3	10		3		19				1

Two own goals

F.A. Cup

#		Date	Opponent	Res	Scorers	Att	Blackburn G	Butler JH	Comrie J	Cuffe JA	Dearnaley I	Elmore GV	Gettins E	Gould W	Greechan J	Grimes WJ	Harvey EA	Hofton LB	McGregor J	Morrison W	Raine JE	Robertson J	Robertson JT	Sharpe IGA	Smith SE	Stapley HS	Stapley WJ	Underwood AT	Weir A	Wilson C
R1	Jan	16	Chesterfield	2-0	Raine, H.Stapley	6000		1		3			7					2	4	5		8	6			9		10		11
R2	Feb	6	Stockport County	1-1	J.Robertson	13000		1		3			7		10			2	4	5		8				9		11	6	
rep		9	STOCKPORT COUNTY	1-0	Greechan	4500		1		3			7		10			2	4	5		8				9		11	6	
R3		20	Sheffield Wednesday	1-0	Greechan (p)	35019		1		3			7		10			2	4	5		8				9		11	6	
R4	Mar	6	BRISTOL CITY	0-0		4500		1		3			7		10			2	4	5		8				9		11	6	
rep		10	Bristol City	0-1		15932		1		3			7		10			2	4	5		8				9		11	6	

R2 replay a.e.t.

106

1909/10

6th in Division Two

North Road

#		Date	Opponent	Res	Scorers	Att	Butler IH	Craigie CM	Cuffe JA	Dearnaley RH	Fitchie TT	Hampton GH	Henderson GT	Heywood J	Hoare GR	Hodkinson JC	Hofton LB	Law WD	Littlewort HC	McGregor J	Morrison W	Needham A	Porter TC	Pryce-Williams P	Raine IE	Sharpe IGA	Stapley HS	Wall LJ	Wilson C
1	Sep	4	BARNSLEY	3-0	Stapley 2, Sharpe	3000	1		3		10						2			4	5	8				7	11	9	6
2		11	Fulham	0-2		20000	1		3		10						2			4	5	8				7	11	9	6
3		13	Birmingham	2-2	Stapley 2	3000	1		3		10						2			4	5	8				7	11	9	6
4		18	BURNLEY	2-0	Sharpe, Stapley	3000	1		3		10						2			4	5	8				7	11	9	6
5		25	Leeds City	2-1	Needham, Stapley	12000	1		3								2	7		4	5	8	10				11	9	6
6	Oct	2	WOLVERHAMPTON W.	2-0	Needham, Cuffe	4000	1		3								2			4	5	8	10			7	11	9	6
7		9	Gainsborough Trinity	3-1	Needham 2, Stapley	3000	1	4	3								2				5	8	10			7	11	9	6
8		16	GRIMSBY TOWN	3-0	Stapley, Porter, Needham	4000	1	4	3								2				5	8	10			7	11	9	6
9		23	Manchester City	3-3	Porter 2, Morrison	14000	1	4	3								2				5	8	10			7	11	9	6
10		30	LEICESTER FOSSE	1-0	Craigie	5000	1	4	3								2				5	8	10			7	11	9	6
11	Nov	6	Lincoln City	2-1	Needham, Sharpe		1	4	3								2				5	9	8			7	11	10	6
12		13	CLAPTON ORIENT	3-1	Stapley 2, Hofton	3000	1	4	3								2				5	8		6		7	11	9	10
13		20	Blackpool	1-1		7000	1	4	3								2				5	8	10			7	11	9	6
14		27	HULL CITY	2-1	Porter, Craigie	4000	1	4	3								2				5	8	10			7	11	9	6
15	Dec	4	Derby County	1-2	Porter	7000	1	4	3								2				5	8	10			7	11	9	6
16		11	STOCKPORT COUNTY	1-0	Hoare	5000	1	4	3						9		2				5	8	10			7	11		6
17		18	Bradford Park Avenue	3-3	Stapley 2, Raine	10000	1	4	3						8		2				5		10			7	11	9	6
18		25	BIRMINGHAM	4-1	Stapley, Wilson, Porter, Sharpe	5000	1	4	3						8		2				5			6		7	11	9	10
19		27	OLDHAM ATHLETIC	6-2	Stapley 4, Needham, Sharpe	6000	1	4	3								2					8	10	6		7	11	9	5
20	Jan	1	Oldham Athletic	0-1		18000	1	4	3								2					8	10	6		7	11	9	5
21		8	Barnsley	0-3		8000	1	4	3					2							5	8	10			7	11	9	6
22		22	FULHAM	0-1		4000	1	4	3						8			7			5	2					11	9	6
23	Feb	5	LEEDS CITY	2-1	Stapley 2	1000	1	4	2	3	10										5	8				7	11	9	6
24		12	Wolverhampton Wan.	1-3	Needham	10000	1	4	2	3											5	8	10			7	11	9	6
25		19	GAINSBOROUGH TRIN.	4-0	Sharpe, Stapley, Morrison, Craigie		1	4	2	3	10										5	8				7	11	9	6
26		26	Grimsby Town	0-4		4000	1	4	3					2							5	8	10			7	11	9	6
27	Mar	12	Leicester Fosse	1-3	Stapley	11000	1	4	3					2							5	8				7	11	9	6
28		19	LINCOLN CITY	0-1		2000	1	4	3					2							5	8	10			7	11	9	6
29		26	Clapton Orient	0-0		5800	1	4	3		10			2	9						5	8				7	11		6
30		28	West Bromwich Albion	0-0		12360	1	4			10			2	3	8					5	2				7		9	6
31	Apr	2	BLACKPOOL	2-3	Fitchie 2	2000	1	4			10			2	3	8	11				5	3				7		9	6
32		6	MANCHESTER CITY	0-3		5000	1	4	3		10			2	3	8	11				5					7		9	6
33		9	Hull City	2-4	Hoare, Sharpe	6000	1		3			4			2	9	11	7			5	8		6		10			
34		18	Burnley	1-0	Wilson	3000	1		3			2	4				10	7	5			8					11	9	6
35		23	Stockport County	0-5		6000	1		3			2	4								5	8	10			7	11	9	6
36		26	WEST BROMWICH ALB.	3-2	Needham 2, Stapley	3000	1		3			2	4					7	5			8	10				11	9	6
37		28	DERBY COUNTY	1-1	Needham	5000	1		3			2	4								5	8	10			7	11	9	6
38		30	BRADFORD PARK AVE.	3-1	Hodkinson, Fitchie, Stapley	500	1				10	2	4			8	11	7			5	3						9	6
			Apps				38	26	35	3	13	5	6	9	10	4	18	6	2	6	36	31	24	5	30	37	32	5	37
			Goals					3	1		3				2	1	1				2	12	6		1	7	23		2

F.A. Cup

R1	Jan	15	Bury	1-2	Hoare	10460	1	4	3						8						2	10				7	11	9	5

Played at 6: AK Campbell

1910/11

North Road

#		Date	Opponent	Score	Scorers	Att	Berwick WJ	Butler JH	Campbell AK	Carney JM	Craigie CM	Cuffe JA	Dearnaley RH	Fitchie TT	Hampton GH	Herbert WE	Heywood J	Hoare GR	Hodkinson JC	Law WD	Littlewort HC	McDonald E	Milne W	Porter TC	Raine JE	Sharpe JGA	Stapley HS	Stapley WJ	Tomkinson A	Wall LJ	Wilson C
1	Sep	3	Gainsborough Trinity	0-3		5000		1	5		4	3					2			7				8			11	9		10	6
2		5	Burnley	0-0		10000		1			4	3					2			7	5			8			11	9		10	6
3		10	LEEDS CITY	2-1	Fitchie, H.Stapley	8000		1			4			10	2		3			7	5			8			11	9			6
4		14	Lincoln City	2-2	H.Stapley 2	3000		1			4				2		3	8		7	5						11	9		10	6
5		17	Stockport County	1-2	Wilson	7000		1			4			10	2		3			7	5			8			11	9			6
6		24	DERBY COUNTY	2-2	Wall, Porter	4000		1				3					2			7	4			8			11	9	5	10	6
7	Oct	1	Barnsley	0-4				1				3					2				4			8	7	11	9	5	10	6
8		8	LEICESTER FOSSE	1-0	Porter	2000		1				3		10			2			7	4			8			11	9	5		6
9		15	Wolverhampton Wan.	0-2		6000		1				3		10			2			7	4			8			11	9	5		6
10		22	CHELSEA	2-1	H.Stapley, Fitchie	7000		1				3		10			2			7	4			8			11	9	5		6
11		29	Clapton Orient	0-4		15600		1				3		10			2			7	4			8			11	9	5		6
12	Nov	5	BLACKPOOL	3-1	Porter, Law, H.Stapley	3000		1		4		3		10			2			7				8			11	9	5		6
13		12	BOLTON WANDERERS	1-2	H.Stapley	2000		1		4		3		10			2			7				8			11	9	5		6
14		26	HUDDERSFIELD T	5-2	Sharpe, Fitchie 2, Milne, H.Stapley	3000		1				3		10			2			7	4		9				11	8	5		6
15	Dec	3	Birmingham	2-1	H.Stapley, Law	6000		1				3		10			2			7	4		9				11	8	5		6
16		10	WEST BROMWICH ALB.	0-2		4000		1	6			3					2			7	4		9				11	8	5		10
17		17	Hull City	0-1		3500		1						3	10		2		11	7	4						8	9	5		6
18		24	FULHAM	2-1	H.Stapley, Fitchie	2000		1						3	10		2		11	7	4			8				9	5		6
19		26	Bradford Park Avenue	0-6		20000		1						3			2		11	7	4			8				9	5	10	6
20		31	GAINSBOROUGH TRIN.	3-1	Porter, Hodkinson 2			1							10	2	3		11	7	4			8				9	5		6
21	Jan	2	BURNLEY	1-1	Tomkinson		8	1								2			11	7	4							9	5	10	6
22		7	Leeds City	2-0	Porter, H.Stapley	10000	8	1					3			2			11	7	4			10				9	5		6
23		21	STOCKPORT COUNTY	3-0	H.Stapley 2, Sharpe	5000	8	1			3					2			11	7	4					10	9	5			6
24		28	Derby County	1-2	Berwick	7000	8	1			3			10	2				11		4					7	9	5			6
25	Feb	11	Leicester Fosse	1-1	Wilson	7000	8	1			3			10	2				11		4					7	9	5			6
26		18	WOLVERHAMPTON W.	5-1	Berwick 2, H.Stapley 2, Sharpe	5000	8	1			4	3			2				11							7	9	5	10		6
27	Mar	4	CLAPTON ORIENT	1-3	Sharpe	3000	8	1			3			10	2				11							7	9	5			6
28		6	Chelsea	0-2		12000	8	1			3			10	2				11		4					7	9	5			6
29		11	Blackpool	0-1		4000	8	1			3				2				11		4					7	9	5	10		6
30		18	Bolton Wanderers	0-4		10000		1			3			10	2				11		4		9			7	8	5			6
31		25	LINCOLN CITY	2-0	Tomkinson, Sharpe			1			3				2				11		4	8				7	9	5	10		6
32		28	BARNSLEY	1-1	Tomkinson			1			3				2				11		4	8				7	9	5	10		6
33	Apr	1	Huddersfield Town	0-1		6000		1		4			3	10	2	8			11		5					7	9				6
34		8	BIRMINGHAM	2-1	Sharpe, H.Stapley	1500		1					3	10	2	8			11		4					7	9	5			6
35		14	BRADFORD PARK AVE.	0-1		3000		1	3						2	8			11				4			7	9	5	10		6
36		15	West Bromwich Albion	1-3	Tomkinson	18000		1	3						2	8			11	7			4				9	5	10		6
37		22	HULL CITY	0-0		1000		1			6			3		2	8		11		5	4				7	9			10	
38		29	Fulham	2-2	Herbert, Fitchie	8000		1			6			3	10	2	8		11		4					7	9	5			

	Berwick WJ	Butler JH	Campbell AK	Carney JM	Craigie CM	Cuffe JA	Dearnaley RH	Fitchie TT	Hampton GH	Herbert WE	Heywood J	Hoare GR	Hodkinson JC	Law WD	Littlewort HC	McDonald E	Milne W	Porter TC	Raine JE	Sharpe JGA	Stapley HS	Stapley WJ	Tomkinson A	Wall LJ	Wilson C
Apps	9	38	4	5	6	23	8	21	22	6	21	1	22	23	32	5	4	16	1	32	38	31	9	5	36
Goals	3							6		1				2	2			1	5		6	15		4	1	2

F.A. Cup

		Date	Opponent	Score		Att	Butler JH					Fitchie TT	Hampton GH	Herbert WE			Hodkinson JC	Law WD	Littlewort HC			Porter TC		Sharpe JGA	Stapley HS	Stapley WJ			Wilson C
R1	Jan	14	Middlesbrough	0-1		15000	1					3	10	2			11	7	4			8			9	5			6

1911/12

18th in Division Two

North Road

#		Date	Opponent	Result	Scorers	Att	Berwick WJ	Butler JH	Campbell AK	Carney JM	Cuffe JA	Dearnaley RH	Fitchie TT	Goldie JW	Groves FW	Hampton GH	Herbert WE	Heywood J	Hoare GR	Hodkinson JC	Law WD	Littlewort HC	McEwen J	McGeachan J	Monk FV	Moore J	Porter TC	Stapley HS	Stapley WJ	Wilson C
1	Sep	2	BURNLEY	1-3	H.Stapley	2000	8	1			3							2		11	7	4				10		9	5	6
2		9	Hull City	0-2		9000		1			3			4			8	2		11	7				5	10		9		6
3		16	Barnsley	0-2		2000	8	1			3			4				2		11	7				5	10		9		6
4		23	Bradford Park Avenue	1-1	Moore	17000		1				3		4	7		8	2		11		5				10		9		6
5		30	FULHAM	1-1	Herbert	2000		1				3		4	7		8	2		11		5				10		9		6
6	Oct	7	Derby County	0-5		10000		1				3		4	7		8	2		11		5				10		9		6
7		14	STOCKPORT COUNTY	1-1	Hampton	3000		1			3				7	9		2		11		4				10		8	5	6
8		21	Leeds City	1-2	H.Stapley	6000	8	1			3			6	7			2		11		4				10		9		5
9		28	WOLVERHAMPTON W.	0-1		1000		1			3			6	7	2				11		4		10			8	9		5
10	Nov	4	Leicester Fosse	0-1		6000	8	1			3			6	7	2				11		4		10				9		5
11		11	GAINSBOROUGH TRIN.	1-1	Wilson	2000	8	1			3			6	7	2				11		4		10				9		5
12		25	NOTTM. FOREST	0-0		2000	8	1		6	3			5	7	2				11		4				10		9		
13	Dec	2	Chelsea	0-1		20000	8	1		6	3		10	5		2				11	7	4						9		
14		9	CLAPTON ORIENT	3-3	Berwick 2, H.Stapley	1000	8	1		6	3		10	5		2				11	7	4						9		
15		16	Bristol City	0-2		3000	8	1		6	3		10	5		2				11	7	4						9		
16		23	BIRMINGHAM	2-0	Berwick, H.Stapley	2000	8	1		6	3		10	5		2				11	7	4						9		
17		25	Huddersfield Town	1-3	H.Stapley	9000		1		6	3			5		2	8			11	7	4		10				9		
18		26	BLACKPOOL	1-1	Law	2000		1		6	3			5		2	8			11	7	4		10				9		
19		30	Burnley	0-4		7000		1		6	3			5		2	8			11	7	4		10				9		
20	Jan	1	Blackpool	0-2		5000		1		6	3			5		2	8			11	7	4		10				9		
21		6	HULL CITY	1-1	Herbert	1000		1		6	3			5		2	8			11	7	4				10		9		
22		27	BRADFORD PARK AVE.	0-0		1000		1		6	3			5		2				11	7	4				10	8	9		
23	Feb	10	DERBY COUNTY	3-1	Berwick, Moore, H.Stapley	5000	8	1		6		3		5		2				11	7	4				10		9		
24		17	Stockport County	0-3		7000	8	1	4	6	3			5		2				11	7					10		9		
25		24	LEEDS CITY	2-1	Moore 2	3000		1		6	3			5		2			9	11	7	4				10		8		
26	Mar	2	Wolverhampton Wan.	1-1	H.Stapley	7000		1		6	3			5		2			9	11	7	4				10		8		
27		9	LEICESTER FOSSE	6-0	Hoare, Littlewort, Moore 2, H.Stapley 2	2000		1		6	3			5		2			9	11	7	4				10		8		
28		16	Gainsborough Trinity	1-1	Moore	5000		1		6	3			5		2			9	11	7	4				10		8		
29		23	GRIMSBY TOWN	5-2	Moore 4, H.Stapley	8000		1		6	3			5		2			9	11	7	4				10		8		
30		30	Nottingham Forest	1-0	Moore	5000		1		6	3			5		2	8			11	7	4				10		9		
31	Apr	1	Fulham	2-0	H.Stapley 2	3000		1		6	3			5		2			9	11	7	4				10		8		
32		5	HUDDERSFIELD T	2-3	H.Stapley, Moore	2000		1		6	3			5		2			9	11	7	4				10		8		
33		6	CHELSEA	1-2	Littlewort	4000		1		6	3			5					9	11	7	4	2			10		8		
34		8	Grimsby Town	0-0		6000	8	1		6	3			5					9	11	7	4	2			10				
35		13	Clapton Orient	1-2	Moore	10000	8	1		6	3			5		2			9	11	7	4				10				
36		20	BRISTOL CITY	3-0	Littlewort, Hoare 2	2000	8	1		6	3			5		2			9	11	7	4				10				
37		27	Birmingham	0-2		10000	8	1		6	3			5		2			9	11	7	4				10				
38		29	Barnsley	0-1		2000	8	1		6	3			5		2			9	11	7	4				10				
			Apps				15	38	1	29	34	4	7	33	9	32	11	9	11	38	29	32	2	7	2	23	4	33	2	13
			Goals				4									1	2		3		1	3				14		13		1

F.A. Cup

#		Date	Opponent	Result	Att	Butler JH	Cuffe JA	Hampton GH	Herbert WE	Hodkinson JC	Law WD	Littlewort HC	Carney JM	Goldie JW	Moore J	Stapley HS
R1	Jan	13	Leeds City	0-1	21000	1	3	2	8	11	7	4	6	5	10	9

109

18th in Division Two

North Road

No	Date	Opponent	Score	Scorers	Att	Bamford HW	Berwick WI	Bowden J	Brennan J	Callender RH	Campbell AK	Carney JM	Causer AH	Cooper E	Crump H	Cuffe JA	Dearnaley RH	Hampton GH	Hoare GR	Hodkinson JC	Law WD	Littlewort HC	Meadowcroft HC	Montgomery J	Moore J	Spittle T	Stapley HS	Stapley WI	Stoodley CH	Thompson R	Toward RH	Williams D
1	Sep 7	Burnley	1-2	Moore	15000	8					9	6	1			3		2		11	7	4			10			5				
2	14	HULL CITY	0-3		3000						9	6	1			3		2	8	11	7	4			10			5				
3	21	BLACKPOOL	2-0	Moore, Hodkinson	3000							6	1		4	3		2	9	11	7	5			10							8
4	28	Clapton Orient	0-1		16000							6	1		4	3			9	11	7	5			10	2						8
5	Oct 5	LINCOLN CITY	0-1		3000					5	9	6	1	7	4	3			8	11		5			10	2						8
6	12	Nottingham Forest	2-3	Williams 2	9000							6	1	7	4	3			9	11		5			10	2						8
7	19	BRISTOL CITY	3-1	Hodkinson, Cooper, Hoare	3000					5		6	1	7		3			8	11		4			10	2						9
8	26	Birmingham	0-0		5000					5		6	1	7		3			8	11		4			10	2						9
9	Nov 2	HUDDERSFIELD T	1-0	Cooper						5		6	1	7		3			8	11		4			9	2			10			
10	9	Leeds City	0-4		12000					5		6	1	7		3	4			11					10	2	8		9			
11	16	GRIMSBY TOWN	2-0	Moore, Stoodley	4000					5		6	1	7		3				11		4			10	2	8		9			
12	23	Bury	1-4	Hoare	5000					5		6	1	7	4	3			9	11					10	2	8					
13	Dec 7	Barnsley	1-2	Moore	4000					5		6	1	7	4			2	8	11					10	3			9			
14	21	Wolverhampton Wan.	1-3	Cooper	10000					5		6	1	7	4			2	8	11					10	3			9			
15	25	Preston North End	0-2		10000							4	1	7			2	6	8	11					10	3		5	9			
16	26	Leicester Fosse	4-1	Moore 4	7000							4	1	7		3		6	10	11					9	2	8	5				
17	28	BURNLEY	1-3	Moore	3000							6	1	7			2	4	10	11					9	3	8	5				
18	Jan 1	PRESTON NORTH END	2-3	Hodkinson, Cooper	4000		5					6	1	7			2	4	8	11					9	3	8					
19	2	FULHAM	2-0	Hoare 2	2000		5		4				1	7			3	2	10	11					9			6			8	
20	18	Blackpool	1-1	Hoare	2000				6				1	7			3	5	2	10	11				9			4			8	
21	25	CLAPTON ORIENT	3-0	Moore 2, H Stapley	3000	6							1	7			3	2	10		11	4			9		8	5				
22	Feb 1	STOCKPORT COUNTY	2-2	H Stapley, Moore	3000	6							1	7			3	2			11	4			9		8	5	10			
23	4	BRADFORD PARK AVE.	4-3	Hoare, H Stapley 2, Law	500	6						4	1	7			3	2	10		11						8	5		9		
24	8	Lincoln City	0-0		8000	6						4	1	7			3	2	10		11				9		8	5				
25	15	NOTTM. FOREST	4-3	Cooper, H Stapley 2, Moore	3000							6	1	7			3	2	10		11	4			9		8	5				
26	22	Bristol City	3-3	H Stapley, Hoare 2	3000	6		5				6	1	7			3	2	10		11				9		8	5				
27	Mar 1	BIRMINGHAM	0-2		3000				4			6	1	7			3	2	10		11			5	9		8					
28	8	Huddersfield Town	0-6		4000			6				5	1	7			3	2	10		11	4			9		8					
29	15	LEEDS CITY	2-1	Hoare, H Stapley	2000				4	11		6	1				3	2	10		7				9		8	5				
30	21	LEICESTER FOSSE	3-0	Moore 3 (1p)	3000				4			6	1				3	2			11				9		8	5	10	7		
31	22	Grimsby Town	0-0		5000				4			6	1				3	2			11				9		8	5	10	7		
32	24	Stockport County	1-1	H Stapley	8000	6			4			5	1				3	2			11				9		8		10	7		
33	29	BURY	1-1	Stoodley	3000	6			4				1				3	2			11						8	5	9	10	7	
34	Apr 5	Fulham	0-2		7000	6			5			4	1				3	2			11				9		8	5		10	7	
35	12	BARNSLEY	1-0	H Stapley	3000				4			6	1				3	2			11				9		8	5		10	7	
36	17	Hull City	0-2		5000				4			6	1				3	2			11				9		8	5		10	7	
37	19	Bradford Park Avenue	0-5		5000	6			5			4	1				3	2			11						8		9	10	7	
38	26	WOLVERHAMPTON W.	1-3	Moore	1000				4			6	1				3	2	10		11			7		9		8	5			
		Apps				9	1	4	20	1	5	33	38	24	6	30	13	25	25	20	22	13	1	1	35	15	24	19	12	8	8	6
		Goals												5					9	3	1				17		10		2			2

F.A. Cup

No	Date	Opponent	Score	Scorers	Att	Bamford HW	Berwick WI	Bowden J	Brennan J	Callender RH	Campbell AK	Carney JM	Causer AH	Cooper E	Crump H	Cuffe JA	Dearnaley RH	Hampton GH	Hoare GR	Hodkinson JC	Law WD	Littlewort HC	Meadowcroft HC	Montgomery J	Moore J	Spittle T	Stapley HS	Stapley WI	Stoodley CH	Thompson R	Toward RH	Williams D
Q4	Nov 30	RIPLEY TOWN & ATH.	2-0	Stoodley, Moore				5				6	1	7			4	2		11					10	3	8		9			
Q5	Dec 14	SOUTHALL	11-1 * see below	1000			5				6	1	7		3	4	2		11					10		8	5	9			
R1	Jan 11	Crystal Palace	0-2		8000			5					1	7			3	2	10	11		4			9		8	6				

Q5 scorers: Cooper 5 (1p), Stoodley 2, Carney (p), Moore, Hodkinson, Cuffe

1913/14

17th in Division Two

North Road

#	Mon	Day	Opponent	Score	Scorers	Att	Bamford HW	Barnett A	Bowden J	Carney JM	Causer AH	Clay G	Costello T	Cuffe JA	Dearnaley RH	Doncaster S	Fletcher AH	Gibbon T	Hampton GH	Henderson JT	Hoare GR	Knight JH	Law WD	Littlewort HC	Montgomery J	Moore J	Stanford J	Stapley HS	Stapley WJ	Thompson AA	Thompson R	Toward RH	Turnell RL
1	Sep	3	Bristol City	1-4	Moore (p)	6000				6	1	8		3					2				11		4	10	9					7	
2		6	Leeds City	0-3		16000				6	1	8		3					2				11		4	9	10	5					7
3		13	CLAPTON ORIENT	0-3		8000				11	1	8		3					2			7			4	6	9	10	5				
4		20	FULHAM	0-1		2000		10		6			2	3				1				8	11		4			5		7			
5		27	Stockport County	1-1	Hoare	10000		10		6	1		2	3							9		11		4			8	5	7			
6	Oct	4	BRADFORD PARK AVE.	2-1	Moore, Hoare	1500	6	10			1			3					2		9		11		4			8	5	7			
7		11	Notts County	2-2	Moore 2	10000	6	10			1			3					2				11		4	8	9		5	7			
8		18	LEICESTER FOSSE	0-2		3000	6	10			1		7	3					2			8	11		4		9		5				
9		25	Wolverhampton Wan.	0-1		7000		7		6	1			3					2				11	5	4		10	8				9	
10	Nov	1	HULL CITY	2-1	Montgomery, H.Stapley	500			10	6	1			3					2			7	11	5	4		9	8					
11		8	Barnsley	0-2		6000			10	6	1			3					2			7	11	5	4			8		9			
12		15	BURY	2-1	A.Thompson 2	2000		9		6	1			3					2			7	11		4			8	5		10		
13		22	Huddersfield Town	1-2	Knight	8000		9		6	1			3					2			7	11		4			8	5			10	
14	Dec	6	BLACKPOOL	1-2	Doncaster	2000		10		6	1	3				9			2				11		4			8	5			7	
15		16	NOTTM. FOREST	3-0	H.Stapley, Doncaster, Carney (p)	1000				6	1			3		9			2				11		4			8	5			10	7
16		20	Woolwich Arsenal	0-2		10000				6	1			3		9			2				11		4			8	5			10	7
17		25	Birmingham	0-6		25000	6		8		1			3		9			2				11		4				5			10	7
18		26	BIRMINGHAM	4-1	Doncaster, H.Stapley 2, Tinkler (og)	2000		10		6	1		7	3		9			2				11		4			8	5				
19		27	LEEDS CITY	1-1	Doncaster	2000		10		6	1			3		9			2				11		4			8	5				
20	Jan	3	Clapton Orient	1-5	Knight	9000		10		6	1			3					2			9	11		4			8	5				
21		17	Fulham	1-2	Barnett	9000		10		6	1			3		9			2				11		4			8	5			7	
22		24	STOCKPORT COUNTY	1-1	Carney	5000		10		6	1		7	3		9			2				11		4			8	5				
23	Feb	7	Bradford Park Avenue	1-2	H.Stapley	12000		10		6	1			3		9	5		2				11		4			8				7	
24		10	LINCOLN CITY	4-0	H.Stapley 3, Toward	1000		10		6	1			3		9			2				11		4			8	5			7	
25		14	NOTTS COUNTY	0-1		2000		10		6	1			3		9			2				11		4			8	5			7	
26		21	Leicester Fosse	3-1	Carney (p), Doncaster 2	4000				6	1			3		9			2			7	11		4			8	5				
27		28	WOLVERHAMPTON W.	1-2	Doncaster	4000				6	1			3		9			2			7	11		4			8	5				
28	Mar	7	Hull City	0-3		9000				6	1	8		3		9			2				11		4				5		10	7	
29		10	BRISTOL CITY	1-1	Carney	1000				6	1			3		9			2				11		4			8	5		10	7	
30		14	BARNSLEY	5-1	R.Thompson 4, Barnett	2000		9		6	1			3					2				11		4			8	5		10	7	
31		21	Bury	0-1		7000	6	9			1			3					2	10			11		4			8	5			7	
32		28	HUDDERSFIELD T	2-3	Toward, Henderson	2000				6	1			3					2	10			11		4			8	5		9	7	
33	Apr	4	Lincoln City	5-1	H.Stapley 2, Henderson 2, R.Thompson	3000				6	1			3					2	10			11		4			8	5		9	7	
34		10	GRIMSBY TOWN	3-0	R.Thompson, H.Stapley 2	3000				6	1		2	3						10			11		4			8	5		9	7	
35		11	Blackpool	1-1	H.Stapley	6000				6	1		2	3						10			11		4			8	5		9	7	
36		13	Grimsby Town	0-3		10000	6				1		2	3						10			11		4			8	5		9	7	
37		18	Nottingham Forest	2-1	Henderson, R.Thompson	7000				6	1		2	3						10			11		4			8	5		9	7	
38		25	WOOLWICH ARSENAL	0-2		3000					1		2	3						10			11		4			8	5		9	7	
					Apps		6	19	3	35	34	6	7	34	9	15	2	4	26	8	4	27	15	3	38	9	4	29	31	7	10	23	4
					Goals			2		4						7				4	2	2			1	4		13		2	7	2	

Played in one game: J Brennan (10, at 4), J Kenyon (7, at 7)
Played in games 26 and 27 at 10: CN Newcombe
Played in games 19 and 20 at 7: H Round

One own goal

F.A. Cup

#	Mon	Day	Opponent	Score	Scorers	Att	Bamford HW	Barnett A	Bowden J	Carney JM	Causer AH	Clay G	Costello T	Cuffe JA	Dearnaley RH	Doncaster S	Fletcher AH	Gibbon T	Hampton GH	Henderson JT	Hoare GR	Knight JH	Law WD	Littlewort HC	Montgomery J	Moore J	Stanford J	Stapley HS	Stapley WJ	Thompson AA	Thompson R	Toward RH	Turnell RL
Q4	Nov	29	HINCKLEY UNITED	5-1																													
Q5	Dec	13	CARLISLE UNITED	4-1																													
R1	Jan	10	EVERTON	2-1	Montgomery, Barnett	5000		10		6	1			3		9			2				11		4			8	5				7
R2		31	PRESTON NORTH END	0-1		10731		10		6	1			3		9			2				11		4			8	5			7	

1914/15

Bottom of Division Two: Not re-elected

North Road

#		Date	Opponent	Result	Scorers	Att.	Allen AJ	Booth C	Bullough DR	Carney JM	Causer AH	Cuffe JA	Dawson G	Dearnaley RH	Gadsby E	Henderson JT	Knight JH	Knighton T	Martin B	Montgomery J	Sharpe H	Sparkes H	Stapley WJ	Sunter J	Thompson R	Toward RW	Ward W
1	Sep	1	Arsenal	0-3		8000				6	1	3		2	10		11			4	8		5		9	7	
2		5	DERBY COUNTY	1-1	Thompson	1000			8	6	1	3		2	10		11			4			5		9	7	
3		8	ARSENAL	0-4		1000			9	4	1			2	10		11			6			5		8	7	3
4		12	Lincoln City	1-2	Henderson	3000				6	1			2		9	11	10		4			5		8	7	3
5		19	BIRMINGHAM	3-3	Carney, Toward, Thompson	1000				6	1	3		2		9	11	10		4			5		8	7	
6		26	Grimsby Town	0-1		6000				6	1	3		2	10	9	11			4			5		8	7	
7	Oct	3	HUDDERSFIELD T	2-2	Carney, Gadsby	2000				6	1	3		2	10		11			4	8		5		9	7	
8		10	Bristol City	1-3	Sharpe	10000				4	1	3		2	10		11			6	8	9	5			7	
9		17	BURY	3-0	Gadsby 2, Thompson	2000				6	1	3			10		11			4	8		5		9	7	2
10		24	Preston North End	0-1		8000				6	1	3			10		11			4	8		5		9	7	2
11		31	NOTTM. FOREST	1-0	W Stapley	2000				6	1	3			10		11			4	8		5		9	7	2
12	Nov	7	Leicester Fosse	2-3	Thompson, Cuffe	5000				6	1	3			10		11			4	8		5		9	7	2
13		14	BARNSLEY	0-1		2000				6	1			3	10		11			4	8		5		9	7	2
14		21	Blackpool	0-3		3000				6	1	3		2	10	9	11			4	8		5			7	
15		28	Wolverhampton Wan.	0-4		6000				11	1	3		6	10	8	7			4	9		5				2
16	Dec	5	FULHAM	1-0	Knight	500	2			6	1		7	3	10		11			4	9		5		8		
17		12	Stockport County	1-2	Sharpe	5000	2			6	1		7		10		11			4	8		5		9		3
18		25	LEEDS CITY	0-3		3000	2			6	1			3		9	11		10	4	8		5			7	
19		26	Leeds City	0-3		10000	2			4	1				10		11			6	8		5		9	7	3
20	Jan	2	Derby County	1-1	Sharpe	7000	2			6	1				10		11			4	8		5		9	7	3
21		16	LINCOLN CITY	1-2	Henderson	8000	2			6	1	3			10	9	11			4	8		5			7	
22		23	Birmingham	1-1	Sharpe	1000	2				1			4	10		11		6	5	8				9	7	3
23		30	GRIMSBY TOWN	0-0		500	2			6	1	3			10		11			4	8		5		9	7	
24	Feb	6	Huddersfield Town	1-0	Thompson	4500	2			6	1	3			10		11			4	8		5		9	7	
25		13	BRISTOL CITY	2-1	Toward, Sharpe	300	2			6	1	3			10		11			4	8		5		9	7	
26		20	Bury	0-5		2582	2			6	1	3			10		11			4	8	9	5			7	
27		27	PRESTON NORTH END	0-1		8000	2			6	1				10		11			4	8	9	5			7	3
28	Mar	6	Nottingham Forest	0-1		4000	2	6			1				10		11			4	8	9	5			7	3
29		13	LEICESTER FOSSE	2-3	Thompson 2	1000	2	4		6	1				10	9	11						5		8	7	3
30		16	HULL CITY	0-5		500	2	4		6	1			3	10	9	11				8		5			7	
31		20	Barnsley	0-2				2			6	1			3	10	8	11		4				5			7	9
32		27	BLACKPOOL	1-3	Sharpe	6000	2			5	1			4	10	8	11		6		9					7	3
33	Apr	2	CLAPTON ORIENT	3-1	Gadsby 2, Knight	2100	2			6	1	3			10		11			4	8		5		9	7	
34		3	WOLVERHAMPTON W.	0-2		4000	2			6	1	3			10		11			4	8		5		9	7	
35		5	Clapton Orient	2-5	Henderson, Knight	6000	2			6	1			3		10	11			4	9		5		8	7	
36		10	Fulham	0-2		6000	2			6	1				10		11			4	9		5		8	7	3
37		17	STOCKPORT COUNTY	1-1	Knight	2000	2			6	1				10		11			4	9		5		8	7	3
38		24	Hull City	0-2		2000	2			6	1				9	10	11			4			5		8	7	3
			Apps				23	3	2	36	38	19	2	18	32	15	38	2	10	28	30	3	36	1	27	35	20
			Goals							2		1			5	3	4				6		1		7	2	

F.A. Cup

#		Date	Opponent	Result	Scorers	Att.	Allen AJ	Booth C	Bullough DR	Carney JM	Causer AH	Cuffe JA	Dawson G	Dearnaley RH	Gadsby E	Henderson JT	Knight JH	Knighton T	Martin B	Montgomery J	Sharpe H	Sparkes H	Stapley WJ	Sunter J	Thompson R	Toward RW	Ward W
Q6	Dec	19	COVENTRY CITY	3-1	Toward, Thompson, Gadsby	600									10		11								9	7	
R1	Jan	9	Queen's Park Rangers	1-2	Toward	7000	2			6	1				10		11			4	8		5		9	7	3

GLOSSOP'S LEAGUE RECORD TO 1914-15

1894-95 The Combination

		p	w	d	l	f	a	pts
1	Ashton North End	20	14	3	3	62	32	31
2	Glossop North End	20	14	2	4	49	19	30
3	Chester	20	12	2	6	53	35	26
4	Dresden United	20	9	7	4	52	25	25
5	Stalybridge Rovers	20	8	5	7	41	35	21
6	Macclesfield	20	8	3	9	44	38	19
7	Leek	20	7	4	9	36	47	18
8	Hurst Ramblers	20	7	1	12	35	61	15
9	Hanley Town	20	6	2	12	37	62	12
10	Buxton	20	4	3	13	22	48	11
11	Northwich Victoria	20	4	2	14	26	55	10

1895-96 The Combination

		p	w	d	l	f	a	pts
1	Everton Reserves	14	11	2	1	34	12	24
2	Macclesfield	14	11	2	1	37	13	24
3	Glossop North End	14	9	3	2	33	13	21
4	Oldham United	14	5	1	8	24	19	11
5	Chester	14	4	2	8	27	29	10
6	Northwich Victoria	14	4	1	9	14	35	9
7	Leek	14	3	3	8	15	35	7
8	Buxton	14	1	2	11	15	43	4

1896-97 Midland League

		p	w	d	l	f	a	pts
1	Doncaster Rovers	28	17	5	6	77	40	39
2	Glossop North End	27	15	4	8	67	39	36
3	Long Eaton Rangers	28	15	2	11	55	39	32
4	Chesterfield	28	13	6	9	74	53	32
5	Kettering Town	28	13	5	10	51	40	31
6	Wellingborough	28	12	7	9	52	46	31
7	Burslem Port Vale	28	14	3	11	62	56	31
8	Heanor Town	28	12	6	10	55	47	30
9	Ilkeston Town	28	11	7	10	60	57	29
10	Dresden United	28	12	5	11	48	63	29
11	Barnsley St Peters	28	10	4	14	57	71	24
12	Rushden	28	9	5	14	43	53	23
13	Mexborough	28	7	7	14	39	50	21
14	Worksop Town	28	6	5	17	27	63	17
15	Grantham Rovers	27	6	3	18	26	76	15

GNE v Grantham Rovers not played: GNE awarded the points

1897-98 Midland League

		p	w	d	l	f	a	pts
1	Mexborough	22	15	3	4	53	30	33
2	Barnsley	22	14	3	5	47	29	31
3	Chesterfield	22	11	7	4	54	23	29
4	Ilkeston Town	22	9	6	7	37	39	24
5	Burslem Port Vale	22	10	3	9	46	32	23
6	Rushden	22	9	5	8	35	44	23
7	Kettering Town	22	7	5	10	19	28	19
8	Long Eaton Rangers	22	7	5	10	26	44	19
9	Glossop North End	22	8	2	12	41	47	18
10	Doncaster Rovers	22	5	6	11	33	35	16
11	Burton Wanderers	22	5	6	11	31	44	16
12	Wellingborough	22	5	3	14	21	48	13

1898-99 Division Two

			home:					away:					Total goals:		
		p	w	d	l	f	a	w	d	l	f	a	f	a	Pts
1	Manchester City	34	15	1	1	64	10	8	5	4	28	25	92	35	52
2	GLOSSOP	34	12	1	4	48	13	8	5	4	28	25	76	38	46
3	Leicester Fosse	34	12	5	0	35	12	6	4	7	29	30	64	42	45
4	Newton Heath	34	12	4	1	51	14	7	1	9	16	29	67	43	43
5	New Brighton Tower	34	13	2	2	48	13	5	3	9	23	39	71	52	43
6	Walsall	34	12	5	0	64	11	3	5	7	15	25	79	36	42
7	Woolwich Arsenal	34	14	2	1	55	10	4	3	10	17	31	72	41	41
8	Small Heath	34	14	1	2	66	17	3	6	8	19	33	85	50	41
9	Burslem Port Vale	34	12	2	3	35	12	5	3	9	21	22	56	34	39
10	Grimsby Town	34	10	3	4	39	17	5	2	10	32	43	71	60	35
11	Barnsley	34	11	4	2	44	18	1	3	13	8	38	52	56	31
12	Lincoln City	34	10	5	2	31	16	2	2	13	20	40	51	56	31
13	Burton Swifts	34	7	5	5	35	25	3	3	11	16	45	51	70	28
14	Gainsborough Trinity	34	8	4	5	40	22	2	1	14	16	50	56	72	25
15	Luton Town	34	8	1	8	37	31	2	2	13	14	64	51	95	23
16	Blackpool	34	6	3	8	35	30	2	1	14	14	60	49	90	20
17	Loughborough	34	5	4	8	31	26	1	2	14	7	66	38	92	18
18	Darwen	34	2	4	11	16	32	0	1	16	6	109	22	141	9

1899-1900 Division One

			home:					away:					Total goals:		
		p	w	d	l	f	a	w	d	l	f	a	f	a	Pts
1	Aston Villa	34	12	4	1	45	18	10	2	5	32	17	77	35	50
2	Sheffield United	34	11	5	1	40	11	7	7	3	23	22	63	33	48
3	Sunderland	34	12	2	3	27	9	7	1	9	23	26	50	35	41
4	Wolverhampton Wan.	34	8	4	5	28	16	7	5	5	20	21	48	37	39
5	Newcastle United	34	10	5	2	34	15	3	5	9	19	28	53	43	36
6	Derby County	34	11	2	4	32	15	3	6	8	13	28	45	43	36
7	Manchester City	34	10	3	4	33	15	3	5	9	17	29	50	44	34
8	Nottingham Forest	34	12	3	2	42	16	1	5	11	14	39	56	55	34
9	Stoke	34	9	5	3	24	15	4	3	10	13	30	37	45	34
10	Liverpool	34	9	4	4	31	19	5	1	11	18	26	49	45	33
11	Everton	34	11	1	5	30	15	2	6	9	17	34	47	49	33
12	Bury	34	12	2	3	29	14	1	4	12	11	30	40	44	32
13	West Bromwich Albion	34	8	6	3	27	11	3	2	12	16	40	43	51	30
14	Blackburn Rovers	34	12	2	3	38	22	1	2	14	11	39	49	61	30
15	Notts County	34	5	7	5	29	22	4	4	9	17	38	46	60	29
16	Preston North End	34	9	3	5	28	20	3	1	13	10	28	38	48	28
17	Burnley	34	10	2	5	28	17	1	3	13	6	37	34	54	27
18	GLOSSOP	34	4	6	7	19	22	0	4	13	12	52	31	74	18

1900-01 Division Two

		p	w	d	l	f	a	w	d	l	f	a	f	a	Pts
1	Grimsby Town	34	14	3	0	46	11	6	6	5	14	22	60	33	49
2	Small Heath	34	14	2	1	41	8	5	8	4	16	16	57	24	48
3	Burnley	34	15	0	2	39	6	5	2	10	14	23	53	29	44
4	New Brighton Tower	34	12	5	0	34	8	5	3	9	23	30	57	38	42
5	GLOSSOP	34	11	2	4	34	9	4	6	7	17	24	51	33	38
6	Middlesbrough	34	11	4	2	38	13	4	3	10	12	27	50	40	37
7	Woolwich Arsenal	34	13	3	1	30	11	2	3	12	9	24	39	35	36
8	Lincoln City	34	12	3	2	39	11	2	4	12	4	28	43	39	33
9	Burslem Port Vale	34	8	6	3	28	14	3	5	9	17	33	45	47	33
10	Newton Heath	34	11	3	3	31	9	1	1	13	11	29	42	38	28
11	Leicester Fosse	34	9	5	3	30	15	2	5	10	9	22	39	37	32
12	Blackpool	34	7	6	4	20	11	5	1	11	13	43	33	58	31
13	Gainsborough Trinity	34	8	4	5	26	18	2	6	9	19	42	45	60	30
14	Chesterfield	34	6	5	6	25	22	3	5	9	21	36	46	58	28
15	Barnsley	34	9	3	5	34	23	2	2	13	13	37	47	60	27
16	Walsall	34	7	7	3	29	23	0	6	11	11	33	40	56	27
17	Stockport County	34	9	2	6	25	21	2	1	14	13	47	38	68	25
18	Burton Swifts	34	7	3	7	16	21	1	1	15	18	45	34	66	20

1901-02 Division Two

		p	w	d	l	f	a	w	d	l	f	a	f	a	Pts
1	West Bromwich Albion	34	14	2	1	52	13	11	3	3	30	16	82	29	55
2	Middlesbrough	34	15	1	1	58	7	8	4	5	32	17	90	24	51
3	Preston North End	34	12	3	2	50	11	6	3	8	21	21	71	32	42
4	Woolwich Arsenal	34	13	2	2	35	9	5	4	8	15	17	50	26	42
5	Lincoln City	34	11	6	0	26	4	3	7	7	19	31	45	35	41
6	Bristol City	34	11	3	3	39	12	4	5	8	13	23	52	35	40
7	Doncaster Rovers	34	12	3	2	39	12	1	5	11	10	46	49	58	34
8	GLOSSOP	34	7	6	4	22	15	3	6	8	14	25	36	40	32
9	Burnley	34	9	6	2	30	8	1	4	12	11	37	41	45	30
10	Burton United	34	8	6	3	32	23	3	2	12	14	31	46	54	30
11	Barnsley	34	9	3	5	36	33	3	3	11	15	30	51	63	30
12	Burslem Port Vale	34	7	7	3	26	17	3	2	12	17	42	43	59	29
13	Blackpool	34	7	5	5	27	21	2	4	13	13	40	40	61	27
14	Leicester Fosse	34	11	2	4	26	14	1	3	13	12	42	38	56	29
15	Newton Heath	34	10	2	5	27	12	1	4	12	11	42	38	54	28
16	Chesterfield	34	10	4	3	35	18	1	3	13	12	50	47	68	28
17	Stockport County	34	8	3	6	25	20	0	4	13	11	52	36	72	23
18	Gainsborough Trinity	34	4	9	4	26	25	0	2	15	4	55	30	80	19

1902-03 Division Two

		p	w	d	l	f	a	w	d	l	f	a	f	a	Pts
1	Manchester City	34	15	1	1	64	15	10	3	4	31	14	95	29	54
2	Small Heath	34	17	0	0	57	11	7	3	7	17	25	74	36	51
3	Woolwich Arsenal	34	14	2	1	46	9	6	6	5	20	21	66	30	48
4	Bristol City	34	12	3	2	43	18	5	5	7	16	20	59	38	42
5	Manchester United	34	9	4	4	32	15	6	4	7	21	23	53	38	38
6	Chesterfield	34	11	4	2	43	10	3	5	9	24	30	67	40	37
7	Preston North End	34	10	5	2	39	12	3	5	9	17	28	56	40	36
8	Barnsley	34	9	4	4	32	13	4	4	9	23	38	55	51	34
9	Burslem Port Vale	34	11	5	1	36	16	2	3	12	21	46	57	62	34
10	Lincoln City	34	9	4	4	32	16	3	3	11	16	31	48	47	31
11	GLOSSOP	34	9	1	7	26	19	2	6	9	17	38	43	57	29
12	Gainsborough Trinity	34	9	4	4	28	20	2	3	12	13	39	41	59	29
13	Burton United	34	9	4	4	26	20	2	3	12	13	39	39	59	29
14	Blackpool	34	7	5	5	32	24	2	5	10	12	35	44	59	28
15	Leicester Fosse	34	5	5	7	20	23	5	3	9	21	42	41	65	28
16	Doncaster Rovers	34	8	5	4	27	11	1	2	14	8	55	35	72	25
17	Stockport County	34	6	4	7	26	24	1	2	14	12	50	38	74	20
18	Burnley	34	6	7	4	25	25	0	1	16	5	52	30	77	20

1903-04 Division Two

			home:					away:					Total goals:		
		p	w	d	l	f	a	w	d	l	f	a	f	a	Pts
1	Preston North End	34	13	4	0	38	10	7	6	4	24	14	62	24	50
2	Woolwich Arsenal	34	15	2	0	67	5	6	5	6	24	17	91	22	49
3	Manchester United	34	14	2	1	42	14	6	6	5	23	19	65	33	48
4	Bristol City	34	14	2	1	53	12	4	4	9	20	29	73	41	42
5	Burnley	34	12	2	3	31	20	3	7	7	19	35	50	55	39
6	Grimsby Town	34	12	5	0	39	12	2	3	12	11	37	50	49	36
7	Bolton Wanderers	34	10	3	4	38	11	2	7	8	21	30	59	41	34
8	Barnsley	34	10	5	2	25	12	1	5	11	13	45	38	57	32
9	Gainsborough Trinity	34	10	2	5	34	17	4	1	12	19	43	53	60	31
10	Bradford City	34	8	5	4	30	25	4	2	11	15	34	45	59	31
11	Chesterfield	34	8	5	4	22	12	3	3	11	15	33	37	45	30
12	Lincoln City	34	9	4	4	25	18	2	4	11	16	40	41	58	30
13	Burslem Port Vale	34	10	3	4	44	20	0	6	11	10	32	54	52	29
14	Burton United	34	8	6	3	33	16	3	1	13	12	45	45	61	29
15	Blackpool	34	8	2	7	25	27	3	3	11	15	40	40	67	27
16	Stockport County	34	7	7	3	28	23	1	4	12	12	49	40	72	27
17	GLOSSOP	34	7	4	6	42	25	3	2	12	15	39	57	64	26
18	Leicester Fosse	34	5	8	4	26	21	1	2	14	16	61	42	82	22

1904-05 Division Two

1	Liverpool	34	14	3	0	60	12	13	1	3	33	13	93	25	58
2	Bolton Wanderers	34	15	0	2	53	16	12	2	3	34	16	87	32	56
3	Manchester United	34	16	0	1	60	10	8	5	4	21	20	81	30	53
4	Bristol City	34	12	3	2	40	12	7	1	9	26	33	66	45	42
5	Chesterfield	34	9	6	2	26	11	5	5	7	18	24	44	35	39
6	Gainsborough Trinity	34	11	4	2	32	15	3	4	10	29	43	61	58	36
7	Barnsley	34	11	4	2	29	13	3	1	13	9	43	38	56	33
8	Bradford City	34	8	5	4	31	20	4	3	10	14	29	45	49	32
9	Lincoln City	34	9	4	4	31	16	3	3	11	11	24	42	40	31
10	West Bromwich Albion	34	8	2	7	28	20	5	2	10	28	28	56	48	30
11	Burnley	34	10	1	6	31	21	2	5	10	12	31	43	52	30
12	GLOSSOP	34	7	5	5	23	14	3	5	9	14	32	37	46	30
13	Grimsby Town	34	9	3	5	22	14	2	5	10	11	32	33	46	30
14	Leicester Fosse	34	8	3	6	30	25	3	4	10	10	30	40	55	29
15	Blackpool	34	8	5	4	26	15	1	5	11	10	33	36	48	28
16	Burslem Port Vale	34	7	4	6	28	25	3	3	11	19	47	47	72	27
17	Burton United	34	7	2	8	20	29	1	2	14	10	55	30	84	20
18	Doncaster Rovers	34	3	2	12	12	32	0	0	17	11	49	23	81	8

1905-06 Division Two

1	Bristol City	38	17	1	1	43	8	13	5	1	40	20	83	28	66
2	Manchester United	38	15	3	1	55	13	13	3	3	35	15	90	28	62
3	Chelsea	38	13	4	2	58	16	9	5	5	32	21	90	37	53
4	West Bromwich Albion	38	13	4	2	53	16	9	4	6	26	20	79	36	52
5	Hull City	38	10	5	4	38	21	9	1	9	29	33	67	54	44
6	Leeds City	38	11	5	3	38	19	6	4	9	21	28	59	47	43
7	Leicester Fosse	38	10	3	6	30	21	5	9	5	23	27	53	48	42
8	Grimsby Town	38	11	7	1	33	13	4	3	12	13	33	46	46	40
9	Burnley	38	9	4	6	26	23	6	4	9	16	30	42	53	38
10	Stockport County	38	11	6	2	36	16	2	3	14	8	40	44	56	35
11	Bradford City	38	7	4	8	21	22	6	4	9	25	38	46	60	34
12	Barnsley	38	11	4	4	45	17	1	5	13	15	45	60	62	33
13	Lincoln City	38	10	1	8	46	29	2	5	12	23	43	69	72	30
14	Blackpool	38	8	3	8	22	21	2	6	11	15	41	37	62	29
15	Gainsborough Trinity	38	10	2	7	35	22	2	2	15	9	35	44	57	28
16	GLOSSOP	38	9	4	6	36	28	1	4	14	13	43	49	71	28
17	Burslem Port Vale	38	10	4	5	34	25	2	0	17	15	57	49	82	28
18	Chesterfield	38	8	4	7	26	24	2	4	13	14	48	40	72	28
19	Burton United	38	9	4	6	26	20	1	2	16	8	47	34	67	26
20	Clapton Orient	38	6	4	9	19	22	1	3	15	16	56	35	78	21

1906-07 Division Two

1	Nottingham Forest	38	16	2	1	43	13	12	2	5	31	23	74	36	60
2	Chelsea	38	18	0	1	55	10	8	5	6	25	24	80	34	57
3	Leicester Fosse	38	15	3	1	44	12	5	5	9	18	27	62	39	48
4	West Bromwich Albion	38	15	2	2	62	15	6	3	10	21	30	83	45	47
5	Bradford City	38	14	2	3	46	21	7	3	9	24	32	70	53	47
6	Wolverhampton Wan.	38	13	4	2	49	16	4	3	12	17	37	66	53	41
7	Burnley	38	12	4	3	45	13	5	2	12	17	34	62	47	40
8	Barnsley	38	14	2	3	56	21	1	6	12	17	34	73	55	38
9	Hull City	38	11	2	6	41	20	4	5	10	24	37	65	57	37
10	Leeds City	38	10	5	4	38	26	3	5	11	17	37	55	63	36
11	Grimsby Town	38	13	2	4	34	16	3	1	15	23	46	57	62	35
12	Stockport County	38	8	8	3	26	12	4	3	12	16	40	42	52	35
13	Blackpool	38	9	4	6	25	19	2	7	10	8	32	33	51	33
14	Gainsborough Trinity	38	12	3	4	33	20	2	2	15	12	52	45	72	33
15	GLOSSOP	38	10	4	5	32	21	3	2	14	21	58	53	79	32
16	Burslem Port Vale	38	11	5	3	45	26	1	2	16	15	57	60	83	31
17	Clapton Orient	38	9	7	3	25	13	2	1	16	20	54	45	67	30
18	Chesterfield	38	10	3	6	36	26	1	4	14	14	40	50	66	29
19	Lincoln City	38	10	2	7	29	24	2	2	15	17	49	46	73	28
20	Burton United	38	7	3	9	24	23	1	4	14	10	45	34	68	23

1907-08 Division Two

			home:					away:					Total goals:		
		p	w	d	l	f	a	w	d	l	f	a	f	a	Pts
1	Bradford City	38	15	2	2	58	16	9	4	6	32	26	90	42	54
2	Leicester Fosse	38	14	2	3	41	20	7	8	4	31	27	72	47	52
3	Oldham Athletic	38	15	4	0	53	14	7	2	10	23	28	76	42	50
4	Fulham	38	12	2	5	50	14	10	3	6	32	35	82	49	49
5	West Bromwich Albion	38	13	3	3	38	13	6	6	7	23	26	61	39	47
6	Derby County	38	15	1	3	50	13	6	3	10	27	32	77	45	46
7	Burnley	38	14	3	2	44	14	6	3	10	23	36	67	50	46
8	Hull City	38	15	1	3	50	23	6	3	10	23	39	73	62	46
9	Wolverhampton Wan.	38	11	4	4	34	11	4	3	12	16	34	50	45	37
10	Stoke	38	11	5	3	43	13	5	0	14	14	39	57	52	37
11	Gainsborough Trinity	38	9	4	6	31	28	5	3	11	16	43	47	71	35
12	Leeds City	38	9	6	4	33	18	3	2	14	20	47	53	65	32
13	Stockport County	38	9	4	6	35	26	3	4	12	13	41	48	67	32
14	Clapton Orient	38	10	5	4	28	13	1	5	13	12	52	40	65	32
15	Blackpool	38	11	3	5	33	19	0	6	13	18	39	51	58	31
16	Barnsley	38	8	3	8	41	31	4	3	12	13	37	54	68	30
17	GLOSSOP	38	9	5	5	36	26	2	3	14	18	48	54	74	30
18	Grimsby Town	38	8	5	6	27	24	3	3	13	16	47	43	71	30
19	Chesterfield	38	6	6	7	33	38	0	5	14	13	54	46	92	23
20	Lincoln City	38	7	2	10	27	28	2	1	16	19	55	46	83	21

1908-09 Division Two

1	Bolton Wanderers	38	14	3	2	37	8	10	1	8	22	20	59	28	52
2	Tottenham Hotspur	38	12	5	2	42	12	8	6	5	25	20	67	32	51
3	West Bromwich Albion	38	13	5	1	35	9	6	8	5	21	18	56	27	51
4	Hull City	38	14	2	3	44	15	5	4	10	19	24	63	39	44
5	Derby County	38	13	5	1	38	11	3	6	10	17	30	55	41	43
6	Oldham Athletic	38	14	4	1	39	9	3	2	14	16	34	55	43	40
7	Wolverhampton Wan.	38	10	6	3	32	12	4	5	10	24	36	56	48	39
8	GLOSSOP	38	11	5	3	35	17	4	3	12	22	36	57	53	38
9	Gainsborough Trinity	38	12	3	4	30	20	3	5	11	19	50	49	70	38
10	Fulham	38	8	4	7	39	26	5	7	7	19	22	58	48	37
11	Birmingham	38	10	6	3	35	21	4	3	12	23	40	58	61	37
12	Leeds City	38	12	3	4	35	19	2	4	13	8	34	43	53	35
13	Grimsby Town	38	9	5	5	23	14	5	2	12	18	40	41	54	35
14	Burnley	38	8	4	7	33	28	5	3	11	18	30	51	58	33
15	Clapton Orient	38	7	7	5	25	19	5	2	12	12	30	37	49	33
16	Bradford Park Avenue	38	9	2	8	30	25	4	4	11	21	34	51	59	32
17	Barnsley	38	11	3	5	36	19	0	7	12	12	38	48	57	32
18	Stockport County	38	11	2	6	25	19	3	1	15	14	52	39	71	31
19	Chesterfield	38	10	3	6	30	28	1	5	13	7	39	37	67	30
20	Blackpool	38	9	6	4	30	22	0	5	14	16	46	46	68	29

1909-10 Division Two

1	Manchester City	38	15	2	2	51	17	8	6	5	30	23	81	40	54
2	Oldham Athletic	38	15	2	2	47	9	8	5	6	32	30	79	39	53
3	Hull City	38	13	4	2	52	19	10	3	6	28	27	80	46	53
4	Derby County	38	15	2	2	46	15	7	7	5	26	32	72	47	53
5	Leicester Fosse	38	15	2	2	60	20	5	2	12	19	38	79	58	44
6	GLOSSOP	38	14	1	4	42	18	4	6	9	22	39	64	57	43
7	Fulham	38	9	7	3	28	13	5	6	8	23	30	51	43	41
8	Wolverhampton Wan.	38	14	3	2	51	22	3	3	13	13	41	64	63	40
9	Barnsley	38	15	3	1	48	15	1	4	14	14	44	62	59	39
10	Bradford Park Avenue	38	12	1	6	47	28	5	3	11	17	31	64	59	38
11	West Bromwich Albion	38	8	5	6	30	23	8	0	11	28	33	58	56	37
12	Blackpool	38	7	7	5	24	18	7	1	11	26	34	50	52	36
13	Stockport County	38	9	6	4	37	20	4	2	13	13	27	50	47	34
14	Burnley	38	12	2	5	43	21	2	4	13	19	40	62	61	34
15	Lincoln City	38	7	6	6	27	24	3	5	11	15	45	42	69	31
16	Clapton Orient	38	10	4	5	26	15	2	2	15	11	45	37	60	30
17	Leeds City	38	8	4	7	30	33	2	3	14	16	47	46	80	27
18	Gainsborough Trinity	38	8	3	8	22	21	2	3	14	11	54	33	75	26
19	Grimsby Town	38	8	3	8	31	19	1	3	15	19	58	50	77	24
20	Birmingham	38	7	4	8	28	26	1	3	15	14	52	42	78	23

1910-11 Division Two

1	West Bromwich Albion	38	14	2	3	40	18	8	7	4	27	23	67	41	53
2	Bolton Wanderers	38	17	2	0	53	12	4	7	8	16	28	69	40	51
3	Chelsea	38	17	2	0	48	7	3	7	9	23	28	71	35	49
4	Clapton Orient	38	14	4	1	28	7	5	3	11	16	28	44	35	45
5	Hull City	38	8	10	1	38	21	6	6	7	17	18	55	39	44
6	Derby County	38	11	5	3	48	24	6	3	10	25	28	73	52	42
7	Blackpool	38	10	5	4	29	15	6	5	8	20	23	49	38	42
8	Burnley	38	9	9	1	31	18	4	6	9	14	27	45	45	41
9	Wolverhampton Wan.	38	10	5	4	26	16	5	3	11	25	36	51	52	38
10	Fulham	38	12	3	4	35	15	3	4	12	17	33	52	48	37
11	Leeds City	38	11	4	4	35	18	4	3	12	23	38	58	56	37
12	Bradford Park Avenue	38	12	4	3	44	18	2	5	12	9	37	53	55	37
13	Huddersfield Town	38	10	4	5	35	21	3	4	12	22	37	57	58	34
14	GLOSSOP	38	11	4	4	36	21	2	4	13	12	41	48	62	34
15	Leicester Fosse	38	12	3	4	37	19	2	2	15	15	43	52	62	33
16	Birmingham	38	10	4	5	23	18	2	4	13	19	46	42	64	32
17	Stockport County	38	10	4	5	27	26	1	4	14	20	53	47	79	30
18	Gainsborough Trinity	38	9	5	5	26	16	0	6	13	11	39	37	55	29
19	Barnsley	38	5	7	7	36	26	2	7	10	16	36	52	62	28
20	Lincoln City	38	5	7	7	16	23	2	3	14	12	49	28	72	24

1911-12 Division Two

			home:					away:					Total goals:		
		p	w	d	l	f	a	w	d	l	f	a	f	a	Pts
1	Derby County	38	15	2	2	55	13	8	6	5	19	15	74	28	54
2	Chelsea	38	15	2	2	36	13	9	4	6	28	21	64	34	54
3	Burnley	38	14	5	0	50	14	8	3	8	27	27	77	41	52
4	Clapton Orient	38	16	0	3	44	14	5	3	11	17	30	61	44	45
5	Wolverhampton Wan.	38	12	3	4	41	10	4	7	8	16	23	57	33	42
6	Barnsley	38	10	5	4	28	19	5	7	7	17	23	45	42	42
7	Hull City	38	12	3	4	36	13	5	5	9	18	38	54	51	42
8	Fulham	38	10	3	6	42	24	6	4	9	24	34	66	58	39
9	Grimsby Town	38	9	6	4	24	18	6	3	10	24	37	48	55	39
10	Leicester Fosse	38	11	4	4	34	18	4	3	12	15	48	49	66	37
11	Bradford Park Avenue	38	10	5	4	30	16	3	4	12	14	29	44	45	35
12	Birmingham	38	11	3	5	44	29	3	3	13	11	30	55	59	34
13	Bristol City	38	11	4	4	27	17	3	2	14	14	43	41	60	34
14	Blackpool	38	12	4	3	24	12	1	4	14	8	40	32	52	34
15	Nottingham Forest	38	9	3	7	26	18	4	4	11	20	30	46	48	33
16	Stockport County	38	8	5	6	31	22	3	6	10	16	32	47	54	33
17	Huddersfield Town	38	8	5	6	30	22	5	1	13	20	42	50	64	32
18	GLOSSOP	38	6	8	5	33	23	2	4	13	9	33	42	56	28
19	Leeds City	38	7	6	6	21	22	3	2	14	29	56	50	78	28
20	Gainsborough Trinity	38	4	6	9	17	22	1	7	11	13	42	30	64	23

1912-13 Division Two

1	Preston North End	38	13	5	1	34	12	6	10	3	22	21	56	33	53
2	Burnley	38	13	4	2	58	23	8	4	7	30	30	88	53	50
3	Birmingham	38	11	6	2	39	18	7	4	8	20	26	59	44	46
4	Barnsley	38	15	3	1	46	18	4	4	11	11	29	57	47	45
5	Huddersfield Town	38	13	5	1	49	12	4	4	11	17	28	66	40	43
6	Leeds City	38	12	3	4	45	22	3	7	9	25	42	70	64	40
7	Grimsby Town	38	10	8	1	32	11	5	2	12	19	39	51	50	40
8	Lincoln City	38	10	6	3	31	16	5	4	10	19	36	50	52	40
9	Fulham	38	13	5	1	47	16	4	0	15	18	39	65	55	39
10	Wolverhampton Wan.	38	10	6	3	34	16	4	4	11	22	38	56	54	38
11	Bury	38	10	6	3	29	14	5	2	12	24	43	53	57	38
12	Hull City	38	12	2	5	42	18	3	4	12	18	37	60	55	36
13	Bradford Park Avenue	38	12	4	3	47	18	2	4	13	13	42	60	60	36
14	Clapton Orient	38	8	6	5	25	20	2	8	9	9	27	34	47	34
15	Leicester Fosse	38	12	2	5	34	20	1	5	13	15	45	49	65	33
16	Bristol City	38	7	9	3	32	25	2	6	11	14	47	46	72	33
17	Nottingham Forest	38	9	3	7	35	25	3	5	11	23	34	58	59	32
18	GLOSSOP	38	11	2	6	34	26	1	6	12	15	42	49	68	32
19	Stockport County	38	8	4	7	32	23	0	6	13	24	55	56	78	26
20	Blackpool	38	8	4	7	22	22	1	4	14	17	47	39	69	26

1913-14 Division Two

			home:					away:					Total goals:		
		p	w	d	l	f	a	w	d	l	f	a	f	a	Pts
1	Notts County	38	16	2	1	55	13	7	5	7	22	23	77	36	53
2	Bradford Park Avenue	38	15	1	3	44	20	8	2	9	27	27	71	47	49
3	Woolwich Arsenal	38	14	3	2	34	10	6	6	7	20	28	54	38	49
4	Leeds City	38	15	2	2	54	16	5	5	9	22	30	76	46	47
5	Barnsley	38	14	1	4	33	15	5	6	8	18	30	51	45	45
6	Clapton Orient	38	14	5	0	38	11	2	6	11	9	24	47	35	43
7	Hull City	38	9	5	5	29	13	7	4	8	24	24	53	37	41
8	Bristol City	38	12	5	2	32	10	4	4	11	20	40	52	50	41
9	Wolverhampton Wan.	38	14	1	4	33	16	4	4	11	18	36	51	52	41
10	Bury	38	12	6	1	30	14	3	4	12	9	26	39	40	40
11	Fulham	38	10	3	6	31	20	6	3	10	15	23	46	43	38
12	Stockport County	38	9	6	4	32	18	4	4	11	23	39	55	57	36
13	Huddersfield Town	38	8	4	7	28	22	5	4	10	19	31	47	53	34
14	Birmingham	38	10	4	5	31	18	2	6	11	17	42	48	60	34
15	Grimsby Town	38	10	4	5	24	15	3	4	12	18	43	42	58	34
16	Blackpool	38	6	10	3	24	19	3	4	12	9	25	33	44	32
17	GLOSSOP	38	8	3	8	32	24	3	3	13	19	43	51	67	28
18	Leicester Fosse	38	7	2	10	29	28	4	2	13	16	33	45	61	26
19	Lincoln City	38	8	5	6	23	23	2	1	16	13	43	36	66	26
20	Nottingham Forest	38	7	7	5	27	23	0	2	17	10	53	37	76	23

1914-15 Division Two

1	Derby County	38	14	3	2	40	11	9	4	6	31	22	71	33	53
2	Preston North End	38	14	4	1	41	16	6	6	7	20	26	61	42	50
3	Barnsley	38	16	2	1	31	10	6	1	12	20	41	51	51	47
4	Wolverhampton Wan.	38	12	4	3	47	13	7	3	9	30	39	77	52	45
5	Arsenal	38	15	1	3	52	13	4	4	11	17	28	69	41	43
6	Birmingham	38	13	3	3	44	13	4	6	9	18	26	62	39	43
7	Hull City	38	12	2	5	36	23	7	3	9	29	31	65	54	43
8	Huddersfield Town	38	12	4	3	36	13	5	4	10	25	29	61	42	42
9	Clapton Orient	38	12	5	2	36	17	4	4	11	14	31	50	48	41
10	Blackpool	38	11	3	5	40	22	6	2	11	18	35	58	57	39
11	Bury	38	11	5	3	39	19	4	3	12	22	37	61	56	38
12	Fulham	38	12	0	7	35	20	3	7	9	18	27	53	47	37
13	Bristol City	38	11	2	6	38	19	4	5	10	24	37	62	56	37
14	Stockport County	38	12	4	3	33	19	3	3	13	21	41	54	60	37
15	Leeds City	38	9	3	7	40	25	5	1	13	25	39	65	64	32
16	Lincoln City	38	9	4	6	29	23	2	5	12	17	42	46	65	31
17	Grimsby Town	38	10	4	5	36	24	1	5	13	12	52	48	76	31
18	Nottingham Forest	38	9	7	3	32	24	1	2	16	11	53	43	77	29
19	Leicester Fosse	38	6	4	9	31	41	4	0	15	16	47	47	88	24
20	GLOSSOP	38	5	5	9	21	33	1	1	17	10	54	31	87	18

and today's club, recent seasons in the North West Counties League, Premier Division

	2009-10	p	w	d	l	f	a	Pts
1	Newcastle Town	42	37	3	2	121	21	114
2	New Mills	42	27	9	6	108	38	90
3	Bootle	42	26	7	9	92	41	85
4	Ramsbottom United	42	24	9	9	92	69	81
5	Congleton Town	42	24	8	10	90	46	80
6	Maine Road	42	21	7	14	82	59	70
7	GLOSSOP NORTH END	42	19	12	11	74	49	69
8	Colne	42	19	10	13	70	65	67
9	St Helens Town	42	20	6	16	74	75	66
10	Padiham	42	18	6	18	71	71	60
11	Runcorn Linnets	42	17	6	19	75	78	57
12	Bacup Borough	42	15	12	15	63	75	57
13	Squires Gate	42	15	8	19	61	74	53
14	Silsden	42	13	7	22	53	75	46
15	Formby	42	14	3	25	57	81	45
16	Flixton	42	12	8	22	54	85	44
17	Nelson	42	12	8	22	47	87	44
18	Alsager Town	42	11	7	24	60	79	40
19	Winsford United	42	11	7	24	53	79	40
20	Atherton LR	42	10	7	25	53	96	37
21	Ashton Athletic	42	8	8	26	51	101	32
22	Abbey Hey	42	7	6	29	49	106	27

2010-11

1	New Mills	42	32	6	4	102	38	102	
2	Ramsbottom United	42	29	4	9	101	45	91	
3	Winsford United	42	26	5	11	99	50	83	
4	Padiham	42	21	10	11	84	62	73	
5	Colne	42	21	10	11	90	73	73	
6	Bootle	42	21	9	12	78	56	72	
7	Barnoldswick United	42	19	12	11	81	58	69	
8	Congleton Town	42	18	10	14	70	60	64	
9	Squires Gate	42	18	10	14	74	70	64	
10	Atherton LR	42	19	6	17	75	72	63	
11	Bacup Borough	42	17	10	15	68	55	61	
12	Runcorn Linnets	42	16	8	18	68	77	56	
13	Maine Road	42	15	9	18	69	64	54	
14	GLOSSOP NORTH END	42	14	11	17	68	55	53	
15	Flixton	42	13	9	20	78	91	48	
16	Silsden	42	13	9	20	47	74	48	
17	St Helens Town	42	14	5	23	79	116	47	
18	Formby	42	11	10	21	67	95	43	
19	Stone Dominoes	42	12	6	24	60	90	42	
20	Alsager Town	42	10	8	24	57	94	38	
21	Rossendale United (-1)	42	6	11	25	63	106	28	D
22	Ashton Athletic	42	5	6	31	45	122	21	

	2011-12	p	w	d	l	f	a	Pts	
1	Ramsbottom United	42	31	3	8	108	43	96	
2	Runcorn Town	42	29	5	8	111	49	92	
3	Bootle (-1)	42	24	13	5	87	43	84	D
4	Barnoldswick United	42	26	5	11	73	38	83	
5	Runcorn Linnets	42	22	10	10	70	62	76	
6	GLOSSOP NORTH END	42	22	7	13	76	42	73	
7	Winsford United	42	21	6	15	88	69	69	
8	Colne	42	19	4	19	68	60	61	
9	AFC Blackpool	42	17	10	15	67	64	61	
10	Flixton	42	18	5	19	69	68	59	
11	Congleton Town	42	18	5	19	56	64	59	
12	Silsden	42	16	9	17	59	59	57	
13	Alsager Town	42	16	9	17	63	65	57	
14	Ashton Athletic	42	15	6	21	70	80	51	
15	Padiham	42	14	9	19	51	65	51	
16	Squires Gate	42	14	8	20	74	89	50	
17	Bacup Borough (-3)	42	15	7	20	59	77	49	D
18	Maine Road (-4)	42	13	9	20	58	69	44	D
19	AFC Liverpool (-3)	42	13	6	23	60	73	42	D
20	Stone Dominoes	42	10	6	26	39	92	36	
21	St Helens Town	42	6	8	28	50	105	26	
22	Atherton LR	42	5	6	31	36	116	21	

2012-13

1	Padiham	42	26	10	6	92	45	88	
2	Maine Road	42	28	3	11	99	57	87	
3	Bootle	42	26	8	8	79	43	86	
4	Runcorn Town (-3)	42	26	9	7	105	45	84	D
5	Winsford United	42	25	8	9	85	45	83	
6	Runcorn Linnets	42	21	9	12	82	58	72	
7	Congleton Town	42	20	9	13	85	55	69	
8	Colne	42	19	10	13	93	60	67	
9	Barnoldswick Town	42	19	9	14	77	57	66	
10	AFC Blackpool	42	19	9	14	60	58	66	
11	AFC Liverpool	42	18	6	18	69	64	60	
12	Wigan Robin Park	42	17	5	20	66	71	56	
13	GLOSSOP NORTH END	42	14	11	17	73	71	53	
14	Norton United (-3)	42	16	7	19	69	83	52	D
15	Alsager Town	42	14	8	20	66	78	50	
16	Stockport Sports (-6)	42	14	13	15	72	69	49	D
17	Bacup Borough	42	13	8	21	51	71	47	
18	Silsden	42	11	6	25	58	98	39	
19	St Helens Town	42	9	9	24	54	91	36	
20	Ashton Athletic	42	10	5	27	58	91	35	
21	Squires Gate	42	8	6	28	47	95	30	
22	Stone Dominoes	42	3	4	35	31	166	13	

GLOSSOP IN F.A. CUP COMPETITIONS

The year is the final year of the season.

FA CUP

Year	Round	Opponent	H/A	Score	
1895	Q1	Tonge	H	4-0	
	Q2	Barnton Rovers	H	5-0	
	Q3	Wrexham	A	2-1	
	Q4	Fairfield	A	1-4	
1896	Q1	Macclesfield (1)	H	5-1	
	Q2	Northwich Victoria	A	4-1	
	Q3	Fairfield	H	0-2	
1897	Q3	Macclesfield (1)	H	5-0	
	Q4	Druids	H	5-2	
	Q5	Fairfield	H	2-1	
	R1	Stoke	A	2-5	
1898	Q3	Aberystwyth	A	0-1	
1899	Q3	New Brighton Tower	H	4-2	
	Q4	Crewe Alexandra	H	1-0	
	Q5	Stockport County	A	2-0	
	R1	Newcastle United	H	0-1	
1900	Q3	Stockport County	H	2-2	
	Q3 r	Stockport County	A	0-3	
1901	IR	Stoke	A	0-1	
1902	Q3	St Helens	H	5-2	
	Q4	Nantwich	A	3-1	
	Q5	Stockport County	H	2-0	
	IR	Leicester Fosse	A	1-0	
	R1	Nottingham Forest	H	1-3	
1903	Q3	Crewe Alexandra	A	3-0	
	Q4	Wrexham	H	4-0	
	Q5	St Helens Recreation	H	5-0	
	IR	New Brompton	H	2-1	
	R1	Stoke	H	2-3	
1904	Q2	Heywood	A	scr	
1905	Q3	Nantwich	A	2-1	
	Q4	Stockport County	H	1-1	
	Q4 r	Stockport County	A	0-0	
	Q4 r2	Stockport County	A	0-1	
1906	Q4	Brighton & Hove Albion	H	0-1	
1907	Q5	Newhall Swifts	A	2-1	
	R1	Brentford	A	1-2	
1908	Q5	West Stanley	A	3-0	
	R1	Manchester City	H	0-0	
	R1 r	Manchester City	A	0-6	
1909	R1	Chesterfield	A	2-0	
	R2	Stockport County	A	1-1	
	R2 r	Stockport County	H	1-0	e
	R3	Sheffield Wednesday	A	1-0	
	R4	Bristol City	H	0-0	
	R4 r	Bristol City	A	0-1	
1910	R1	Bury	A	1-2	
1911	R1	Middlesbrough	A	0-1	
1912	R1	Leeds City	A	0-1	
1913	Q4	Ripley Town & Athletic	H	2-0	
	Q5	Southall	H	11-1	
	R1	Crystal Palace	A	0-2	
1914	Q4	Hinckley United (1)	H	5-1	
	Q5	Carlisle United	H	4-1	
	R1	Everton	H	2-1	
	R2	Preston North End	H	0-1	
1915	Q6	Coventry City	H	3-1	
	R1	Queen's Park Rangers	A	1-2	
1920	Q1	Altrincham	H	1-1	
	Q1 r	Altrincham	A	4-5	
1921	PR	Eccles United	A	0-10	
1922	EP	Atherton	H	1-4	
1923	PR	Eccles United	A	0-2	
1924	EP	Orrell	A	1-0	
	PR	New Mills	A	1-3	
1925	PR	Hurst	H	2-2	
	PR r	Hurst	A	2-0	
	Q1	Manchester North End	H	3-0	
	Q2	Burscough Rangers	H	3-2	
	Q3	Buxton	A	1-4	
1926	PR	Whiston	H	4-1	
	Q1	Stalybridge Celtic	A	2-5	
1927	PR	Manchester North End	H	4-1	
	Q1	Stalybridge Celtic	A	0-4	
1928	PR	Manchester North End	A	3-4	
1929	PR	Whiston	A	1-4	
1930	PR	Bootle Celtic	A	1-4	
1931	Q1	Whiston	H	1-1	
	Q1 r	Whiston	A	1-1	e
	Q1 r2	Whiston	N	2-4	
1932	PR	Timperley	A	2-3	
1933	PR	Whiston	A	1-3	
1934	PR	Droylsden	H	1-0	
	Q1	Seaforth Albion	H	6-2	
	Q2	Marine	A	1-2	
1935	PR	Manchester North End	H	3-1	
	Q1	Earle	A	1-0	
	Q2	Denton United	A	1-2	
1936	PR	Droylsden	A	1-1	
	PR r	Droylsden	H	5-2	
	Q1	Northern Nomads	A	1-1	
	Q1 r	Northern Nomads	H	1-0	
	Q2	Denton United	H	3-0	
	Q3	Prescot Cables	H	5-2	
	Q4	Kells United	H	2-4	
1937	PR	Droylsden	H	2-2	
	PR r	Droylsden	A	2-1	e
	Q1	Manchester North End	A	2-3	
1938	PR	Droylsden	H	w/o	
	Q1	Urmston	A	3-4	
1939	PR	Rhyl	A	2-3	
1946	Q1	Witton Albion	A	2-8	
1947	Q1	Rhyl	H	2-6	
1949	EP	Harrowby	A	11-2	
	PR	Winsford United	A	1-3	
1950	PR	Hyde United	H	1-2	
1951	PR	Altrincham	H	1-4	
1952	PR	Congleton Town	A	scr	
1972	Q1	Worksop Town	H	0-1	
1973	PR	Rawmarsh Welfare	A	1-0	
	Q1	Mexborough Town	H	3-2	
	Q2	Macclesfield Town	A	0-3	
1974	Q1	Altrincham	A	1-3	
1975	Q1	Emley	A	1-4	
1976	Q1	Fleetwood	A	0-2	
1977	Q1	Droylsden	A	2-3	
1978	Q1	Winsford United	H	0-2	
1979	Q1	Buxton	A	1-3	
1980	Q1	New Mills	A	2-1	
	Q2	Winsford United	A	0-2	
1981	PR	Formby	A	2-0	
	Q1	Prescot Cables	A	0-2	
1982	Q1	Bangor City	A	0-6	
1983	Q1	Worksop Town	H	2-5	
1984	PR	Witton Albion	A	1-1	
	Q1 r	Witton Albion	H	2-0	
	Q2	Goole Town	H	4-0	
	Q3	Frickley Athletic	H	2-3	
1985	PR	Appleby Frodingham Athletic	A	0-2	
1986	PR	Nantwich Town	A	0-1	
1987	PR	Penrith	A	2-6	
1988	PR	Heanor Town	H	2-3	
1989	PR	Prescot Cables	H	0-0	
	PR r	Prescot Cables	A	0-1	
1990	PR	Maine Road	H	0-4	
1991	PR	Skelmersdale United	H	1-1	
	PR r	Skelmersdale United	A	2-0	
	Q1	Maine Road	A	0-1	
1992	PR	Newtown (2)	A	2-4	
1993	Q1	Macclesfield Town	H	0-1	
1994	PR	Glasshoughton Welfare	A	2-0	
	Q1	Goole Town	H	2-2	
	Q1 r	Goole Town	A	0-1	
1995	PR	Goole Town	A	2-0	
	Q1	Eastwood Town	A	2-2	
	Q1 r	Eastwood Town	A	1-1	e
	Q1 r2	Eastwood Town	H	3-5	e
1996	PR	Nantwich Town	H	1-2	
1997	PR	Blakenall	A	0-3	
1998	PR	Belper Town	A	2-2	
	PR r	Belper Town	H	1-2	
1999	Q1	Bourne Town	A	2-1	
	Q2	Cambridge City	A	1-1	
	Q2 r	Cambridge City	H	1-1	P
	Q3	Grantham Town	H	2-3	

Year	Round		Opponent		Venue	Score	
2000	PR		Stafford Rangers		A	0-2	
2001	PR		Spalding United		A	0-4	
2002	PR		Stourbridge		H	0-1	
2003	PR		Boldmere St Michaels		H	1-0	
	Q1		Solihull Borough		A	0-9	
2004	PR		Spalding United		A	0-3	
2005	PR		Ludlow Town		H	2-3	
2006	EP		Stourbridge		N	0-3	
2007	EP		North Shields		H	2-0	
	PR		Seaham Red Star		H	2-1	
	Q1		New Mills		H	3-1	
	Q2		Trafford		A	0-5	
2008	EP		Eccleshall		H	2-0	
	PR		Malvern Town		A	0-3	
2009	EP		Pegasus Juniors		A	4-1	
	PR		Belper Town		H	1-2	
2010	EP		Formby		A	1-1	
	EP	r	Formby		H	3-1	
	PR		Rossington Main		A	2-1	
	Q1		Chorley		H	2-3	
2011	EP		Wigan Robin Park		H	2-2	
	EP	r	Wigan Robin Park		A	1-0	
	PR		St Helens Town		A	1-1	
	PR	r	St Helens Town		H	3-1	e
	Q1		Mossley		H	0-4	
2012	EP		Boston Town		H	2-4	
2013	EP		Louth Town		H	0-0	
	EP	r	Louth Town		A	2-1	e
	PR		Loughborough Dynamo		H	0-3	
2014	EP		Armthorpe Welfare		A	4-1	
	PR		Runcorn Town		A	1-0	
	Q1		Runcorn Linnets		A	1-2	

FA TROPHY

Year	Round		Opponent		Venue	Score	
1972	Q1		Belper Town		A	0-2	
1973	Q1		Congleton Town		A	0-1	
1974	Q1		Woolley MW		H	0-1	
1983	Q1		Arnold		H	1-1	
	Q1	r	Arnold		A	3-2	
	Q2		Rhyl		A	1-3	
1984	Q1		Oswestry Town		H	1-2	
1985	PR		Belper Town		H	3-0	
1985	Q1		Curzon Ashton		A	0-2	
1986	PR		Leyland Motors		A	1-3	
1987	Q1		Workington		H	1-1	
	Q1	r	Workington		H	1-0	
	Q2		Whitley Bay		A	0-2	

FA VASE

Year	Round		Opponent		Venue	Score	
1975	R1		Northern Nomads		A	2-1	
	R2		Chloride Recreation		A	0-0	
	R2	r	Chloride Recreation		H	1-0	
	R3		Middlewich Athletic		H	2-4	
1976	PR		Sheffield		A	0-3	
1977	PR		Liversedge		H	2-0	
	R1		Hoylake Athletic		H	2-0	
	R2		Congleton Town		A	0-2	
1978	PR		Rawmarsh Welfare		A	1-2	
1979	PR		Chadderton		H	2-3	
1980	R1		Normanby Park Works		A	2-1	
	R2		Harworth CI		H	1-2	e
1981	PR		Arnold Kingswell		H	4-1	
	R1		Stapenhill		H	3-0	
	R2		Winterton Rangers		H	3-0	
	R3		Norton Woodseats		A	0-3	
1982	R1		Lytham		H	1-0	
	R2		Waterloo Dock		H	0-1	e
1988	PR		Colne Dynamoes		A	4-5	
1989	PR		Newcastle Town		A	2-2	
	PR	r	Newcastle Town		H	0-1	
1990	PR		Irlam Town		H	1-2	
1991	PR		Waterloo Dock		H	2-1	
	R1		Curzon Ashton		H	6-1	
	R2		Winterton Rangers		H	4-0	
	R3		North Ferriby United		H	1-0	
	R4		Cammell Laird		H	2-2	
	R4	r	Cammell Laird		A	1-2	
1992	R1		Newcastle Town		H	0-1	
1993	PR		Rocester		H	2-3	e

Year	Round		Opponent		Venue	Score	
1994	PR		Hatfield Main		H	2-1	
	R1		Newcastle Town		A	4-3	
	R2		Rocester		A	2-1	
	R3		Cammell Laird		A	3-2	
	R4		Bridgnorth Town		A	2-3	
1995	R1		Worsbrough Bridge MW		A	4-2	
	R2		Bootle		H	2-0	
	R3		Stocksbridge Park Steels		H	0-5	
1996	R1		Flixton		A	0-3	
1997	Q2		Burscough		A	0-0	e
	Q2	r	Burscough		H	0-3	
1998	Q1		Vauxhall Motors		H	2-4	e
1999	Q2		Sandwell Borough		H	2-1	
	R1		Birstall United		A	0-3	
2000	Q2		Blackstones		A	2-0	
	R1		Bolehall Swifts		H	4-2	
	R2		Malvern Town		A	2-2	e
	R2	r	Malvern Town		H	3-0	
	R3		Brigg Town		H	3-2	
	R4		Chippenham Town		H	0-1	e
2001	R2		Squires Gate		A	2-3	
2002	Q2		Kirby Muxloe		A	2-0	
	R1		Raunds Town		H	1-2	
2003	Q2		Sutton Town		A	6-5	e
	R1		Ford Sports Daventry		H	1-2	
2004	Q2		Rainworth MW		A	1-2	
2005	Q2		Holbrook MW		A	3-2	
	R1		Barwell		A	2-0	
	R2		Quorn		A	1-1	e
	R2	r	Quorn		H	1-3	
2006	Q2		Staveley MW		H	3-2	e
	R1		Romulus		H	6-4	
	R2		Carlton Town		H	3-4	
2007	Q2		Biddulph Victoria		A	1-2	
2008	Q1		Pershore Town		A	2-1	
	Q2		Racing Club Warwick		H	2-0	
	R1		Coventry Sphinx		A	3-4	
2009	Q1		Sporting Khalsa		H	5-0	
	Q2		Calverton Miners Welfare		A	4-1	
	R1		New Mills		A	4-1	
	R2		Biddulph Victoria		H	4-0	
	R3		Winterton Rangers		H	2-1	
	R4		Stewarts & Lloyds (2)		H	2-1	
	R5		Bitton		A	2-0	
	R6		Marske United		H	5-2	
	SF	1	Chalfont St Peter		A	3-3	
	SF	2	Chalfont St Peter		H	2-2	P
	F		Whitley Bay		N	0-2	
2010	R2		Dunston UTS		H	1-0	
	R3		Barwell		A	0-2	
2011	Q2		Blackstones		A	0-0	e
	Q2	r	Blackstones		H	3-1	e
	R1		Gedling Town		A	1-2	
2012	Q2		Shirebrook Town		A	3-1	
	R1		Blidworth Welfare		H	5-0	
	R2		Billingham Town		A	4-2	
	R3		Runcorn Town		H	1-2	
2013	Q1		Barton Town Old Boys		H	2-1	
	Q2		Winsford United		H	1-1	e
	Q2	r	Winsford United		A	1-4	
2014	Q1		Nostell MW		H	3-2	
	Q2		Formby		H	1-0	
	R1		Kinsley Boys		H	7-0	
	R2		Staveley MW		A	0-2	

KEY

e	extra time played
P	won on penalties
N	played on a neutral ground

TODAY'S GLOSSOP NORTH END

The modern Glossop football club, with its 'North End' suffix proudly restored in 1992, is a very different animal to the club that existed prior to the First World War. It would now take five promotions for the club to get back to the Football League, and many ground improvements. However, these are not the ambitions of the modern club. The aim is to provide regular football for local players and spectators, and to place the club at the heart of the community. If, in achieving this, they go up a couple of leagues... well, that would be nice.

Between the wars the club played in the Lancashire Combination and the Manchester League, of which they were champions in 1927/28. They also won the Gilgryst Cup on three occasions. Matches ceased during the Second World War, then Glossop re-joined the Manchester League afterwards. They won the Gilgryst Cup for a fourth time in 1949. In 1955 they moved from their original ground at North Road to their present home at Surrey Street. Ok, they were evicted. Although 'Surrey Street' is the name used by all Glossopians, the stadium is officially named 'The Arthur Goldthorpe Stadium' after a Glossop estate agent who provided much of the finance for the move. Since moving to Surrey Street they have played in the Lancashire Combination, the Manchester and the Cheshire leagues, before becoming founder members of the North West Counties League in 1982.

The Hillmen – the nickname evolved from 'Hillsmen' as it was under Samuel Hill-Wood – spent much of the next three decades in financial strife, in times (as one Director liked to put it) "so dark you couldn't see your hand in front of your face". The majority of the problems were brought on by a criminally corrupt owner in the 1980s. It was only the hard work of board members and supporters that kept the club afloat after the disgraced regime departed. Lack of finance meant that they spent the majority of their time in the North West Counties League battling relegation from the First (now Premier) Division, indeed suffering the drop in 1988 and only returning in 1992. All this time the club itself was fighting for survival. However, there was a little success — the club was Manchester Premier Cup winners in 1997 and 1998, and Derbyshire Cup winners in 2000-01.

More recently though, things have improved for the Hillmen. 2008-09 saw the biggest day in the history of the club after Steve Young & Terry Hincks' side embarked on a terrific FA Vase run which saw North End reach the final at Wembley. They played in every single round of the competition, leaving some fantastic memories for supporters along the way. None more dramatic perhaps than the 123rd minute equalizer in the semi-final against Chalfont St. Peter. This led to a penalty shootout, where the Hillman seized the opportunity to head down Wembley Way.

Whilst the final saw a disappointing result — losing 0-2 to Whitley Bay — the run awakened interest in the Hillmen throughout the town. It is estimated that 5,000 Glossopians made the trip to London. There were numerous coaches from the club itself and from pubs around the town. A local policeman arranged with the railway companies for a special service to run from Glossop Station to Wembley, its assortment of 12 elderly coaches earning it the nickname 'Hogwarts Express'. It took hundreds of fans to the game.

As a result of the renewed interest there is now a thriving Supporters Club, which has funded makeovers to a ground that had become rather ramshackle, and helped generate interest in the club home and away. Indeed, the finance provided by that FA Vase run has funded a refurbishment of changing rooms, a new clubhouse and a new covered standing area. North End have finally achieved the necessary ground grading for the league above and the club feels it is ready to progress up the football pyramid. In new manager Chris Willcock they hope to have found the man to take the first steps on that path. They are not dreaming of former glories – that is a long way and a huge financial injection away. However they are dreaming of building on the recent success to give Glossop a football team to be proud of once again.

Jonathan Haggart
November 2013

The Vase semi-final 2009: Kelvin Lugsden scores the goal to make the score 2-2 (5-5 on agg.) and take the game into extra time...

...then wheels away in celebration.

Goalkeeper Ash Gotham is chaired around Surrey Street on the shoulders of supporters after his heroic penalty shoot-out performance helped the Hillmen reach Wembley.

The FA Vase final 2009. Glossop number 8 Dave Morris holds his head in his hands (as do thousands of GNE fans) after his early near miss and "what might have been?" moment at Wembley against Whitley Bay.

GNE's Surrey Street ground. The former Ferro Alloys chimney stands 250 feet tall; opinion is divided in the town as to whether it is an eyesore or a landmark.

20 August 2011 - FA Cup, Extra Preliminary Round - Glossop North End v Boston Town. Sam Hind of GNE chases the ball wearing the celebratory kit for the 125th season of the club. The kit references the one worn by the 1899-1900 team that graced the Football League's First Division.

5 October 2013 – NWCFL Premier Division – GOAL: Tom Bailey of GNE scores past Ciaran Gibson of St Helens Town to make it 1-0.

19 October 2013 – GNE v Kinsley Boys – FA Vase First Round: Sam Hare of GNE celebrates with Harry Bockarie after combining to score the fourth goal in a 7-0 result.

ABOUT THE AUTHOR

Garth Dykes was born at Mellor, near Blackburn, and was educated at Chadderton Grammar School. Qualifications in cotton spinning followed, and employment in yarn sales commenced in 1957, a career move taking Garth to Leicester in 1961. A keen, if not very successful footballer in his youth, Garth fondly remembers scoring two goals, on a very wet afternoon in 1951, for the Grammar School Old Boys Reserves against Old Hulmeians, when one of the Chadderton eleven, who arrived without boots, played the 90 minutes wearing a pair of wellingtons! A member of the Football Writers' Association, Garth's lifelong love of football, which commenced when he attended his first match at Boundary Park, Oldham, in season 1945-46, has seen his involvement in twenty books to date. A number of caricatures drawn by the author appear within the pages of this book. This aspect of his work has appeared in several of his earlier titles, as well as in football programmes, national magazines and in several sets of trade cards produced and marketed by David Rowland of Bury.

BY THE SAME AUTHOR

Oldham Athletic – A Complete Record, 1899 -1988 (Breedon Books, 1988)
Exeter City – A Complete Record, 1904 – 1990, with Alex Wilson and Maurice Golesworthy
(Breedon Books 1990)
New Brighton – A Complete Record of the Rakers in the Football League, 1922 – 1951 (Breedon Books 1990)
Accrington Stanley – A Complete Record, 1894 – 1962, with Mike Jackman (Breedon Books 1991)
The United Alphabet – A Complete Who's Who of Manchester United F.C.
(ACL and Polar Publishing (UK) Ltd. 1994)
All The Lads – A Complete Who's Who of Sunderland A.F.C., with Doug Lamming (Polar Publishing, 1999)
Latics Lads – The Official Who's Who of Oldham Athletic A.F.C., 1907 – 2002 (Yore Publications, 2002)
Meadow Lane Men – The Complete Who's Who of Notts County F.C., 1888 – 2005 (Yore Publications, 2005)
The Legends of Oldham Athletic (Breedon Books, 2006)
The Who's Who of Oldham Athletic (Breedon Books, 2008)
A Who's Who of Barrow A.F.C. – Barrow's Football League Players 1921 – 1972 (Soccerdata, 2009)
Nelson F.C. in the Football League. A Complete Record and Who's Who 1921-31 (Soccerdata 2009)
Durham City in the Football League. A Complete Record and Who's Who 1921-28 (Soccerdata 2010)
A Spinner's Yarn. High Crompton St Mary's C.C. The Official History 1904-1910, with Allan Cadman
(Soccerdata 2010)
Ashington A.F.C. in the Football League. A Complete Record and Who's Who 1921-1929. (Soccerdata 2011)
Wigan Borough in the Football League. A Complete Record and Who's Who 1921-31 (Soccerdata 2011)
A Spinner's Yarn Over and Out. High Crompton St Mary's C.C. The Official History 1904-2011,
with Allan Cadman (Soccerdata 2012)
New Brighton in the Football League. A Complete Record and Who's Who 1923-51 (Soccerdata 2012)
Oldham Athletic A.F.C. 1895-1915 (Soccerdata 2012)
Oldham Athletic A.F.C. 1915-1939 (Soccerdata 2013)

 ## The English National Football Archive
www.enfa.co.uk

All Glossop's Football League line-ups and scorers form part of the English National Football Archive. The ENFA database holds more than 400,000 line-ups, 600,000 goal scorers, and 41,000 players. It includes every League and cup game from 1888-89 onwards. It is fully indexed, so that a player's career can be followed match by match and club by club.